THE FEASTS UNLOCKED

THE FEASTS UNLOCKED
A Practical Understanding of God's Holy Days

These are my appointed festivals, the appointed festivals of the LORD, which you are to proclaim as sacred assemblies.
Leviticus 23:2 (NIV)

ALLAN R. AGUIRRE

CHAMELEON CHURCH RESOURCE SERIES
PLANET BLUE MEDIA
PARK CITY

The Feasts Unlocked – A Practical Understanding of God's Holy Days
Copyright © 2018 by Allan R. Aguirre

Published by Planet Blue Media
2100 Park Ave., #684147, Park City, UT 84068
planetBlueMedia.com

For speaking engagements / business inquiries: info@chameleonChurch.com

All rights reserved. No part of this publication may be reproduced without written permission from the publisher. The only exception is brief quotations in printed reviews.

Paperback Unabridged "Understanding": ISBN 978-0-9991300-0-1
Paperback Abridged "How To": ISBN 978-0-9991300-1-8
Workbook: 978-0-9991300-2-5

Cover photo by Allan R. Aguirre
"Young Olive Tree in Cardo - Old City of Jerusalem"
Cover Design: Saltar Media

Unless otherwise indicated: Scripture quotations are from the ESV® Bible (The Holy Bible, English Standard Version®), copyright 2001 by Crossway, a publishing ministry of Good News Publishers. Used by permission. All rights reserved.

Scripture quotations marked CJB are taken from the Complete Jewish Bible by David H. Stern. Copyright © 1998. All rights reserved. Used by permission of Messianic Jewish Publishers, 6120 Day Long Lane, Clarksville, MD 21029. www.messianicjewish.net.

Scripture quotations marked (NIV) are taken from the Holy Bible, New International Version®, NIV®. Copyright © 1973, 1978, 1984, 2011 by Biblica, Inc.™ Used by permission of Zondervan. All rights reserved worldwide. www.zondervan.com. The "NIV" and "New International Version" are trademarks registered in the United States Patent and Trademark Office by Biblica, Inc.™

Scripture from the New Revised Standard Version Bible, copyright © 1989 the Division of Christian Education of the National Council of the Churches of Christ in the United States of America. Used by permission. All rights reserved.

Scripture quotations marked KJV are taken from the King James Version. The KJV is in the Public Domain.

Scripture taken from the New King James Version®. Copyright © 1982 by Thomas Nelson. Used by permission. All rights reserved.

Chameleon Church Resource Series
web | facebook | twitter | instagram | youtube: chameleonChurch

INTRODUCTION

I'm at a prophetic conference in Las Vegas; I'm asking the Lord for strategies on how to take my literal mountain and praying for insight on how to go forward when I get a comment on a Facebook post from a friend of mine:

"So... speaking of feasts... I truly get overwhelmed when trying to learn more about and how to celebrate them; when, what and where. I would love to even understand the lessons in the Feasts. Is there a very simple, introductory version / book / website, etc., that I can access to start and then learn and grow each year? I am really bad about analysis paralysis. I go to websites and people start to contradict each other and then I get confused and frustrated. It would be great if I had a friend (hint, hint) who could notify me when a feast is coming up. And then point me to a page that would line upon line tell me what to do. At least until I feel like I have my training wheels off. Is that the silliest, laziest question you have ever heard?!"

"Nope," I replied. "It's more common than you think. In fact, the work in figuring it out and knowing and seeking etc., is all a part of it. I would be more than happy to discuss it with you and point you in the right direction."

"Sunday would be great, unless there is a feast before then!"

"Sunday is good" I commented back. "And no, the last feast day was *last* Sunday for the New Moon."

"Awwww man!" she exclaimed. "I need like a *Feast for Dummies* - a 'how to.' And more importantly, I would like to know more of the meaning behind it, rather than just doing a ritual."

"That actually sounds like a great idea," I commented about the *Feasts for Dummies* idea. "Absolutely. It won't just be ritual. Paul said the Torah is Spiritual. That means it's a living organism. It's the Word, and the Word is alive, and the Feasts are the celebratory / worship / holy rehearsals of tomorrow in the *now*. It's amazing..." I was getting excited.

And so was she: "YES! That's what I am looking for. And so much of what is lacking in everything I have found thus far! THEN I could teach others in my community how to celebrate them! That would be soooo fun! I'm excited!"

Wow... I've talked about and pondered teaching in book form to the extent that I've started on a couple two or three titles but I fizzled out on them (it takes a lot of discipline for me to write like this.)

> "Ideas are easy. Execution is everything"
> - Casey Neistat

I now have an inquiry about a book while asking for insightful strategies at a prophetic conference, and this could be a direct vehicle for duplication and discipleship. Thank you, Abba.

Before going any further, I want to strongly suggest that you watch an independent documentary called "*The Way* – A documentary about leaving 'churchianity' to live like the Savior." I've known about it since before its release but only just now watched it five weeks into this book. I love that many of the points I make in this book you'll also find in this film: http://thewaydoc.com

Before we begin, agree with me in prayer if you will:

Father, I ask for Your Spirit of Wisdom and Revelation to fall upon the readers; I ask that the eyes of their understanding be opened to the reality of Your Word as we unlock and open the truths within.

I pray, Holy Spirit, that readers would allow You to open their ears to have ears to hear You and that they would allow You to open their eyes to have eyes to see You.

Any spirit of confusion or religion that would attempt to pervert Your Word, Father, during this process we bind and cast out from hearts and minds; you have no authority or influence here!

Father, we ask for your Grace and Mercy as we unlock the blessings of your Feasts, that we would continually desire to be in alignment with You and with Your everlasting Word.

In the name of Your Son, Jesus of Nazareth.
Amen

Assumptions

> *By this we may know that we are in him: whoever says he abides in him ought to walk in the same way in which he walked.*
> 1 John 2:5b-6

"Whoever says they are in Jesus, a 'Christian,' should walk in the same way Jesus walked," says John, Jesus' beloved disciple. John was in the top three; he was at the Mount of Transfiguration, he outlived everybody else, and it was John that received the Revelation on Patmos for the End Time Church. I think John would know...

Jesus ate according to His Father's dietary instruction. Jesus walked in the instruction His Father gave to Moses, the instructions on how to live for God on planet earth exclusively. Jesus obeyed the "Law," the Word, because He was and is that Word. Jesus kept the doctrine His Father established on Mount Sinai through His Prophet Moses. This is what we are to emulate, as John clearly stated, *if* we say we abide in Jesus. *This* is how others will know that we are "Christians" – *this* is how others will know that we are truly in Him: by imitating Jesus.

So Jesus answered them, "My teaching is not mine, but his who sent me. If anyone's will is to do God's will, he will know whether the teaching is from God or whether I am speaking on my own authority. The one who speaks on his own authority seeks his own glory; but the one who seeks the glory of him who sent him is true, and in him there is no falsehood. Has not Moses given you the law? Yet none of you keeps the law..."
John 7:16-19a

This book has been written with the assumption in mind that you, the reader, have somehow, in some way and to some extent, received the revelation or are in the process of receiving the revelation that the Scriptures, the TaNaKh, the "Old Testament" – and the information and instructions therein – haven't been *"done away with"* or made obsolete and somehow, in some way and to some extent, must apply to those calling upon the name of ADONAI, today; i.e. "Christians." You.

Writing this book in no way suggests that I've figured everything out or that I am an expert. On the contrary, I am simply providing a resource on the subject matter based on my present understanding and convictions. My present position could very well be modified as I continue going "further up and further in."

I also know that there are multiple positions and a myriad of conclusions regarding any and all of the information in this book. This writing is not meant to be an exhaustive study but a comprehensive approach to the Feasts in hopes of clarifying contradictions, confusion and frustration many experience when approaching the topic. I hope to bring understanding to your desire to participate in the Feasts as you go deeper in His Word.

Again, I go forward with the assumption that you have received or are in the process of receiving the revelation that the instructions found in the Old Testament haven't been eliminated from the equation for those of us that call upon the name of ADONAI.

With that, I want to clearly state from the very beginning that observing "the Law" / Torah, that keeping God's Commandments, is obedience for blessing – not salvation.

Old / New Testament – TaNaKh – Torah

Many of us have been taught that this Old Testament... Stop right there! Let's start with the proper names and titles now.

It's not the *"Old Testament."* It's called the *"TaNaKh,"* the Word or the Scriptures. *TaNaKh* is an acronym of the first Hebrew letter of each of the Masoretic Text's three traditional subdivisions:

- The Torah (Genesis – Deuteronomy, also known as the Five Books of Moses), the "T" in **T**a**N**a**K**h
- The Prophets (Hebrew: *"Nevi'im"*) The "N" in Ta**N**aKh, and
- The Writings, i.e. the Proverbs and the Psalms (Hebrew: *"Ketuvim"*), the "K" in TaNa**Kh**

So when you read the words "scripture(s)" or "Word" in the New Testament, it's referring to the actual scriptures: the TaNaKh, the "Old Testament," the scriptures only. There was no "New Testament" (weird that we still need to clarify that...) nor was there the compilation known as "The Bible" when the New Testament was written, so it couldn't possibly be referring to that either.

The TaNaKh, the Scriptures, were the text that Jesus and His disciples – the writers of the New Testament – had, obeyed and followed. The New Testament – outside of the Gospels, Acts and Revelation – is instruction and a breakdown *of* these Scriptures. The unpacking of those Scriptures by Rabbi Sha'ul (Paul the Apostle), for example, were primarily for the benefit of Gentiles, a pagan people group with absolutely no reference experience in regards to the Hebraic Faith of the One True

God of Abraham, Isaac and Jacob or the Scriptures of that faith.

This is why Paul – "circumcised the eighth day, of the nation of Israel, of the tribe of Benjamin, a Hebrew of Hebrews; as to the Law, a Pharisee; as to zeal, a persecutor of the church; as to the righteousness which is in the Law, blameless" (Philippians 3:4-6) – was the Apostle to the Gentiles. Besides this amazing Jewish pedigree, Paul, possibly an up-and-comer for the Jewish high council and more than likely on a fast track for High Priest, was also a Roman citizen. Who else could unpack this nebulous "Old Testament" to pagan Gentiles? The fishermen or tax collector? I think not.

There is a common and popular position of disregarding (or rather discrediting) Paul's Jewish pedigree based on Philippians 3:7-10, which only lends to a collective misunderstanding of what Paul actually writes in his letters in support of keeping God's covenant commandments. Contextually, I don't see Philippians 3:7-10 as an emphasis discrediting Paul's Jewishness or role in Rabbinical Judaism, pre- or post-Jesus, exclusively, but rather the importance of Messiah over *all things*, especially legalism and a religious spirit. It's *because* of this specific pedigree and knowledge of the scriptures – not just his Roman citizenry – that God chose him to be the Apostle to the Gentiles. What other reason had He?

Paul is teaching Gentiles in his letters / epistles the proper way to live out the Scriptures in light of the Messianic fulfillment of Jesus as a Jewish Rabbi would, *not* as a Roman Citizen. The Law… Stop! Proper name and title correction:

The Hebrew word *"Torah"* was erroneously and, in my opinion, deliberately translated into the negative connotation "Law." The word Torah actually means "teaching" and/or "instruction" and is known and referred to as the Teachings of Moses. Torah is also known as The Commandments of God (Think "The Ten Commandments") and the Covenant(s). So depending on what Bible translation you use, Torah is translated as teaching(s), instruction(s), covenant(s), the Word, command(s) and/or commandments.

The Torah, given to Moses by God on Mount Sinai, is the covenant instruction on how to live this life for, with and in God; also known as The Commandments, and are an essential part of the Scriptures. You not only find them in Deuteronomy and Leviticus from the Five Books of Moses, you also find references and instructions to obey the Torah in the Prophets, the Proverbs and the Psalms.

That's just about your entire "Old Testament," and they would have us believe that Jesus, this same "Word made flesh," did away with Himself, the Torah and the Scriptures, through His death and resurrection? That makes absolutely no sense whatsoever, especially when you look at the actual "red letters" on the subject matter! (Have you read Matthew 5 recently?)

Many of us have been taught that the TaNaKh, the Scriptures, have been deemed obsolete; that they don't apply to us for a variety of reasons. Many of those differing reasons are rooted in our various denominational backgrounds:

- The Old Testament? That's the "old covenant"
- We're "'New Testament' believers"
- The Old Testament applies to Jews not Gentiles

And so on...

A huge cross-section of the Mainstream Western Church believes that the OT (Old Testament) is irrelevant and doesn't apply to them in any practical, real-life scenario. That's 60% of the Bible! Add to that the position that this same Bible is not to be taken literally and that even whole chunks of the NT (New Testament) are not applicable to us in any practical, real-life scenario due to the ever-convenient "that's not for today" mentality, and it's no wonder that none of this makes any sense or is working properly. How can it when we've eliminated more than half of the biblical text?

Yet, the Western Church will still tell us that the Bible is the infallible, the inerrant, and the absolute Word of God and that God is "the same yesterday, today and tomorrow." Really?

So then, is it any wonder that the Romanized Mainstream Western Church would be so vehemently opposed to anything and everything regarding the potentiality that the "Law of Moses" (Mosaic Law) is still a binding covenant for those that call on the name of ADONAI? It shouldn't be a surprise when the Western Church is straining at the gnat of the literal and contextual Bible and its lifestyle application in today's modern world. Unless, of course, Gentile Christianity doesn't regard itself as "Called of God" or in covenant with Him. Then in that case, the matter is moot.

(On a side note, you'll also find that the New Testament makes references to and instructs us in obeying the Torah. Jesus refers to the

Psalms as "Torah" in John 10:34 and John 15:25. In 1 Corinthians 14:21, Paul references Isaiah 28:11-12 as "Torah" and cites Psalms 143:2 as "Torah" in Romans 3:20.)

I ask these hard questions, because that's what the Torah is. It's God's written Covenant with His people, and as a general whole, the Romanized Western Church has rejected this covenant reality for 1800+ years.

We have doctrinally demonized and eliminated the instructions on how to do any of this correctly: the Scriptures – the very Word that is the total and absolute essence of Jesus – and the covenant instructions of God for His people – the Torah; the very reasons for His Feasts! How can we possibly understand what anyone is actually referring to in the New Testament, completely and in its contextual entirety, when we have no idea what the Old Testament is saying? The reality is that we can't and don't.

As I was saying...

Paul is teaching his Gentile churches, through his letters, epistles and covenant lifestyle the proper way to live out the Scriptures / Torah in light of the Messianic fulfillment of Jesus. If Torah wasn't applicable to Gentile Believers, then the word "Torah" should never have come out of Paul's mouth with any sort of instructional reference. The word "Torah" would simply be a passing reference warning against the false teachings of the Judaizers that were subverting his work, don't you think? Instead, Paul is unpacking – unlocking, if you will – the scriptures, Torah, in his letters and epistles to Gentiles that have no reference experience to or with the scriptures. This third generation Rabbi of the Pharisaical sect *is*, after all, the Apostle to the Gentiles.

Are We Capable of Keeping Torah?

Here's the Million Dollar Question: Are we, as Christians, regardless of Jewish or Gentile lineage and/or denominational background, obligated to follow "the Law"? Since we're working with the assumption that you're past that point, I'll have to think about the best way to address that in some later form or fashion. Right now we're going to address whether or not we're even capable of keeping Torah, let alone are we supposed to, which is actually a silly question when you think about it.

"Are we, as followers of God in Jesus, obligated to obey God by keeping His commandments?" See how silly that is?

Many of us were taught that man could never fully meet "the requirements of the 'Law;'" that no man could ever fully accomplish obeying "the whole 'Law'" and for that reason, God sent Jesus to earth; to fully live out and accomplish all of the requirements of the "Law" on our behalf, because we would never be able to, and so now – because of Jesus – we don't have to!

"So now, because of Jesus, we don't have to keep God's commandments"?!? Yes, that's what many of us are actually taught...

There are some serious fundamental and foundational problems with that teaching. Besides being an extreme form of replacement theology, our Bibles never actually state or even suggest that line of reasoning. In fact, Biblically, the exact opposite is true! To suggest that Father God would instruct us to obey His commands – or any of His instructions for that matter – teachings that He knew we would "never be able to accomplish" is simply not in His nature (Matt. 7:9-11; Luke 11:11-13). God isn't in the business of giving us stones instead of bread or snakes instead of fish. Technically, obeying God or His commandments has never been an issue of "could we." It's always been an issue of "would we."

Besides, to suggest that man could never keep God's commandments is a false narrative. Paul himself states in the passage regarding his pedigree that he was blameless when it came to the righteousness of Torah. Noah, Abraham, David (except in the case of Uriah), Job, Daniel, Zechariah and his wife Elizabeth (the parents of John the Baptist), John the Baptist, Simeon, Joseph of Arimathea and Jesus were all listed as being perfect, blameless and righteous in regard to obedience to God and His instructions.

Here's what the actual Torah says about keeping Torah: Moses and the Children of Israel, after 40 years in the wilderness, are assembled in the land of Moab – east of the Jordan River and the Dead Sea – to hear the words of the covenant (Torah) and to make a contract between themselves and God Himself. We catch up with Moses after promising Israel blessings:

> However, all this will happen... *"when you obey the voice of the LORD your God, to keep his commandments and his statutes that are written in this Book of the Law, when you turn to the LORD your God with all your heart and with*

*all your soul [sound familiar?]. For this commandment that I command you today **is not too hard for you, neither is it far off** [beyond your reach]. It is not in heaven, that you should say, 'Who will ascend to heaven for us and bring it to us, that we may hear it and do it?' Neither is it beyond the sea, that you should say, 'Who will go over the sea for us and bring it to us, that we may hear it and do it?' **But the word is very near you. It is in your mouth and in your heart, so that you can do it!"***
Deuteronomy 30:10-14 [Emphasis mine]

Wow... that's the exact opposite of what many of us have been told. This is also the very reason why I've been teaching *"Christianity vs The Bible"* for decades. They haven't been entirely honest with us. But don't just take my word for it. What does the Apostle John, Jesus' beloved, say about it?

*By this we know that we love the children of God, when we love God and obey his commandments [Torah]. For this is the love of God, that we **keep his commandments**. And **his commandments are not burdensome**.*
1 John 5:2-3 [Emphasis mine]

Just in case you're not completely convinced that the NT actually tells us to obey "the Law," the Strong's Greek word for "commandments" in this passage is Strong's #G1785 "*entolē*", which means command, ordinance, and/or Torah ("law"). So, just like Deuteronomy 30 says, keeping His Torah commands "are not burdensome." You can do it!

Paul tells us specifically that the Torah is holy, righteous and good (Romans 7:12) and that the Torah is also spiritual (Romans 7:14). Because the Torah is spiritual, it requires a spiritual revelation to understand and grasp it. Walking in obedience to God, His commandments, also requires walking in the Spirit in order to accomplish that obedience, much like salvation does. Attempting to keep Torah (obedience to His instructions) or attempting to walk out salvation (Christianity) in or by our own power; in or by our own reasoning; through works of the flesh or by walking in the flesh versus walking in, living by and abiding in God's Spirit has a guaranteed end result: a religious spirit and/or legalism. Neither is of God, neither is a "blessing," and Torah, obedience, is for blessing. We will touch on this "identity crisis" later.

So yes! We are capable of keeping Torah. We are capable of keeping God's commandments!

What Does Jesus Say About It?

If you're thinking of verses right now that seemingly state otherwise (I've heard quite a few of them), we need to then defer to the established understanding that the Bible doesn't contradict or oppose itself. Whatever it is we *think* those conflicting verses say, they can't be saying what we've been *told* they say. And these verses are more than likely out of context as a whole. Even Jesus stated as much:

> You search the Scriptures [the TaNaKh] because you think that in them you have eternal life; and it is they that bear witness about me... Do not think that I will accuse you to the Father. There is one who accuses you: Moses, on whom you have set your hope. For if you believed Moses, you would believe me; for he wrote of me. But if you do not believe his writings [Torah], how will you believe my words?"
> John 5:39, 45-47

Jesus shared a parable in Luke 16:19-31 about an unnamed rich man and a poor man named Lazarus. This Lazarus was so poor that he would beg for the scraps from the rich man's table of daily elaborate meals. Both men die with the poor man being carried by the angels to Abraham's Bosom (considered a temporal paradise) while the rich man was sent to be tormented in Hades.

The rich man called out for mercy to Abraham asking him to allow Lazarus to bring him some water so that he could cool his tongue while in the anguishing flames. Even now he looked at the poor man as subservient.

Abraham replied explaining that the tables had turned. Lazarus, who had experienced a lifetime of woes, was now experiencing comfort; whereas, the rich man who had enjoyed the good things in life was now to experience punishing torment. Besides, continued Abraham, the gaping chasm between them was designed to keep both sides separated. How was Lazarus to accommodate his request?

The rich man, continuing with his entitled opinion of Lazarus, then begs Abraham to send Lazarus to the rich man's family to warn them of the realities of this afterlife. Abraham tells the rich man,

"They have Moses and the Prophets. They have all that they need to avoid the horrible situation that you find yourself in."

The rich man answered,

"No! If someone were to rise from the dead and go to them they would repent!"

The Abraham character in Jesus' parable countered,

"If they aren't listening to Moses and the Prophets, they're not going to listen to someone that rises from the dead…"

Again. Jesus had no need to accuse those He was speaking to in John 5 before the Father, because Moses is taking care of that. Jesus, the Prophet unto Moses, completely submits, defers and adheres to the authority of Moses constantly throughout the Gospels. Aren't we to be imitators of Jesus, and aren't we being transformed into His likeness by our obedience to Him and that transformational process?

"If you don't believe Moses, you won't believe Me," Jesus says. Yikes! What does this say about everyone that confesses Jesus but doesn't believe that the writings of Moses and/or the prophets apply to them?

> "Do not think that I have come to abolish the Law [Torah] or the Prophets; I have not come to abolish them but to fulfill them. For truly, I say to you, until heaven and earth pass away, not an iota, not a dot, will pass from the Torah until all is accomplished. Therefore, whoever disobeys one of the least of these commandments and teaches others to do the same will be called least in the kingdom of heaven, but whoever does them and teaches them will be called great in the kingdom of heaven.
> Mathew 5:17-19

This passage is huge and somehow incorrectly taught across the board. Jesus clearly states in Matthew 5:17 that He **did not** come to abolish, "do away with," destroy or eliminate, depending on your translation, the Torah and/or the Prophets. End of story. End of discussion.

I had a seminary professor argue what has become a popular position as of late, that because Jesus was speaking to Jews and not Gentiles, this passage regarding Torah observance doesn't apply to Gentile believers. In fact, according to this seminary professor, only around 10 percent of what Jesus actually spoke and taught applied to

Gentiles. I suggested that if that was the case, then only 10 percent of His atoning death and resurrection would apply to Gentiles. He didn't like that very much and proceeded to tell me how 100 percent of His atoning death and resurrection applied to him. I chuckled and suggested that he couldn't have it both ways. (Funny how that's always the case.)

"If only 10 percent of what Jesus actually spoke and taught applied to Gentiles," I concluded, "Then only 10 percent of His atoning death and resurrection applied."

"Now, it might be true that only 10 percent of Jesus applied to this man," I added, "But I was no bastard!"

One hundred percent of what Jesus spoke and taught applied to me and so did 100 percent of His atoning death and resurrection! I am a full son – a full joint heir – with full rights and privileges as such in regards to my Father because of what my Brother Jesus did on my behalf. This is the definition of the Spirit of Adoption. It's the full and complete work of His life, death and resurrection. Not just 10 percent!

I've had others on numerous occasions contest and argue Jesus' instruction to us to observe Torah by (mis)quoting Paul. You're going to argue the Words of Jesus with Paul?!? Yes, this really does occur! Is it any wonder that Paul is preached more than Jesus on any given Sunday, in Any Town, USA?

Anything we can come up with to contest this proclamation by Jesus in Matthew 5 would clearly be completely out of context and futile. It's as clear as "Jesus wept." You can't misinterpret it, and there's also no need for "scholarly exegesis." It's also not an issue of a doctrine or a theology being created from one or two lone verses like so many are so fond of doing. A simple contextual reading of the rest of the chapter proves the contextual integrity of what I'm suggesting. But just to be perfectly clear, the Greek word for abolish, "do away with," destroy or eliminate, depending on your translation, is the Strong's #G2647 "*katalyō*":

1. to dissolve, disunite
    a. (what has been joined together), to destroy, demolish
    b. metaph. to overthrow i.e. render vain, deprive of success, bring to naught
        i. to subvert, overthrow
            a. of institutions, forms of government, laws, etc., to deprive of force, annul, abrogate, discard

c. *of travelers, to halt on a journey, to put up, lodge (the figurative expression originating in the circumstance that, to put up for the night, the straps and packs of the beasts of burden are unbound and taken off; or, more correctly from the fact that the traveler's garments, tied up when he is on the journey, are unloosed at its end)*

Jesus said that He did not come to "*katalyō*" the Torah and the Prophets, but that He came to "complete" or "fulfill," depending on your translation; whereas the Western Church teaches that "fulfill" in this passage means to "do away with" (*katalyō*). In all reality, the word "fulfill" here is actually the Strong's #G4137 Greek word: "*plēroō*".

1. *to make full, to fill up, i.e. to fill to the full*
   a. *to cause to abound, to furnish or supply liberally*
      i. *I abound, I am liberally supplied*
2. *to render full, i.e. to complete*
   a. *to fill to the top: so that nothing shall be wanting to full measure, fill to the brim*
   b. *to consummate: a number*
      i. *to make complete in every particular, to render perfect*
      ii. *to carry through to the end, to accomplish, carry out, (some undertaking)*
   c. *to carry into effect, bring to realisation, realise*
      i. *of matters of duty: to perform, execute*
      ii. *of sayings, promises, prophecies, to bring to pass, ratify, accomplish*
      iii. *to fulfil, i.e. to cause God's will (as made known in the law) to be obeyed as it should be, and God's promises (given through the prophets) to receive fulfilment*

I mentioned that the passage of Matthew 5:17 is incorrectly taught and used to support the "doctrine" that Jesus did away with the Torah. So how do we determine what meaning of the word *plēroō* is being used here? Well, it can't be #2: to complete, as to finish or terminate, as we have been led to believe because then we would have a double negative:

"*Don't think that I have come to abolish / terminate / do away with the Torah or the Prophets. I have come not to abolish / terminate / do away with but to abolish / terminate / do away with."*

This is what many of us have been and continue to be taught to believe this declaration of Jesus is saying. But it simply doesn't jive by itself or contextually. Let's continue reading the chapter to determine the proper and contextual use of the Greek word for "fulfill," *plēroō*, in verse 17. In verses 18-19 Jesus says:

"For truly, I say to you, until heaven and earth pass away, not an iota, not a dot, will pass from the Torah until all is accomplished. Therefore, whoever disobeys one of the least of these commandments and teaches others to do the same will be called least in the kingdom of heaven, but whoever does them and teaches them will be called great in the kingdom of heaven."

I live in beautiful Utah, and I just looked out my window. Guess what? Heaven and earth haven't passed away. They're still there! So then neither *an iota or a dot* of the Torah have passed away either – they're still here!

Also, contrary to popular belief, Jesus isn't speaking of His own death when He says *"...until all is accomplished."* That's another angle some of us have been told, because it plays into their false narrative that Torah was eliminated by Jesus. That's not what's "passing," and that's not what He's referring to. The following verse and the rest of the chapter make that clear, otherwise, Jesus wouldn't continue by addressing Torah in the future tense after His physical death. But even if Jesus *was* speaking of His death, He still made it clear that Torah wouldn't pass until *heaven and earth passed* – not *His* passing.

Do you want to know why He mentions the passing of heaven and earth? ImaGonnaTellYaAnyWays...

We're back with Moses after 40 years in the wilderness and he's assembled Israel on the first day of the Eleventh month. He's recounting their journeys, their victories, their defeats, their times of disobedience and obedience; he's been foretold of his death and that Joshua is to succeed him as Israel's leader, and he begins to read to them the Torah and how God is taking them for a nation unto Himself. If they will obey Gods commandments, the Torah, they'll be blessed, but when they fail to obey His commandments, the Torah, they'll be cursed. And in verse 26 of Deuteronomy 4, Moses calls on heaven and earth as a witness against Israel when, not *if*, but *when* they choose to disobey the Torah. He repeats this charge in chapter 30:

> *"For this commandment that I command you today is not too hard for you, neither is it far off. It is not in heaven, that you should say, 'Who will ascend to heaven for us and bring it to us, that we may hear it and do it?' Neither is it beyond the sea, that you should say, 'Who will go over the sea for us and bring it to us, that we may hear it and do it?' But the word is very near you. It is in your mouth and in your heart, so that you can do it. "See, I have set before you today life and good, death and evil. If you obey the commandments of the LORD your God that I command you today, by loving the LORD your God, by walking in his ways, and by keeping his commandments and his statutes and his rules, then you shall live and multiply, and the LORD your God will bless you in the land that you are entering to take possession of it. But if your heart turns away, and you will not hear, but are drawn away to worship other gods and serve them, I declare to you today, that you shall surely perish. You shall not live long in the land that you are going over the Jordan to enter and possess.* **I call heaven and earth to witness against you today**, *that I have set before you life and death, blessing and curse. Therefore choose life, that you and your offspring may live, loving the LORD your God, obeying his voice and holding fast to him, for he is your life and length of days, that you may dwell in the land that the LORD swore to your fathers, to Abraham, to Isaac, and to Jacob, to give them."*
> Deuteronomy 30:11-20 [Emphasis mine]

That is so beautiful and amazing.

Before going to die, Moses caused a contract between Israel and God: That Israel would keep God's commandments, to live in obedience to the Torah, and he swore that oath against heaven and earth. That's why Jesus, a Prophet unto Moses, declared that heaven and earth will pass away before Torah will.

> *Assemble to me all the elders of your tribes and your officers, that I may speak these words [the Torah] in their ears*

and call heaven and earth to witness against them.
Deuteronomy 31:28 [Emphasis mine]

I asked the question earlier, "What about Christians that confess Jesus but don't believe that the writings of Moses and/or the prophets apply to them?" I'm asked that a lot, and a judgmental answer regarding that person's eternal destination is always anticipated. Instead, I give them Jesus' answer on the matter found in Matthew 5:19:

"Therefore, whoever disobeys one of the least of these commandments and teaches others to do the same will be called least in the kingdom of heaven, but whoever does them and teaches them will be called great in the kingdom of heaven."

If Jesus was going to "do away" with Torah after His death, why would obeying or disobeying Torah – teaching or not teaching Torah – be an issue and a posthumous status qualification? It wouldn't be! In fact, there wouldn't have been another mention of it in the NT except to say, "No. We don't do that no mo." But then that's not the case now, is it?

Back to Matthew 5:

We're told that as humans it is impossible to keep God's commandments successfully, that it's unreasonable to believe that we can live out the Torah, even though both the OT and NT say otherwise. Does Jesus have an opinion on the matter?

In verses 21-47 of this same chapter 5 of Matthew, Jesus explains how He's going to "fulfill," "complete" the Torah, concluding that the correct and contextual definition of the use of the Greek word for "fulfill," *plēroō*, in verse 17 must be the Greek definitions 1. a., 2. a., 2. b. i., 2. c., and especially 2. c. iii. by utilizing anger, lust, divorce, oaths, retaliation, and loving your enemies as examples. Let's look at lust for our example:

"You have heard that it was said, 'You shall not commit adultery.' But I say to you that everyone who looks at a woman with lustful intent has already committed adultery with her in his heart."
Mathew 5:27-28

We've been told that it is impossible for man to keep the requirements of the "Mosaic Law," in this example, *"You shall not commit adultery"* – a physical act of lust. So how does Jesus "fulfill" this Torah commandment? How does Jesus "cause God's will (as made known in the law) to be obeyed as it should be?"

By "making it harder!"

By taking it from a *physical* act to an *invisible intention of the heart* act: *"everyone who **looks** at a woman **with lustful intent** has already committed adultery."*

Whose Torah is *"impossible"* for man to keep the requirements of?!? I promise you, it's a lot easier to say no to physical sexual immorality (Moses) then it is to say no to your thoughts (Jesus). Ask any man. In all actuality, Jesus only brought His Father's instruction back to where it was always intended to reside: the heart.

A simple and contextual reading of Matthew 5 shows us that the Greek word for "fulfill," *plēroō*, in verse 17 cannot and does not mean the Greek word *katalyō* used for abolish, "do away with," destroy or eliminate, depending on your translation. It should be understood that two entirely different Greek words are used in this single passage that many insist on teaching have the same meaning.

We should also note that the Scripture uses words like "forever" (Exod. 12:24), "perpetual" (Exod. 31:16), and "throughout your generations" (Lev. 23:31) in regards to the longevity of obeying God's commandments, the Torah. It never states "until the arrival and/or death and resurrection of My Promised Messiah..."

"Forever," "perpetual," "throughout your generations," and "until heaven and earth pass away" mean exactly what you know they mean and say. Jesus, the author and finisher of our faith, Messiah, the one we claim allegiance to, teaches us that His Father's Commandments – the same Commandments given to Moses for mankind, Torah – are a standing covenant for as long as you, your son and your grandson walk the earth (Deut. 6).

I want to take one last look at whether or not man is capable of keeping Torah, and did Jesus truly "do away with the 'Law'" by His complete and finished work on Calvary as so many of us have been taught.

Let's take a look at Luke 24: Jesus has resurrected from the dead to the surprise of all His disciples. He spends 40 days on earth after His resurrection in His new body with which He can eat fish and walk through walls. He has the ability to appear and disappear. He appears to many of them at various times. He appears to many of them, in different places, at the same *exact* time.

He has just spent hours walking seven miles with two of these disciples where they explained to Him all that had been happening in Jerusalem regarding the death, burial and resurrection of a Jesus of Nazareth. He's rebuked them for their lack of understanding (not very "Christian" of Him) and explains to them everything that's been written about this Jesus starting with the Torah and the Prophets (verses 13-27).

They arrive at their destination, and as He raises the matzah to bless it (*matzah* is unleavened bread – He raised matzah because it was the Feast of Unleavened Bread), their eyes are opened and they recognize that it's Him (verses 28-31).

These disciples rush back to Jerusalem to where everyone else is gathered (hiding actually), and as they're discussing all of these things:

> ...Jesus himself stood among them, and said to them, "Peace to you!" But they were startled and frightened and thought they saw a spirit [you think?]. And he said to them, "Why are you troubled, and why do doubts arise in your hearts [because you're dead, and you just materialized out of thin air maybe?!?]? See my hands and my feet, that it is I myself. Touch me, and see. For a spirit does not have flesh and bones as you see that I have." And when he had said this, he showed them his hands and his feet.
>
> Then he said to them, "These are my words that I spoke to you while I was still with you, that everything written about me in the Law of Moses and the Prophets and the Psalms must be fulfilled." Then he opened their minds to understand the Scriptures.
> Luke 24:36-40, 44-45

In Luke's Gospel, the last thing Jesus did to His disciples before leading them to Bethany and blessing them was to open up their minds to the TaNaKh: the Torah, the Prophets and the Psalms... maybe He wanted them, wanted us, to understand so that we could also do...

In Summary

This book is written with the assumption in mind that you have, in some way and to some extent, received the revelation or are in the process of receiving the revelation, that the Scriptures, the TaNaKh, the "Old Testament" – and the information and instructions therein – haven't been *"done away with,"* and somehow, in some way, and to some extent, must apply to those calling upon the name of ADONAI, today; i.e. "Christians." You.

That the instructions found in the TaNaKh, the literal covenant outline for how to live in obedience to the God we claim to confess allegiance to – through the life exemplified and the finished work of Jesus on Golgotha – was not eradicated by the death and resurrection of Jesus but rather empowered by that sacrifice. That it is a perpetual covenant applicable to us today and, because we love Jesus, we will keep His commandments.

That, in fact, at one time you [Gentiles] had no Messiah. You were estranged from the national life of Isra'el. You were foreigners to the covenants [Torah] embodying God's promise. You were in this world without hope and without God.

But now, you who were once far off have been brought near through the shedding of the Messiah's blood. For he himself is our shalom [peace] — he has made us both one and has broken down the m'chitzah [wall of separation] which divided us [Jew and Gentile] by destroying in his own body the enmity occasioned by the Torah, with its commands set forth in the form of ordinances. He did this in order to create in union with himself from the two groups a single new humanity [One New Man] and thus make shalom, and in order to reconcile to God both in a single body by being executed on a stake as a criminal and thus in himself killing that enmity.

Also, when he came, he announced as Good News shalom to you far off and shalom to those nearby, [Isaiah 57:19] news that through him we both [Jew and Gentile] have access in one Spirit to the Father.

So then, you are no longer foreigners and strangers. On the contrary, you are fellow-citizens with God's people and members of God's family. You have been built on the founda-

> tion of the emissaries [Apostles] and the prophets, with the cornerstone being Yeshua [Jesus] the Messiah himself. In union with him the whole building is held together, and it is growing into a holy temple in union with the Lord. Yes, in union with him, you yourselves are being built together into a spiritual dwelling-place [succah] for God!
> Ephesians 2:12-22 (CJB)

Before we continue, agree with me again in prayer, if you will:

Father, we thank you for your Spirit of Wisdom and Revelation. We ask that the eyes of our understanding be opened to the reality of Your Word.

I pray, Holy Spirit, that this reader would welcome You and allow You to open their ears to hear You and allow You to open their eyes to see You.

Any spirit of confusion or religion, you have no authority or influence here!

Father we ask for your Grace and Mercy as we unlock the blessings of your Feasts, that we would continually desire to be in alignment with You and Your Word.

In the name of Your Son, Jesus of Nazareth.

Amen.

TABLE OF CONTENTS

THE BIBLICAL FEASTS OF OUR GOD	1
THE NEW MOON - ROSH CHODESH	15
THE SABBATH - SHABBAT	43
PASSOVER (PESACH) AND THE FEAST OF UNLEAVENED BREAD	87
FEAST OF FIRSTFRUITS / FEAST OF WEEKS (THE OMER COUNT)	133
SHAVUOT (WEEKS) / PENTECOST	165
FEAST OF TRUMPETS (YOM TERUAH) / DAY OF ATONEMENT (YOM KIPPUR)	181
FEAST OF TABERNACLES (SUKKOT)	203
IN CONCLUSION	221
FEAST OF DEDICATION (HANUKKAH) / PURIM	247
BIBLIOGRAPHY	261
INDEX	263

CHAPTER 1

THE BIBLICAL FEASTS OF OUR GOD
Leviticus 23 wants to be your BFF

> *These are the appointed feasts of the LORD that you shall proclaim as holy convocations; they are my appointed feasts.*
> Leviticus 23:2

Leviticus 23 is going to serve as our general guide. We will also be using additional scripture passages as we narrow down each feast and/or instruction. I say "feast and/or instruction" because, for example, Passover (Pesach) and Tabernacles (Sukkot) are "feasts," but the Sabbath and the Counting of the Omer are more "instructions" and not "feasts" per se.

The individual Chapters will breakdown each feast and/or instruction.

Fundamentally and foundationally, the Feasts are designed to assist us as individuals, families and communities in experiencing and visualizing annually the life God intends for us to live with, in and for Him. Essentially, the act of keeping the Feasts represents alignment with Father God by way of keeping His appointed times for specific purposes. This is crucial to understand for living an actual scriptural lifestyle. Let me repeat this: Keeping the Feasts, His appointed times, is how we align our lives and lifestyles with God for His specific Kingdom purposes "on earth as it is in heaven." Let's begin.

The Hebrew word for "feast" is *mo'ed* (Strong's #H4150) meaning "appointed place," "appointed time," or "appointed meeting;" a fixed time or season. And what are the purposes for these "holy convocations," these "holy gatherings" of a "solemn assembly"? Well, the answer to that is found in my personal favorite definition for the Feasts: "convocation," which in the Hebrew means "a rehearsal": *miqra'* (Strong's #H4744). The Appointed Feasts of our God are *Holy Rehearsals!* Rehearsals for what, you might ask? Rehearsals for us to practice today to prepare us for tomorrow. They also serve as reminders of the past (Exod. 12:24-27). The Feasts are mandated appointed times and places of meeting – to meet with our God – for which we are required to assemble. Isn't that wonderfully amazing?!?

It's simple: if you and I are going to have a lunch date and it was my turn to pick and I decided on Original Tommy's on Beverly and Rampart in Los Angeles at 1:00 pm on Tuesday, there's no way that we're going to have lunch together if you go to In-N-Out in Burbank at 3:00 pm on Thursday. If you *truly* want to be when and where I am, you're going to be at Tommy's on Tuesday at 1:00 pm. Problem is, the Romanized Western Church believes that it actually doesn't matter *where* they go or *when* they go or even *if* they go to have lunch with me. Meanwhile, I'm at Tommy's every Tuesday at 1:00 pm waiting for you, but you never show up.

> *"Because these people approach me with empty words, and the honor they bestow on me is mere lip-service; while in fact they have distanced their hearts from me, and their 'fear of me' is just a mitzvah (commandment) of human origin..."*
> Isaiah 29:13 (CJB)

Remember when Jesus told the Pharisees that they were exactly like the Prophet Killers and they adamantly said, "No way!" and how they insisted that they would *never* have aligned themselves with them, ever, and how they would have believed the Prophets had they lived back then, and yet all the while they were scheming to murder Messiah?

I am constantly trying to be convinced by others that they too would have been at the Jordan to listen to John or how they too would have been where Jesus would have been had they lived back then, etc. Really? My Bible tells me exactly when and where God will be, All-Year-Long, yet these same people don't believe they actually need to be there. But I digress...

God said, "Let there be lights in the dome of the sky to divide the day from the night; let them be for signs, seasons [mo'ed], days and years;
Genesis 1:14

As we go forward and deeper into unlocking the Feasts, you'll start to appreciate how Father God establishes things from the very beginning for His people. You'll start to see the character and Person of Messiah and the Father's heart toward the "ingathering" of His people unto Himself – very much like a mother hen.

Because God's calendar is an agricultural one, the Feasts are intricately connected to the land. This is why Jesus used agricultural metaphors as often as He did in the Gospels. Words like planting, seeds and reaping within concepts of sowing, seasons and harvesting, etc.

The first three Spring Feasts are connected to barley, the first crop in Israel's yearly harvest. Seven weeks later (50 days) the assembly is gathered for the wheat harvest and to participate in the receiving of Torah and the baptism of Pentecost on their way to the ingathering of the produce harvest of Tabernacles.

The Feasts are a massive part of Israel's identity; individually, corporately, physically and spiritually. Imagine the richness these yearly experiences brought to families and individuals. Jesus knew this, so the agricultural symbolism in His discourses rang true to His listeners. Look for it in your studies.

I've included the majority of Leviticus 23 below for an easy reference as we go forward. I have removed instructions regarding animal sacrifices and some offerings such as "offer a male lamb a year old without blemish as a burnt offering," "seven lambs a year old without blemish, and one bull from the herd and two rams. They shall be a burnt offering to the LORD, with their grain offering..." etc., etc., because we can't offer lambs and bulls due to the fact that there isn't a Temple at which to sacrifice nor a Levitical Priesthood to administer such things. I've kept the offerings we can observe such as food offerings, drink offerings, etc.

Critics, or those who don't agree that Torah is applicable to Christians today because of Jesus...

NOTE: I want to make it excruciatingly clear right now that I do not look down upon or judge those who may believe that Torah is not applicable to Christians today because of Jesus. As I stated clearly in the

Introduction, in the same way that Salvation is a spiritual revelation from God, obeying the scriptural instructions of Torah are also a spiritual revelation from God. Salvation is through the Blood of Jesus, and obeying God's commandments is for blessing. We choose to obey the commandments of God, because we love Jesus. Jesus clearly stated that if we loved Him, we would keep His commandments, but I do not judge those that have made the choice not to observe "the law" in the same way I don't judge those that don't speak in tongues, for example.

Back to our original programming:

Because we can't offer lambs and bulls due to the fact that there isn't a Temple at which to sacrifice nor a Levitical Priesthood to administer such sacrifices, I've kept the offerings we can observe and that we're instructed to administer such as food offerings, drink offerings, etc.

Those that don't agree that Torah is applicable to Christians in the Western Church today because of Jesus, do the "Aha!" out of Psalms right about here...

"You see", they'll say, "You can't fully observe the Torah instruction because there *is* no Temple and there *is* no Levitical Priesthood. You can't observe *any* of the sacrificial requirements of the Law fully and correctly because you're not *supposed* to be following the Law!" or something quite close to that.

It's a valid position, but it's stated out of ignorance and scriptural illiteracy. Not all "laws" apply to all of us. There are Torah instructions specifically for women. There are Torah instructions specifically for farmers. There are Torah instructions specifically for government officials, and there are Torah instructions specifically for Levites. The Torah instructions regarding the Temple sacrifices are Levite specific. This is where I also remind these "critics" of what the Bible says about Israel being taken into Babylonian captivity for not keeping the Sabbath Year, a commandment in the Torah. As punishment for not keeping the Law, God destroyed His Temple and had Israel taken away to where they wouldn't be able to fully and correctly observe close to two-thirds of the Torah (like today), and yet they were still expected to keep His commandments in Babylon without a Temple.

Thus says the LORD of hosts, the God of Israel: "Add your burnt offerings to your sacrifices, and eat the flesh. For in the day that I brought them out of the land of Egypt, I did

not speak to your fathers or command them concerning burnt offerings and sacrifices. But this command I gave them: 'Obey my voice, and I will be your God, and you shall be my people. And walk in all the way that I command you, that it may be well with you.' But they did not obey or incline their ear, but walked in their own counsels and the stubbornness of their evil hearts, and went backward and not forward. From the day that your fathers came out of the land of Egypt to this day, I have persistently sent all my servants the prophets to them, day after day. Yet they did not listen to me or incline their ear, but stiffened their neck. They did worse than their fathers.
Jeremiah 7:21-26

I threw that in there to show that it's *not* about the animal sacrifices; it has never *been* about the animal sacrifices, then, now or tomorrow. It has *always* been about obedience to God's voice and walking in His ways as He has commanded us. That's basically the simple point of this book: obey ADONAI's voice and walk in His ways as He has commanded us. Why? So that He can be our God and so that we can be His people. Remember that, because you're going to hear it again and again: Obey ADONAI's voice and walk in His ways as He has commanded us. So that He can be our God and so that we can be His people...

Ezekiel and his wife lived on the bank of the Chebar River in Tel Abib, on the Kebar Canal, near Nippur in what is now Iraq. Ezekiel kept the commandments (Torah) of God while in Babylon without a Temple:

*"...And you shall eat it as a barley cake, baking it in their sight on **human dung**." And the LORD said, "Thus shall the people of Israel **eat their bread unclean**, among the nations where I will drive them." Then I said, "Ah, Lord GOD! Behold, **I have never defiled myself. From my youth up till now I have never eaten what died of itself or was torn by beasts, nor has tainted meat come into my mouth.**" Then he said to me, "See, I assign to you cow's dung instead of human dung, on which you may prepare your bread."*
Ezekiel 4:12-16 [Emphasis mine]

Ezekiel kept the dietary instructions before and during the Babylonian exile. Daniel, another exile from Jerusalem in Babylon, also kept the commandments during his exile:

> *The king assigned them [the Jewish exiles in his court] a daily portion of the food that the king ate, and of the wine that he drank. But Daniel resolved that he would not defile himself with the king's food, or with the wine that he drank. Therefore, he asked the chief of the eunuchs to allow him not to defile himself. And God gave Daniel favor and compassion in the sight of the chief of the eunuchs [...] Then Daniel said to the steward whom the chief of the eunuchs had assigned over Daniel, Hananiah, Mishael, and Azariah, "Test your servants for ten days; let us be given vegetables to eat and water to drink. Then let our appearance and the appearance of the youths who eat the king's food be observed by you, and deal with your servants according to what you see." So he listened to them in this matter, and tested them for ten days. At the end of ten days it was seen that they were better in appearance and fatter in flesh than all the youths who ate the king's food.*
> Daniel 1:5a, 8-9a, 11-15

In chapter 3 of Daniel, the Babylonian King erects a statue that all the people must worship. Daniel's Jewish companions, Hananiah, Mishael, and Azariah, refuse to worship the graven image, because it would be sinful to do so – the New Testament clearly states that sin is the breaking of Torah (1 John 3:4). Daniel and his companions observed Torah in Babylon without a Temple.

Daniel's favor was ever increasing, so his peers were devising a plot to subvert him. These men knew that they would never find any basis for charges against Daniel unless it had something to do **with the law of his God**. So they convinced the king to sign a decree that anyone who prayed to any god or human being during the next thirty days, except to the king himself, should be thrown into a lions' den. You can read the entire account of how Daniel observed Torah in Babylon without a Temple in chapter 6 of Daniel's book.

And finally, in chapter 9, when Daniel determined through the scriptures that Israel's exile would be 70 years, he pleaded with God in prayer and petition, in fasting, and in sackcloth and ashes. Daniel writes in verses 20-21:

> While I was speaking and praying, confessing my sin and the sin of my people Israel and making my request to the LORD my God for his holy hill – while I was still in prayer, Gabriel, the man I had seen in the earlier vision, **came to me in swift flight about the time of the evening sacrifice** [offering]. (NIV)

Yes, dear reader. During the Babylonian exile, just as it is today, Israel didn't have a Temple or an acting Levitical priesthood to administrate close to two-thirds of the commandments written in the Torah. But they were expected to observe the commandments that they could keep/observe without adding to or taking away from the Torah just as we are also expected to do today.

The Appointed Feasts – Leviticus 23

The LORD spoke to Moses, saying, "Speak to the people of Israel and say to them, These are the appointed feasts of the LORD that you shall proclaim as holy convocations; they are my appointed feasts."

The Sabbath / Shabbat

"Six days shall work be done, but on the seventh day is a Sabbath of solemn rest, a holy convocation. You shall do no work. It is a Sabbath to the LORD in all your dwelling places."

Passover (Pesach) / Feast of Unleavened Bread

"These are the appointed feasts of the LORD, the holy convocations, which you shall proclaim at the time appointed for them. In the first month, on the fourteenth day of the month at twilight, is the LORD's Passover. And on the fifteenth day of the same month is the Feast of Unleavened Bread to the LORD; for seven days you shall eat unleavened bread. On the first day you shall have a holy convocation (a High Sabbath); you shall not do any ordinary work. But you shall present a food offering to the LORD for seven days. On the seventh day is a holy convocation (a High Sabbath); you shall not do any ordinary work."

The Feast of Firstfruits

And the LORD spoke to Moses, saying, "Speak to the people of Israel and say to them, When you come into the land that I give you and reap its harvest, you shall bring the sheaf of the firstfruits of your harvest to the priest, and he shall wave the sheaf before the LORD, so that you may be accepted (a Firstfruits Offering). On the day after the Sabbath the priest shall wave it. And on the day when you wave the sheaf, the grain offering shall be of fine flour mixed with oil, a food offering to the LORD with a pleasing aroma, and the drink offering with it shall be of wine. And you shall eat neither bread (no leaven) nor grain parched or fresh until this same day, until you have brought the offering of your God: it is a statute forever throughout your generations in all your dwellings."

Counting of the Omer / Feast of Weeks

You shall count seven full weeks from the day after the Sabbath, from the day that you brought the sheaf of the wave offering. You shall count fifty days to the day after the seventh Sabbath.

Shavuot / Pentecost

Then you shall present a grain offering of new grain to the LORD. You shall bring from your dwelling places two loaves of bread to be waved. They shall be of fine flour, and they shall be baked with leaven, as firstfruits to the LORD. And the priest shall wave the bread of the firstfruits as a wave offering before the LORD. They shall be holy to the LORD for the priest.

And you shall make proclamation on the same day. You shall hold a holy convocation (a High Sabbath). You shall not do any ordinary work. It is a statute forever in all your dwelling places throughout your generations. And when you reap the harvest of your land, you shall not reap your field right up to its edge, nor shall you gather the gleanings after your harvest. You shall leave them for the poor and for the sojourner: I am the LORD your God."

The Feast of Trumpets / Yom Teruah

And the LORD spoke to Moses, saying, "Speak to the people of Israel, saying, In the seventh month, on the first day of the month, you shall observe a day of solemn rest, a memorial proclaimed with blast of trumpets, a holy convocation (a High Sabbath). You shall not do any ordinary work, and you shall present a food offering to the LORD."

The Day of Atonement / Yom Kippur

And the LORD spoke to Moses, saying, "Now on the tenth day of this seventh month is the Day of Atonement. It shall be for you a time of holy convocation (a High Sabbath), and you shall afflict (humble) yourselves and present a food offering to the LORD. And you shall not do any work on that very day, for it is a Day of Atonement, to make atonement for you before the LORD your God. For whoever is not afflicted (does not humble themselves) on that very day shall be cut off from his people. And whoever does any work on that very day, that person I will destroy from among his people. You shall not do any work. It is a statute forever throughout your generations in all your dwelling places. It shall be to you a Sabbath of solemn rest, and you shall afflict (humble) yourselves. On the ninth day of the month beginning at evening, from evening to evening shall you keep your Sabbath."

The Feast of Booths (Tabernacles) / Sukkot

And the LORD spoke to Moses, saying, "Speak to the people of Israel, saying, On the fifteenth day of this seventh month and for seven days is the Feast of Booths to the LORD.

On the first day shall be a holy convocation (a High Sabbath); you shall not do any ordinary work. For seven days you shall present food offerings to the LORD. On the eighth day you shall hold a holy convocation (a High Sabbath) and present a food offering to the LORD. It is a solemn assembly; you shall not do any ordinary work.

"On the fifteenth day of the seventh month, when you have gathered in the produce of the land, you shall celebrate the feast of the LORD seven days. On the first day shall be a solemn rest, and on the eighth day shall be a solemn rest. And you shall take on the first day the fruit of splendid trees, branches of palm trees and boughs of leafy trees and willows of the brook, and you shall rejoice before the LORD your God seven days. You shall celebrate it as a feast to the LORD for seven days in the year. It is a statute forever throughout your generations; you shall celebrate it in the seventh month. You shall dwell in booths for seven days. All native Israelites shall dwell in booths, that your generations may know that I made the people of Israel dwell in booths when I brought them out of the land of Egypt: I am the LORD your God." Thus Moses declared to the people of Israel the appointed feasts of the LORD.

Overview and Summary of the Seven Feasts

As we unlock the Feasts together, we will discover how the first three Spring Feasts are foundational to our deliverance, the fourth feast establishes our relationship with God as His Bride and the Fall Feasts represent the relational and eternal purposes of God through our repentant cleansing and redemption. Notice how each feast points towards Messiah:

Feast	Jesus
Passover Unleavened Bread Firstfruits	Death Burial Resurrection
Shavuot / Pentecost	Covenant / One New Man
Trumpets Atonement Tabernacles	Call to Salvation Holy of Holies / Repentance Indwelling / Sabbath Rest

Three times a year, every first born Israeli male was to present himself before ADONAI in Jerusalem, the three Pilgrimage Festivals. In this passage from Exodus, the Feasts are divided into those three feast cycles:

> *"Three times a year, you are to observe a festival for me. Keep the festival of matzah: for seven days, as I ordered you, you are to eat matzah at the time determined in the month of Abib; for it was in that month that you left Egypt. No one is to appear before me empty-handed. Next, the festival of harvest, the firstfruits of your efforts sowing in the field; and last, the festival of ingathering, at the end of the year, when you gather in from the fields the results of your efforts. Three times a year all your men are to appear before the Lord, ADONAI."*
> Exodus 23:14-17 (CJB)

Festival of Matzah - Unleavened Bread

- Beginning of the scriptural calendar and barley harvest (Exod. 12:6; Lev. 23:5-8; Num. 28:16)
- First month of the year

- Three Spring Feasts:
  - Passover
  - Feast of Unleavened Bread
  - Feast of Firstfruits

Festival of Harvest - Shavuot

- Third month of the year
- Feasts of Weeks / Counting of the Omer, a 7-week wheat harvest (Exod. 34:26; Lev. 23:10-14; Num. 28:26-31) period of thanks for provision culminating in
  - Shavuot (Weeks): His Word
  - Pentecost: Holy Spirit

Festival of Ingathering – Tabernacles / Sukkot

- Seventh month of the year
- End of the Year and produce harvest (Exod. 23:16)
- Feast of Tabernacles / Sukkot

Each feast season is designed to speak to a spiritual exchange between us and the Father.

Passover speaks to our sin and the sacrifice of blood required for atonement and our deliverance from Egypt – "our carnal state". Unleavened Bread speaks to the purging of sin and bad doctrine/leaven from our lives and homes. Firstfruits: the joy of bringing firstfruits to ADONAI after the redemptive process of deliverance.

The seven-week Count of the Omer – Feast of Weeks – keeps our focus on His continued spiritual and physical provision with the anticipation of the wheat harvest. Shavuot (Weeks) itself speaks of the actual wheat harvest of God's physical provision in our lives and the spiritual provision of His Word – Torah – at Mount Sinai. Shavuot also reveals His desire to betroth us as His Bride through the covenant of Torah – His initial "marriage proposal." The giving of His Holy Spirit at Pentecost completes His richness given to us to live life abundantly.

The Fall Feasts speak of our being called to Him with the blast of the shofar; the consecration of our cleansing through repentance and the redemption given us with the ingathering of His people, His Bride, unto Himself, a people that would become His "tabernacle" in which to dwell in their midst in His Sabbath Rest.

Spiritual Application of the Feasts

Feast	Spiritual Application
Passover (Pesach)	Blood atonement for our sin nature Salvation through faith in the shed blood of the Lamb Deliverance from Egypt
Unleavened Bread (Hag HaMatzah)	Death and entombment of "old man" and sin nature Separation and removal of sin and bad doctrine (leaven) from our lives and homes
Firstfruits (Bikkurim)	Resurrected "One New Man" Newness of life
Feast of Weeks (Omer Count & Shavuot (Weeks) / Pentecost	Increase of the harvest of our lives through acceptance of God's Wedding Contract Immersion and indwelling of Holy Spirit
Feast of Trumpets (Yom Teruah)	Call to action Sound of the call on our lives Alignment, assembling, and linking shields
Day of Atonement (Yom Kippur)	Repentance Submission
Feast of Tabernacles (Sukkot)	Ingathering Wedding Feast Messiah's Sabbath Rest

"Therefore, say to the Israelites: 'I am the LORD, and I will bring you out from under the yoke of the Egyptians. I will free you from being slaves to them, and I will redeem you with an outstretched arm and with mighty acts of judgment. I will take you as my own people, and I will be your God. Then

you will know that I am the LORD your God, who brought you out from under the yoke of the Egyptians. And I will bring you to the land I swore with uplifted hand to give to Abraham, to Isaac and to Jacob. I will give it to you as a possession. I am the LORD.'"
Exodus 6:6-8 (NIV)

"'You yourselves have seen what I did to Egypt, and how I carried you on eagles' wings and brought you to myself. Now if you obey me fully and keep my covenant [Torah], then out of all nations you will be my treasured possession. Although the whole earth is mine, you will be for me a kingdom of priests and a holy nation.' These are the words you are to speak to the Israelites."
Exodus 19:4-6 (NIV)

This was the purpose of delivering Israel from Egypt – from delivering *you* from your Egypt – to become God's Treasured Possession from among all the nations – to be a Kingdom of Priests unto Himself – a Holy Nation.

And these are the biblical Feasts of our God. His yearly steps of deliverance, steps that lead us into His presence, steps of transformation into His Treasured Possession – a Kingdom of Holy priests, steps of spiritual power, not legalistic ritual.

CHAPTER 2

THE NEW MOON – ROSH CHODESH
I saw Mr. Moon last night

> Blow the trumpet at the new moon, at the full moon, on our feast day.
> Psalm 81:3

Before we can begin, we need to have a brief discussion about time. We, as in "we" in the West, keep to the Gregorian calendar and time model. The Gregorian calendar, birthed at the Vatican and also known as the Christian calendar (that delineation should tell you something) is solar-based. This basically means the day starts with the rising of the sun and ends with the setting of the sun.

In contrast, God's scriptural calendar and time model, established in written form by Moses after the exodus from Egypt and during Israel's time in the wilderness, is lunar-based. This time model was established in Genesis 1 and basically means that the day starts at sunset and (traditionally) ends at sunset. I say "traditionally," because the actual scripture says "evening, and there was morning" instead of saying "evening, and there was evening," whereas it does say "evening to evening" in Leviticus 23:32 making it widely known and accepted that this is what is meant. The key here is that the day starts in the evening at sunset and not in the morning with the rising of the sun.

> God called the light Day, and the darkness he called Night. So there was evening, and there was morning, one day.
> Genesis 1:5

Now here's where things can start to get a little confusing, but I'm going to explain it as I go along (don't be afraid.)

The Jewish calendar, or the fixed Hebrew calendar, months are determined by the New Moon conjunction. This calendar, credited as being finalized by the Nasi of the Sanhedrin, Hillel II (330-365 CE), though foundationally based on God's calendar, is lunisolar, meaning it keeps in sync with the natural cycles of both the Sun and the Moon. The simplest way to explain the difference between the two is like this: God's calendar is outlined in scripture; whereas, the Jewish calendar has also incorporated dates and methods that are deemed "traditional" and "rabbinical" respectively, as well as various secular modifications. They differ in some ways (I'll explain) but they also fall in line on occasion.

Oral Traditions, Talmud and Rabbinical Judaism vs Scripture

The Jewish calendar, though foundationally based on God's calendar, has seen changes throughout the millennium due to Rabbinical religious and secular modifications. For the sake of ease and definition, the word "Talmud" from here on out will represent the Rabbinical and/or the Pharisees' and Sadducees' religious traditions and the infamous "Traditions of Men." Here's what I mean:

Rabbis and Sages throughout the ages have had commentaries on the Torah in oral and written form since the Third Century. These commentaries, oral traditions and collective writings on Torah observance are typically known as "Talmud." Think of the Talmud as a custodian, a fence, a "guideline," or a "safety net" for understanding and keeping Torah commands. The idea behind Talmud is that you won't break the actual Torah commands if you don't break the extracurricular Talmudic instructions – the "safety net." In other words, by adding additional instructions to Torah by utilizing Talmud as a fail-safe, you won't break Torah. The Catch 22 here is that it is against the Torah itself to add to it or to take away from it (this is where Christianity gets their idea regarding adding to or taking away from the Bible.) Thus, following Talmudic instruction to avoid the breaking of Torah, or better yet, following Talmudic instruction above and beyond Torah, which has become the case, is basically breaking Torah. Does that make sense?

Here's an example of how Talmud "overrides" Torah: In Numbers 15:37-40 we are instructed to wear tassels (Hebrew *"tzitzit".*) There are only two instructions to this command:

1. Wear the tassels on the corner of your garments, and
2. Put a blue thread on each corner of the tassel

Easy enough, right? Well, Talmudic oral tradition states that this blue fringe must be dyed with the blood of a shellfish known as *"chilazon."* Since we don't know the actual identity of this aquatic or semi-aquatic creature or the actual hue of blue that was used or that is meant to be used, so as not to break the commandment by using the wrong blue or deriving a blue from the wrong sea creature, Talmudic thought process concludes that we're not to wear any blue at all in our tassels – all-white tassels without any blue in them. This would be a Talmudic fail-safe so as **not** to break the actual Torah command. But by regulating the commandment with this extracurricular instruction, they break the core instruction of the literal commandment by wearing only all-white tassels.

There are 606 Scriptural Torah commandments. Through the process of oral traditions and additional Rabbinical teachings and time, seven additional "laws" have been added to the original Torah count of 606 for a total of 613 "laws." Here are the seven additional "laws," also known as the Seven Rabbinic Mitzvahs (commands) not found in scripture:

1. Saying Hallel

The reciting of Psalms 113 - 118 on certain special occasions. It's actually more exhaustive than this, but this book isn't about that.

2. Blessings

Rabbinical scripted blessings for various occasions: finding pleasure in eating, drinking or smelling fragrances. Witnessing a natural phenomenon like a meteor shower or going from a mediocre to a better wine... You get the idea.

3. Washing Hands Before Eating

This actually comes up in Mark 7 so we'll unpack it a bit in a few minutes. The rabbis decreed that one must wash one's hands in a prescribed manner before eating bread, ensuring that hands would be washed before sacred foods were eaten. Thus the rabbis stretched out this law and decreed that one should wash one's hands any time bread is eaten.

4. Eruv on the Sabbath / Shabbat

"Eruv" is a technical boundary that allows Jews to carry items in public areas or places on the Sabbath. It's a mechanism that makes these restrictions more permissive with three kinds of *eruvs*... yeah, I'm

not going to get into that.

5. Shabbat Candles

Jewish homes at the beginning of the Sabbath must light at least two candles as well as on Rosh Hashana, Yom Kippur, Sukkot, Pesach and Shavuot.

6. Purim

Purim celebrates the miracle of Israel's salvation via Queen Esther and her adopted father Mordechai from certain extermination by the Persians in 355 BCE. The celebration was established at the request of Queen Esther and/or Mordechai, instructing all Jews to celebrate a joyous festival on the 14th day in the month of Adar.

7. Hanukkah

Hanukkah celebrates the victory of the Maccabees and Israel's salvation from the hands of the Greeks in 165 BCE. It also celebrates the miracle of one day's worth of oil for the Temple menorah that kept on burning for eight days.

The last thing I want to do, and the last thing I want to see anyone else do is replace one set of manmade traditions, such as the ones found in the Romanized Western Church, with another set of manmade traditions, such as the ones found in Rabbinical Judaism. What would be the point of that? Unfortunately, this is a frequent occurrence with many that begin their journey into Torah observance without any responsible guidance or leadership.

Being obedient to the scriptures and keeping and observing God's Sabbaths and Feasts are not about "being Jewish." Stop! Proper name correction for the purposes of this book:

- "Jew" / "Jewish" = the race / ethnicity (physical) and religion
- "Hebrew" = genetics / genealogical
- "Israelite" = ancient political
- "Israel" = modern political and,
- The "Israel of God" (spiritual)

Being obedient to the scriptures and keeping and observing God's Sabbaths and Feasts isn't about "being Jewish." It's about being the Israel of God; it's about being obedient. Nothing that we're discussing or going to discuss is about "trying to be Jewish." That's also ridiculous (Rev. 2:9, 3:9).

God's Feast Days and Sabbaths being "Jewish" is a common false narrative in the Romanized Western Church dating as far back as the second and third centuries and the birth of the Roman Catholic Church (more specifics in Chapter 3). This false delineation was intended to control and discourage Gentile believers from observing Torah. Added to this was the "discouraging" of the reading of the scriptures by anyone not of the clergy. Also implementing "canons" outlawing actual Torah commands like the observance of Passover, eating unleavened bread and scriptural Sabbath observance created a winning combination that the enemy was more than happy to pervert – on both sides of the aisle – for centuries to come. Remember: Protestant Christianity is "re-formed" Catholicism.

We've been told that the Biblical Sabbath and God's Biblical Feasts Days are the "Jewish Sabbath" and "Jewish Holidays." No. They're not. The scriptures actually never say that. What the scriptures *do* say is that the Sabbath is actually God's, not "Jewish," and that the Sabbath of God is a covenant sign between Him and His people (Exodus 31:13). The scriptures also say that the Feasts days are *His* Holy Days, not "Jewish," and that these Feasts are mandated appointed times for His people. Now, if you don't consider yourself one of God's covenant people, then by all means, don't participate, but the Bible also tells us not to judge those of us that do participate (Col. 2:16). You see, I want to be "*His* people!" I want to be counted in that number! I want to be the Bride of Christ!!

I do realize that some New Testament translations make the delineation of certain feasts as "Jewish," but their origins found in Deuteronomy, Leviticus, Exodus and Numbers clearly state that they are "Adonai's" – God's Feasts, not "Jewish."

With that in mind, making the decision to eat biblically (notice that I said "biblically" and that I didn't say "kosher;" kosher is Rabbinical), or making the decision to keep and observe the scriptural Sabbath and God's Feasts doesn't require anyone to start wearing kippahs, head coverings or tallits! Kippahs are skull caps for men, aka yarmulkes (Yiddish), while head coverings are scarves or shawls that women place over their heads. We understand the New Testament teaching of head coverings to represent "spiritual covering" and are only required to be worn when a woman lacks spiritual covering such as a father or husband, and a tallit is a prayer shawl for men. Kippahs and tallits are Rabbinical and traditional. Torah observance also doesn't require you to wear white linen outfits with colored scarves around your waist at church or the carrying around of an imitation-gold encrusted shofar.

Just to be perfectly clear: I am not anti-kippahs, anti-head coverings, anti-tallits, or anti-shofars. I'm simply anti-goofiness.

Do I own a kippah? Yes. If not wearing a head covering is going to keep me out of a situation, I'd rather have one than not. But since I have dreadlocks, I'm usually wearing a head covering anyways.

Do I own a tallit? Yes. Two of them. One is a priceless, prophetic and sentimental gift, and the other is the one I usually wear when I actually wear a tallit.

Do I own a shofar? Absolutely! A very large "war" one.

Again, this isn't about exchanging one set of traditions for another, and this also isn't cosplay! This isn't about getting weird or being weird. This is about being scriptural – I just want to be scriptural! I don't want to be "weird."

Le sigh...

I say all this, because there are four traditional things that we, as a community / as a church, do and they're not done for any of the reasons just mentioned:

- Shabbat Candles
- Passover Seder
- Purim, and
- Hanukkah

Each of these will be covered in their respective Chapters as to why and how we observe them.

Now back to the examples of how religious and manmade traditions have usurped God's calendar and God's Word.

In Mark 7, Jesus is challenged and confronted by *the Pharisees with some of the scribes who saw that some of his disciples ate with hands that were defiled, that is, unwashed. (For the Pharisees and all the Jews do not eat unless they wash their hands,* **holding to the tradition of the elders,** *and when they come from the marketplace, they do not eat unless* *they wash.* ***And there are many other traditions that they observe****, such as the washing of cups and pots and copper vessels and dining couches.)*

*And the Pharisees and the scribes asked him, "Why do your disciples not walk **according to the tradition of the elders**, but eat with defiled hands?" And he said to them, "Well did Isaiah prophesy of you hypocrites, as it is written, "'This people honors me with their lips, but their heart is far from me; in vain do they worship me, **teaching as doctrines the commandments of men.'** [Isaiah 29:13]* ***You leave the commandment of God and hold to the tradition of men."***

And he said to them, ***"You have a fine way of rejecting the commandment of God in order to establish your tradition thus making void the word of God by your tradition*** *that you have handed down. And many such things you do."*

Mark 7:1-9, 13 [Emphasis mine]

"Their worship of Me is useless, because they teach manmade rules as if they were doctrines." Sound familiar? "Because of the traditional teachings you uphold you make the scriptures, the Word of God (Torah), null and void…"

The Romanized Western Church has been teaching for centuries that Jesus opposed the Pharisees because they observed Torah, not that Jesus opposed the Pharisees because of their observance and teaching of manmade traditions as if they were theologies and doctrines *trumping* the Torah.

- The Torah doesn't make the Scriptures null and void. The Torah *is* the scripture!
- The Torah isn't manmade rules. The Torah is *God's* rules

So where would the Western Church get this idea that Jesus opposed the Pharisee's because of Torah observance and why?

Quick note because those that would be against Torah "post Jesus" have already thought about it. Mark 7:

Jesus gives an example of how the Pharisees and Torah-teachers taught manmade traditions as doctrine in verses 10-13. Some of you might be on the verge of exploding right about now because of verses

14-23, which is why I have to address it.

There are those that would say that verses 14-23 make a clear case for anti-Torah and especially the dietary restrictions. Really? After what we just read? Yup. Really...

> And he called the people to him again and said to them, "Hear me, all of you, and understand: There is nothing outside a person that by going into him can defile him, but the things that come out of a person are what defile him."
>
> And when he had entered the house and left the people, his disciples asked him about the parable. And he said to them, "Then are you also without understanding? Do you not see that whatever goes into a person from outside cannot defile him, since it enters not his heart but his stomach, and is expelled?" (Thus he declared all foods clean.)
>
> And he said, "What comes out of a person is what defiles him. For from within, out of the heart of man, come evil thoughts, sexual immorality, theft, murder, adultery, coveting, wickedness, deceit, sensuality, envy, slander, pride, foolishness. All these evil things come from within, and they defile a person."

Some will point out verses 18-19 where Jesus "declared all foods clean." They'll erroneously and adamantly conclude that with these standalone verses Torah observance was done away with, generally, and that the dietary restrictions were done away with, specifically, (this is also done with Acts 10 as well). Here's why I say "erroneously": *context*.

In order for anyone to come to this conclusion they have to take verses 18 and 19 out of context. You'll hear me say "context" all the time, and I say that because we have a really bad habit of tossing out context to support our various agendas. The context for Mark 7 is found in the first 5 verses where Jesus is asked in verse 5:

> "Why do your disciples not walk according to the tradition of the elders, but eat with defiled hands?"

1. The questioning isn't about Torah; the questioning is about tradition: *ritual hand washing*
2. The questioning isn't about *what* is permissible to eat, the questioning is about whether or not eating is

permissible *without ritual handwashing*

Remember that contextually Jesus is advocating for the *keeping* of the scriptural commandments against traditions and manmade doctrines (Mk. 7:6-9, 13), not *neglecting* them (doing away with them.) We see that in verses eight and nine:

> *"You leave the commandment of God and hold to the tradition of men." And he said to them, "You have a fine way of rejecting the commandment of God in order to establish your tradition!"*

Jesus is obviously not going to circumvent scripture (the commandments) regarding eating in verse 19 when He's clearly criticizing the Pharisees and Torah-teachers for doing that very thing: circumventing scripture. Remember, the context is traditional hand washing, *not* Torah observance or the dietary instructions.

Compare this same discussion in Matthew's account (15:1-20) where Jesus concludes by saying,

> *"...but to eat with unwashed hands does not defile the man."*

Because the subject of Mark 7:1-19 is ritual handwashing and *not* the dietary Torah commands, Mark 7:1-19 is also *not* about *abolishing* the dietary Torah commands! Look at the context.

Furthermore, the Western Church's definition of "food" isn't *God's* definition of "food," and it wouldn't have been Jesus' definition of food. Remember, Jesus only says what He hears the Father say, and Jesus only does what He sees the Father do. Jesus' definition of "food" is *God's* definition of food, and it's most definitely not the *Western Church's* definition of "food." So even if Jesus *is* talking about food, which He's not, He most definitely isn't supporting the eating of pork and lobster!

When you take into consideration what is scripturally deemed "clean" or "unclean" regarding food for human consumption (Lev. 11; Deut. 14), contextually Mark 7:19 correctly says, "Thus He declared all foods (*things considered "food" by God as fit for human consumption*) clean – regardless of ritual hand washing."

How do I know for certain that Jesus isn't actually talking about "food" in verse 19? Because He tells us what He *is* talking about in verses 20-23!

> "What comes **out** of a person **is what defiles him**. For **from within, out of the heart of man**, come evil thoughts, sexual immorality, theft, murder, adultery, coveting, wickedness, deceit, sensuality, envy, slander, pride, foolishness. All these evil things come from within, and they defile a person."

[Emphasis mine]

You see, Mark 7 is not an argument for the abolishment of the dietary commandments. It's in support of keeping God's commandments over manmade rules and traditions taught as doctrines...

We have a similar convoluted discrepancy in Acts 15.

Acts 15 is regarding whether or not Gentiles should be ritually circumcised for salvation. To dispute the instruction by the Council of Jerusalem – that Gentiles are indeed expected to observe Torah but they do not have to undergo ritual circumcision for salvation – the Western Church has twisted the text in verses 10 and 19, similar to the way that they've twisted Mark 7:19. They take the reference to tradition, the context, and erroneously call it Torah! Here's Acts 15:10:

> Now, therefore, why are you putting God to the test by placing a yoke on the neck of the disciples that neither our fathers nor we have been able to bear?

The "yoke" of this verse is the context of the chapter: ritual circumcision / tradition – *not* Torah observance. We, as in "we the Church," instead teach that this "yoke" is Torah, therefore, Gentiles were not instructed to observe Torah, and verses 10 and 19 are used as their proof text citing Torah as the "yoke" that was troubling and unbearable! Here's what your mind *should* be remembering when you read that:

- Deuteronomy 30 says the Torah is not too hard, it's not beyond my reach and I can do it
- 1 John 5 says that keeping Torah is not burdensome, and
- Jesus said in Matthew 11:30 that His yoke is easy and His burden is light

It's obvious that the Council of Jerusalem isn't referencing Torah in verses 10 and 19 simply because of the chapter's context, and because the biblical texts clearly teach that Torah isn't a burdensome yoke! Furthermore, contextually, the Council isn't discussing or contesting Torah – exactly like in the case of Mark 7. They're discussing whether or not Gentiles need to be circumcised *ritually, for salvation.* That's the entire reason for this meeting. Even when it's suggested in verse five that Gentiles need to be circumcised (not for salvation) and directed to observe Torah in verse five, it is never contested by the Council. In fact, the conclusion of the matter is thus: In order for Gentiles to even qualify for salvation, they must observe two Torah commands and two instructions also based on Torah, known as "*halakhah*" (more in a minute on that.) Did you see that? In order for Gentiles to even *qualify for salvation* they must observe two Torah commands and two instructions also based on Torah. James, the brother of Jesus and the leader of the church, came to this conclusion in verses 19-20, and James instructs the Gentiles to follow this ruling in a letter as seen in verses 28-29. Read it for yourself:

> "Therefore my judgment is that we should not trouble those of the Gentiles who turn to God, but should write to them to abstain from the things polluted by idols, and from sexual immorality, and from what has been strangled, and from blood."

> "For it has seemed good to the Holy Spirit and to us to lay on you no greater burden than these requirements: that you abstain from what has been sacrificed to idols, and from blood, and from what has been strangled, and from sexual immorality. If you keep yourselves from these, you will do well. Farewell."

Two of these regulations, abstain from sexual immorality (Exod. 20:14; Lev. 18:6-20, 22-23; 20:10-16) and abstain from blood (Gen. 9:4; Lev. 17:10, 12-14) are direct Torah commands. The other two rulings, abstain from strangled meats (see the scripture references to blood) and abstain from the things polluted by idols (more on this in the next section), are considered *halakhah*: "rulings derived from Torah." Take note: these four foundational instructions for Gentiles who desire to come to salvation speak directly to their paganism. The instructions for Gentile salvation continues in verse 21:

"For from ancient generations Moses has had in every city those who proclaim him, for he is read every Sabbath in the synagogues."

Translation: Since the time Torah was given to Moses, every city has had Torah-observant believers who meet on the Sabbath in the synagogues where the Torah is taught.

Q. When and where are these Gentile converts going to meet?
A. On the Sabbath in the synagogue.

Q. What are these Gentile converts going to be taught?
A. The Torah and the Prophets.

Q. Why were prospective Gentile believers instructed to abstain from blood, meat offered to idols, strangled meats and sexual immorality?
A. Because these actions spoke of their paganism. Being a Gentile didn't just mean they were non-Jews. It also meant that they were pagans. And as pagans, their beliefs consisted of ritual fornication, idol worship, the eating of pagan-sacrificed meats and ritual blood eating. You can't really be a disciple of Jesus if you're going around doing that! So, if you're seriously considering Christianity...

Q. What does the Book of Acts say Paul's ministry was?
A. It states that he taught the Torah and the Prophets in the synagogue on the Sabbath to Jews and Gentiles.

Halakhah and the Gentile Converts

Halakhah (Hebrew) literally means "the way to behave" or "the way of walking." Halakhah are instructions derived from Torah – this is *not* "adding" to the Torah – and the ruling by James and the Council of Jerusalem in Acts 15 is a great example of how "additional" instruction (think "amendments") was needed to accommodate this new and exciting chapter in the church: The Gentiles had been granted access to Messiah!

By the time Peter was sent to Cornelius in Acts 10, the church was roughly 20 – 25 years old and it was exclusively Jewish. The church was so new, in fact, that when the Judaizers infiltrated Paul and Barnabas' work among the Gentiles with their flawed teaching that these new Gentile converts had to undergo ritual circumcision in order to be saved, Paul and Barnabas didn't have the answer! This is why they went to Jerusalem in Acts 15 to seek counsel and instruction from the leadership in regards to the Judaizers' teaching of ritual circumcision among Gentiles for salvation.

As we're seeing, opening the doors of faith to Gentiles was proving to have its own challenges. The Council of Jerusalem not only addressed the matter regarding ritual circumcision for Gentile salvation, they also "adapted" four key instructions that would directly speak to Gentile paganism:

1. Abstain from the things polluted by idols
2. Abstain from sexual immorality
3. Abstain from what has been strangled, and
4. Abstain from blood

Abstaining from the things polluted by idols, be it items used in and for pagan rituals, ceremonies, and/or food or meats, etc., would be considered a halakhah instruction derived from Torah. James, the brother of Jesus and the leader of the church, along with the Council members would have made this ruling based on scripture. Chances are they had Exodus 34:12-16 in mind:

> Take care, lest you make a covenant with the inhabitants of the land to which you go, lest it become a snare in your midst. **You shall tear down their altars and break their pillars and cut down their Asherim** (for you shall worship no other god, for the LORD, whose name is Jealous, is a jealous God), lest you make a covenant with the inhabitants of the land, **and when they whore after their gods and sacrifice to their gods and you are invited, you eat of his sacrifice**, and you take of their daughters for your sons, and their daughters whore after their gods and make your sons whore after their gods.
> [Emphasis mine]

Eating, or partaking of a pagan sacrifice, is not permissible even though there isn't a standalone commandment that states "Thou shalt not..." The implication here is clear: Do not make covenant with pagans and eat of their food sacrifice that is made to their pagan gods. This is also known as "spiritual adultery." To avoid this sin, tear down their pagan places of worship. Thus, abstinence from things polluted by idols is a logical and scripturally based ruling: Halakhah.

Another scriptural reference the Council more than likely had in mind was Numbers 25:1-3:

> While Israel lived in Shittim, the people began to whore with the daughters of Moab. **These invited the people to the sacrifices of their gods, and the people ate and bowed down to their gods.** So Israel yoked himself to Baal of Peor. And the anger of the LORD was kindled against Israel.

[Emphasis mine]

Here the eating of food sacrificed to pagan idols is mixed with sexual immorality and pagan worship. We've already looked at the stand-alone commandments that state "Thou shalt not..." in regards to sexual immorality and the worship of false gods. Lacking a direct "Thou shalt not..." in regards to the eating of food sacrificed to idols doesn't mean it's a good idea to do so. Again, abstaining from the things polluted by idols is a logical and scripturally-based ruling for these new Gentile converts with a pagan background. Remember, the instructions for new Gentile converts in Acts 15 were speaking directly to their pagan roots:

> The converted gentiles just came out of a system that engaged in pagan sun god worship. Active worship included going to the Temple, sacrificing, eating of that sacrifice, drinking its blood and engaging in Temple prostitution. That is why James mentions all of these things. James is telling converted gentiles that a true believer must first stop worshipping false gods before learning the Torah which is the next instruction found in verse 21.

(Source: 119 Ministries "Meat Sacrificed to Idols" http://www.119ministries.com/teachings/video-teachings/detail/meat-sacrificed-to-idols)

Romans 14 and 1 Corinthians 8 are frequently cited by those that don't agree with Torah observance for Christians as "proof text" against the dietary instructions found in Torah. Once again, we have to remember that the Western Church's definition of "food" isn't the same definition established by God in Leviticus 11 and Deuteronomy 14, the same definition of food that would have been used by Rabbi Sha'ul (the Apostle Paul.) Besides, contextually, neither Romans 14 nor 1 Corinthians 8 are about the dietary instructions. Contextually, they're about the buying and eating of food / meat that may or may not be sacrificed to idols.

The real question you should be asking yourself right about now is why would Paul be needing to instruct his Gentile churches regarding "eating meat offered to idols" if the Torah instructions forbidding such activity weren't applicable to Gentiles? If Paul himself didn't observe Torah, and if Acts 15 isn't actually saying what we've been taught it says? But that's another conversation...

> One person believes he may eat anything, while the weak person eats only vegetables.
> Romans 14:2

We're discussing the eating habits of the weak individual that has decided to only eat vegetables. Why? Well, to avoid the possible sin, judgment and/or confusion from eating meat that may or may not be scarified to idols many were apparently turning to vegetarianism. Contextually, Romans 14 is also about not stumbling weaker believers.

Verse 14, yet another standalone verse out of context, is used to renounce the dietary Torah instructions because of Paul's statement, "nothing is unclean in itself, but it is unclean for anyone who thinks it unclean." When you put this statement in context with the whole of the Bible, as you should with everything, you cannot conclude that Paul is saying that "pork chops are now on the menu." Here's how he unpacks this statement in 1 Corinthians:

> Therefore, as to the eating of food offered to idols, we know that "an idol has no real existence," and that "there is no God but one." However, not all possess this knowledge. But some, through former association with idols, eat food as really offered to an idol, and their conscience, being weak, is defiled. Therefore, if food makes my brother stumble, I will never eat meat, lest I make my brother stumble.
> 1 Corinthians 8:4, 7, 13

Again, the subject isn't the dietary instructions of Torah. The subject is the eating of food / meat that may or may not be sacrificed to idols and the weaker believer's conviction regarding so. The dialog continues in chapter 9 where Paul quotes Torah to make his point.

Are we to believe that in chapter 8 Paul is teaching "freedom from the dietary law," yet he's quoting "the law" in his defense in the next chapter? That's completely unsound reasoning, and it would be extremely hypocritical of Paul! By the way, quoting verse 20 would be a shallow and inaccurate understanding of the passage considering Paul continues this discourse in chapter 10 where he goes back to Torah. Here's Paul's conclusion of the matter in 1 Corinthians 10 that started in 1 Corinthians 8 (context, context, context!):

> What do I imply then? That food offered to idols is anything, or that an idol is anything? No, I imply that what pagans sacrifice they offer to demons and not to God. **I do not want you to be participants with demons**. You cannot drink the cup of the LORD and the cup of demons. You cannot partake of the table of the LORD and the table of demons.
>
> Eat whatever is sold in the meat market without raising any question on the ground of conscience.
>
> If one of the unbelievers invites you to dinner and you are disposed to go, eat whatever is set before you without raising any question on the ground of conscience. **But if someone says to you, "This has been offered in sacrifice," then do not eat it**, for the sake of the one who informed you, and for the sake of conscience... I do not mean your conscience, but his.
>
> 1 Corinthians 10:19-21, 25, 27-29a [Emphasis mine]

Paul is not circumventing his leadership, James' authority, or James' instruction in Acts 15 regarding abstaining from things polluted by idols with Romans 14 or 1 Corinthians 8. If anything, Paul is supporting and expounding on the instruction.

The Calendar

Where were we again? Oh yeah. Time... he's still waiting in the wings... God's calendar is outlined in scripture, whereas, the Jewish calendar is "traditional." Here is a very brief example:

God's Calendar	Jewish Calendar
Lunar Based: The day starts at sunset and ends at sunset (Gen. 1:5). The key is that the day starts in the evening at sunset	Lunisolar Based: The day also starts and ends at sunset (Gen. 1:5). The calendar keeps in sync with the natural cycles of both the Sun and the Moon
Months are determined by the visible New Moon crescent - Rosh Chodesh (Exod. 12:1-2, Num. 10:10) thus determining the dates of the Feasts days, etc.	By 1178 CE mathematical approximation calculation and the New Moon conjunction replaced the sighting of the New Moon determining both the beginning of a new calendar month and the dates of the Feasts days, etc.
Shavuot / Pentecost will always be on a Sunday based on the Counting of the Omer commencing after the Feast of Firstfruits which is always at the end of the first weekly Sabbath following Passover, during Unleavened Bread, regardless of the date	Shavuot will be on Sivan 6 based on the Omer Count established by the Pharisees, starting at the end of the High Sabbath of the First Day of the Feast of Unleavened Bread
Purim and Hanukkah are traditional not mandated holidays	Purim and Hanukkah are listed as mandated holidays

We adhere to God's scriptural calendar and time model by default. On occasion, the fixed Jewish calendar, based on the New Moon conjunction, will coincide with the Scriptural calendar. We try to stay flexible in this regard so as not to alienate ourselves from our Jewish brethren. After all, we're to provoke Israel to jealousy unto salvation in Messiah (Romans 11).

As we'll see, the Feasts are synonymous with God's agricultural calendar. They also have an important cyclical order to them. You find this cyclical rhythm in the weekly cycle of the Sabbath, a weekly life reboot if you will, in the monthly cycle of the New Moon and in the yearly cycle of the Feasts themselves. The lunar calendar follows the cycle of the moon as it waxes and wanes each month.

To add to the confusion, the fixed Jewish calendar has the Biblical / Hebrew names of the months and their Babylonian renames – the Civil calendar order, a Babylonian-based hybrid, (the civil calendar is used for common dates such as birthdays, contracts, etc.) that starts with Yom Teruah / Rosh HaShanah ("Head of the Year") on Ethanim / Tishrei 1 and, the Religious calendar order (the scriptural / religious calendar is used for the Feasts and festivals) that starts on Abib / Nisan 1:

Jewish Calendar			
Scriptural (Babylonian)	**Gregorian**	**Feast**	**Civil Order**
Abib (Nisan)	March - April	Passover / Feast of Unleavened Bread / Feast of Firstfruits	Tishrei (7)
Ziv (Iyar)	April - May	Feast of Weeks / Counting of the Omer	Kheshvan (8)
Third (Sivan)	May - June	Shavuot / Pentecost	Kislev (9)
Fourth (Tammuz)	June - July		Tevet (10)
Fifth (Av)	July - Aug		Shevat (11)
Sixth (Elul)	Aug - Sept		Adar (12)
Ethanim (Tishrei)	Sept - Oct	Feast of Trumpets / Day of Atonement / Feast of Tabernacles	Nisan (1)
Bul (Kheshvan)	Oct - Nov		Iyar (2)
Ninth (Kislev)	Nov - Dec	Hanukkah	Sivan (3)
Tenth (Tevet)	Dec - Jan		Tammuz (4)

Eleventh (Shevat)	Jan - Feb		Av (5)
Twelfth (Adar)	Feb - March	Purim	Elul (6)

The New Moon

Now that we've gotten all of that out of the way...

The New Moon – Rosh Chodesh ("head of the month") – determines the beginning of the month and in turn the dates for the Feast Days (Numbers 10:10). Because of the lack of conclusive scriptural clarity regarding the "how" in regards to the definitive determination of the New Moon and the absence of a governing body to determine which and when the New Moon is sighted, I'm going to address the three popular New Moon observances:

- Conjunction
- Visible Crescent Jerusalem
- Visible Crescent Present

Conjunction

Technically, a new moon starts in darkness. To be truly accurate, the new moon month starts in the lunar conjunction. A lunar conjunction is when the earth, moon, and sun, in that order, are approximately in a straight line. From conjunction to visible crescent is approximately two to three days. There are those that believe that the New Moon should be calculated based on a lunar conjunction. The following passage shows that Israel had knowledge of the lunar conjunction to determine when their Rosh Chodesh feasting should begin, but it should also be noted that it wasn't until the visible crescent was seen that Rosh Chodesh was officially started:

> David said to Jonathan, "Behold, tomorrow is the new moon, and I should not fail to sit at table with the king. But let me go, that I may hide myself in the field till the third day at evening." Then Jonathan said to him, "Tomorrow is the new moon, and you will be missed, because your seat will be empty. On the third day [...]" And when the new moon came, the king sat down to eat food. But on the second day, the day

after the new moon, David's place was empty.
1 Samuel 20:5, 18-19, 24, 27

They knew when the New Moon was coming but set aside three days for feasting. "And when the new moon came" was it a visible crescent? In *Laws Concerning the Sanctification* by Maimonides, it states that mathematical calculations were used to determine the sighting of the New Moon. These calculations assisted in the gathering of the members of the court that would confirm a visible crescent sighting in order to alert the people that Rosh Chodesh had arrived.

To make matters more confusing, are we to adhere to the lunar conjunction based on Jerusalem time or...?

Visible Crescent Jerusalem (VCJ)

Visible Crescent Jerusalem is exactly what it sounds like. Those that adhere to VCJ await to see the visible crescent over Jerusalem or await the news that the visible crescent has been sighted over Jerusalem before blowing the shofar for Rosh Chodesh.

Visible Crescent Present (VCP)

Those that adhere to VCP look for the visible crescent to appear in their local time zone or await the news that the visible crescent has been sighted. At that time, the shofar is blown for Rosh Chodesh. We adhere to Visible Crescent Present but also take into consideration the New Moon Conjunction in order to estimate the sighting of the crescent for the scheduling of our public gatherings.

Rosh Chodesh

Blow the trumpet at the new moon, at the full moon, on our feast day.
Psalm 81:3

From new moon to new moon, and from Sabbath to Sabbath, all flesh shall come to worship before me, declares the LORD.
Isaiah 66:23

"Thus says the Lord GOD: The gate of the inner court that faces east shall be shut on the six working days, but on the Sabbath day it shall be opened, and on the day of the new moon it shall be opened."
Ezekiel 46:1

On seeing the visible crescent, the elders would declare that Rosh Chodesh, the beginning of the month, had commenced. The entire calendar is dependent on this New Moon declaration. Without it, there would be no way of knowing when the Feasts days are supposed to occur.

Rosh Chodesh is the perfect time for thanksgiving and reflection on the previous month as a family and as a community. Celebrate Rosh Chodesh as a festive family celebration with the blowing of the shofar, worship, and a meal. The New Moon is also the time to look with anticipation toward all that ADONAI is doing physically, financially, spiritually, and prophetically in our lives. Look forward with a teaching on the meaning of the new month. Through prayer and/or inquiring of the prophets, like the Shunammite women had a habit of doing (2 Kings 4:22-23), look forward prophetically for God's revelation for the month to come. Rosh Chodesh is also a great time to bring to ADONAI the first portions of your monthly harvest: Firstfruits (Proverbs 3:9-10).

Firstfruits

"When you come into the land that the LORD your God is giving you for an inheritance and have taken possession of it and live in it, you shall take some of the first of all the fruit of the ground, which you harvest from your land that the LORD your God is giving you, and you shall put it in a basket, and you shall go to the place that the LORD your God will choose, to make his name to dwell there. And you shall go to the priest who is in office at that time and say to him, 'I declare today to the LORD your God that I have come into the land that the LORD swore to our fathers to give us.' Then the priest shall take the basket from your hand and set it down before the altar of the LORD your God. And you shall make response before the LORD your God,
'And behold, now I bring the first of the fruit of the

ground, which you, O LORD, have given me.' And you shall set it down before the LORD your God and worship before the LORD your God. And you shall rejoice in all the good that the LORD your God has given to you and to your house, you, and the Levite, and the sojourner who is among you. You have declared today that the LORD is your God, and that you will walk in his ways, and keep his statutes and his commandments and his rules, and will obey his voice. And the LORD has declared today that you are a people for his treasured possession, as he has promised you, and that you are to keep all his commandments, and that he will set you in praise and in fame and in honor high above all nations that he has made, and that you shall be a people holy to the LORD your God, as he promised."
Deuteronomy 26:1-5a, 10-11, 17-19

You, the Levite and the sojourner, were to put the first portion of their harvest into a basket and offer it to ADONAI by giving their firstfruits to the priest and declaring God's goodness and faithfulness. They would also declare that ADONAI was their God and that they would walk in His statutes and covenants and obey His voice. They recognized His promise that they were a people for His treasured possession and that they were to keep His commandments. If they would honor Him in that way, He would bless them incredibly.

This firstfruits (Hebrew *"bikkurim"*) covenant refers to the seven species of fruits found in the Promised Land: wheat, barley, grapes, figs, pomegranates, olives, and dates (Deut. 8:8). The giving of these monthly firstfruit offerings are not to be confused with the firstfruits brought at the yearly Feast of Firstfruits as you will see in Chapter 5.

Firstfruits is significant. Did you know that the firstborn male received a double inheritance, and every firstborn male child and male animal were to be consecrated unto ADONAI? (Exodus 13:2) Being the first is significant, and honoring the Father with your first, as a sign of your source of blessing, is important to Him and significant to you.

Ask the Father what your monthly firstfruits offering amount should be. It can be a monetary amount from your job, a side venture or a bonus. It can also be actual vegetables and/or fruits from your garden. Your monthly firstfruits is the first of your harvest, be it monetary or otherwise. Honoring the Father with your first and best is the principle behind firstfruits.

Tithing, Offerings and Firstfruits

Giving in the form of firstfruits, offerings and tithes are all Torah instructions. It's important for us to discuss the differences between tithing, offerings and firstfruits, not only because they are three separate forms of giving, but because scripture defines them as three different forms of giving:

In Nehemiah 7, we see the list of returned exiles from Babylon that are back in the Land of Israel. In chapter 8, we see Ezra the priest and scribe reading the Torah of Moses to the Assembly of Israel, just as Moses and Joshua had done hundreds of years before. In chapter 9, we see that the Assembly of Israel confessed their sin and reestablished their covenant in writing with ADONAI. In chapter 10, they list the leaders of the Assembly who sealed that covenant and the list of obligations of that covenant. It is here that we want to look at the three forms of giving:

> *"We obligate ourselves to bring the firstfruits of our ground and the firstfruits of all fruit of every tree, year by year, to the house of the LORD; and to bring the first of our dough, and our contributions [offerings], the fruit of every tree, the wine and the oil, to the priests, to the chambers of the house of our God; and to bring to the Levites the tithes from our ground, for it is the Levites who collect the tithes in all our towns where we labor. For the people of Israel and the sons of Levi shall bring the contribution [offerings] of grain, wine, and oil to the chambers, where the vessels of the sanctuary are, as well as the priests who minister, and the gatekeepers and the singers. We will not neglect the house of our God."*
> Nehemiah 10:35, 37, 39

- Firstfruits (verses 35, 37) are to be brought to the priests
- Contributions / offerings (verses 37, 39) are to be brought to the priests, and
- Tithes (verse 37) are to be brought to the Levites, for it is the Levites who collect the tithes

The Torah defines the duties and compensation of the Priests and Levites. Let's take a look at Numbers 18:21-24:

> *"To the Levites I have given every tithe in Israel for an inheritance, in return for their service that they do, their service in the tent of meeting, so that the people of Israel do not come near the tent of meeting, lest they bear sin and die. But the Levites shall do the service of the tent of meeting, and they shall bear their iniquity. It shall be a perpetual statute throughout your generations, and among the people of Israel they shall have no inheritance. For the tithe of the people of Israel, which they present as a contribution to the LORD, I have given to the Levites for an inheritance. Therefore I have said of them that they shall have no inheritance among the people of Israel."*

You have to ask yourself why the Mainstream Western Church would insist on taking the tithes of God when the tithe doesn't belong to them. It belongs to the Levites exclusively.

Now, I understand that some church leaders today believe that they're in the role that the Levities played in the Temple, thus the continued institution of tithing. But that's just not the case. Chances are your "pastor" isn't from the Tribe of Levi, and chances are your church believes that they're not "under the Law." Well, tithing is a "law," a Torah command, exclusively for Levites. I also doubt that any church leaders today would welcome the stipulation of having no inheritance either. The tithe belongs to the Levite. Leave it alone.

This is why we don't "tithe," per se, but instead give monthly firstfruits and offerings to Israel first (literally) and then to the House (church) that feeds us. It shouldn't be, but I know that this is quite a shocker to many when they first hear of it, that we don't "tithe." Again, we only want to be scriptural...

In Genesis 14:17-24, Abraham receives a blessing from Melchizedek and in turn, Abraham gives Melchizedek a tenth of everything – even though there is no Levite or Temple. Melchizedek trumps a Levitical priest. Jesus is a priest in the order of Melchizedek who, as you know, has no earthly lineage. Abraham not only discerned a ruling supernatural authority, he also sows into this ruling supernatural authority. Abraham receives a blessing that transcends 400 earth years! The writer of Hebrews expounds:

> See how great this man was to whom Abraham the patriarch gave a tenth of the spoils! And those descendants of Levi who receive the priestly office have a commandment in the law to take tithes from the people, that is, from their brothers, though these also are descended from Abraham. But this man who does not have his descent from them received tithes from Abraham and blessed him who had the promises. It is beyond dispute that the inferior is blessed by the superior. In the one case tithes are received by mortal men, but in the other case, by one of whom it is testified that he lives. One might even say that Levi himself, who receives tithes, paid tithes through Abraham, for he was still in the loins of his ancestor when Melchizedek met him.
> Hebrews 7:4-10

This is some heavy stuff, and it covers the teaching and question of tithing and the Levites into the New Testament. If you continue reading, you'll see that the writer is expressly discussing "priesthood." This discussion started in chapter 4 and continues into chapter 9 making erroneous the argument by those that are not in support of Torah for Christians that Hebrews 8:13 proves the dissolving of Torah. The topic is the priesthood, not Torah. And then there's that nagging little dialog of Jesus in the red letters known as Matthew 5. But I digress... again...

This "tenth of everything" from Abraham to Melchizedek could also be looked at as firstfruits giving. The more you think about it, the more examples of how you can participate in firstfruits giving will come up. Awesome, isn't it?

Firstfruits are an act of honoring God with the first of what you receive, whereas offerings are an expression of thanksgiving, an act of worship for God's blessings in your life. Both of these, firstfruits and offerings, are given to the priest of the house (your church, your home church, etc.), and the tithe belongs to the Levites exclusively. Here are a couple passages regarding the blessings of firstfruits giving:

> And the first of all the firstfruits of all kinds, and every offering of all kinds from all your offerings, shall belong to the priests. You shall also give to the priests the first of your dough, that a blessing may rest on your house.

Ezekiel 44:30

> Honor the LORD with your wealth and with the firstfruits of all your produce; then your barns will be filled with plenty, and your vats will be bursting with wine.

Proverbs 3:9-10

Firstfruits giving can also be expressed through the giving of our time. This is why I mentioned earlier that Rosh Chodesh was a great time to bring your monthly firstfruits.

In Summary

Appointed Time: Rosh Chodesh

Significance: The beginning ("head") of a new month

Observance: Rosh Chodesh, like Shabbat, is a monthly "reboot" and the perfect time for thanksgiving and reflection on the past month as a family and as a community. Rosh Chodesh is *not* a day to abstain from ordinary work except in the case of Yom Teruah (more on that in Chapter 7). Celebrate Rosh Chodesh as a festive family celebration with the blowing of the shofar, worship and a meal. The New Moon is also the time to look with anticipation toward all that ADONAI is doing physically, financially, spiritually and prophetically in our lives. Look forward with a teaching on the meaning of the new month. Through prayer and/or inquiring of the prophets, like the Shunammite women had a habit of doing (2 Kings 4:22-23), look forward prophetically for God's revelation for the month to come. Rosh Chodesh is also the time to bring to ADONAI the first portions of your harvest: Firstfruits

Length: 24 hours, sunset to sunset

Earlier in this Chapter, I mentioned cycles. I mentioned how the Feasts are synonymous with God's agricultural calendar with an important cyclical order to them and how we find these cyclical rhythms in the weekly cycle of the Sabbath, in the monthly cycle of the New Moon and in the yearly cycle of the Feasts themselves. These cycles take us from harvest (Passover and Firstfruits) to harvest (Feast of Weeks) towards increase (Shavuot / Pentecost), culminating with the year-end harvest gathering of the Feast of Ingathering – all with an aspect of firstfruits along the way.

This ever-forward, yearly-momentum of "further up and further in" speaks to lifestyle participation. As we grow in our knowledge, worship of giving and in the sowing into of firstfruits, so will our provision and blessing grow. Firstfruits is spiritual in nature, intended to produce a Kingdom mindset in us.

I also mentioned that we don't "tithe." Instead, we give of our firstfruits monthly and we give offerings; to Israel first and then to the House that feeds us. We give to "Israel first" based on the following:

- God's covenant promise to Abraham in Genesis 12:3: *"I will bless those who bless you, and, in you all the families of the earth shall be blessed."*
- *Pray for peace in Jerusalem. May all who love this city prosper.* Psalm 122:6 (NLT)
- *At present, however, I am going to Jerusalem bringing aid to the saints. For Macedonia and Achaia have been pleased to make some contribution for the poor among the saints at Jerusalem. For they were pleased to do it, and indeed they owe it to them. For if the Gentiles have come to share in their spiritual blessings, they ought also to be of service to them in material blessings.* Romans 15:25-27

Salvation and blessing are to the Jew first (Ro. 1:16; 2:10), and my Salvation in Jesus is from the Jews (Jesus in John 4:22). In Acts 10, a Roman centurion of the Italian Regiment was visited by an angel because his prayers and his acts of charity, his gifts to the poor, had gone up and become a memorial before God. These are some of the reasons why we give to "Israel first," and then we give to the House (Church) that feeds us and then to the needs of others.

We keep to God's biblical calendar to determine His Feasts Days. That calendar is based on the sighting of the visible crescent in our local time zone. This determines the New Moon (Rosh Chodesh) and the beginning of the month and, in turn, the days that the Feasts begin and end.

On occasion, the fixed Jewish calendar, based on the New Moon conjunction, will coincide with the Scriptural calendar, so we try to stay flexible in this regard so as not to alienate our Jewish brethren (Romans

11). Again, this is about obeying the commandments because we love Jesus – not the legalistic observance of Torah commands for any reason.

On seeing the visible crescent, the elders would declare that Rosh Chodesh, the beginning of the month and a type of "firstfruits" had commenced. Seeking God's favor and blessing for the month ahead, the people would gather to celebrate in the dedication of the head of the month.

Rosh Chodesh is a time of joyful celebration and treated as a Sabbath. It is a time for worship, celebration and feasting – not fasting. And it is a time to seek the prophets for the coming month as an individual, a family and as a community. (Psa. 81:3; Hos. 2:11; Amos 8:5; Num. 28:11-15; Num. 10:10; Isa. 66:23; 1 Sam. 20:5; 2 Kings 4:23)

Celebrate Rosh Chodesh as a festive family celebration with the blowing of the shofar, worship and a meal. The New Moon is also the time to look with anticipation toward all that ADONAI is doing physically, financially, spiritually and prophetically in our lives. Look forward with a teaching on the meaning of the new month. Through prayer and/or inquiring of the prophets, like the Shunammite women had a habit of doing (2 Kings 4:22-23), look forward prophetically for God's revelation for the month to come.

Download our Calendar to assist you with determining Rosh Chodesh and the Feasts in your own home: http://chameleonchurch.com/pdf/calendarGuide.pdf

CHAPTER 3

THE SABBATH - SHABBAT
"This is a sign that I sanctify you." – God

>And on the seventh day God finished his work that he had done, and he rested on the seventh day from all his work that he had done. So God blessed the seventh day and made it holy, because on it God rested from all his work that he had done in creation.
>Genesis 2:2-3

>Six days shall work be done, but on the seventh day is a Sabbath of solemn rest, a holy convocation. You shall do no work. It is a Sabbath to the LORD in all your dwelling places.
>Leviticus 23:3

A few years ago I reconnected with an old friend of mine that was briefly in a band with my youngest brother back in the mid to late '80's in Los Angeles. We'll call him… "Bill." Bill has known our family from the very beginning; good, bad or indifferent. We continue to treasure his friendship and the friendship of *his* family today.

Bill has had a pretty good vantage point when it came to watching my wife and I navigate the waters of parenthood, let alone the even more precarious waters of raising our children in the Lord. My wife and I were young parents. We were both under 26 when our third and final child was born. Bill watched us not only juggle the realities of raising a family and maintaining our faith, he watched us do the juggle while I was working on breaking into the Hollywood music scene. It was insanely difficult, highly not recommended and rarely pretty.

Bill was married with two small boys when we reconnected, and for both of us it was awesome to catch up. And then he asked me for advice that I wish more young husbands and fathers had the foresight to ask:

"Looking back, what one thing do you wish you had done, as a husband and a father, from the very beginning, to facilitate the success of your family when it came to following the faith and raising your children so that they would serve the Lord when they became older?"

As heavy as a question that it was, the answer was easy.

"That's easy," I said, "I wish that I had kept Shabbat (the Sabbath) sooner with my family."

"Remember the Sabbath day, to keep it holy. Six days you shall labor, and do all your work, but the seventh day is a Sabbath to the LORD your God. On it you shall not do any work, you, or your son, or your daughter, your male servant, or your female servant, or your livestock, or the sojourner who is within your gates. For in six days the LORD made heaven and earth, the sea, and all that is in them, and rested on the seventh day. Therefore the LORD blessed the Sabbath day and made it holy.
Exodus 20:8-11

Like many of us, Bill had no idea what I was talking about. The vast majority of the Romanized Western Church has never been taught in regard to a Sabbath rest; what it looks like, the why's and how's, nor have many of us actually ever taken a Sabbath rest – a Shabbat – a weekly rest from work on a weekly basis as instructed. Yet it's right up there with "You shall not kill" (Exod. 20:13), and it's also one of the first commandments humans ever received from God. In my experience, one of the main reasons the Romanized Western Church avoids the subject of the Sabbath is out of fear of legalism. It's difficult to teach and model what you don't understand, and that will almost always lead to legalism or worse, wackiness.

The Holy Spirit started revealing Torah to me by highlighting specific scriptures on the subject beginning in 1986. He also started showing me the various ways that we as Christians fail to follow God's Word or His commandments. The first thing He showed me was Shabbat and how man didn't have the authority to change His Sabbath day(s), let alone His seasons, feast days or Torah (Daniel 7:25). As much as I knew all this to be true, I didn't have a reference outside of "orthodox Christianity" in regards to keeping the Sabbath, the fourth commandment.

I also didn't have any "Torah-observant" friends to point me in the right direction, and the acquaintances I did have that observed Shabbat mostly fell under the "goofy" category. The Christians I knew and fellowshipped with, including my pastor, observed the traditional Romanized Western Church's endorsed Sabbath of Sunday, as did I, and they knew less than I did regarding the subject. Who was I going to go to with questions or for clarification about these things that didn't have a fear of hard questions or an agenda full of answers? As you can imagine, this is a common story for many that I have spoken with regarding their experience with transitioning from what they've been *told* the Bible says to actually living *what* the Bible says. This may even be your story as you read this.

When the Holy Spirit starts revealing to you the grotesque errors in Christianity vs the truth of actual scripture, it's quite a jolt! You're being told that everything you know to be true or knew to be true or *thought* you knew to be true is, in all actuality, false. And not only is it false, the majority of it is based on traditions rooted in paganism. The walls of your paradigm begin to crumble – the floor of the absolute surety of your theology and doctrine is pulled out from under your feet – now you're in a freefall; a terrifying freefall. I know. I've been there, and I've seen it on the faces of many.

You see, this is war. Spiritual war. Yet many of us can't believe that our God would allow anything like this to actually happen. Really?

- Adam and Eve were immortals, yet they were still able to be seduced by the enemy of your life and soul
- Genesis 6 (that's for another book... literally)
- More than half of the TaNaKh documents Israel's blatant disobedience while murdering Prophets
- Israel had one prime directive: usher in Messiah for the rest of us, yet at the end of the day only 120 Believers – out of an entire people group – sat available, obedient and in anticipation in an upper room
- Christianity is Judaism realized: The one can't survive or succeed without the other, but a false narra-

tive that is 2000 years old keeps them both foundationally divided

Look up these passages if you still don't believe me: Mt. 24:21-24; Rev. 13; 2 Thess. 2:1-12; 2 Tim. 4:3-4. Yeah, our God would allow this to happen...

"But what about Shabbat," you might be asking. Trust me, it's all going to make sense.

Here's a typical case study of what happens when the Holy Spirit brings this spiritual revelation to light, not unlike being unplugged from the matrix (sorry, I had to.)

So you begin to start seeing in the Bible how God instructed His people to live a certain way, eat a certain way, dress a certain way, worship a certain way... and by doing this "Way," an outward reflection of what's happening inside of you, you're delineated by it; it separates you / "sets you apart" from the rest of the guys. You believe in this thing, and you've given your life to it. This Way also says that you are not to add, include, or mix into your worship of God any hint or form of paganism. (Deut. 12:4)

This is the one that stings the most; realizing that a lot of what we've been doing is rooted in... "something else" and not even in the Book for us to do. Yet the things listed in the Book that we're *supposed* to be doing, we're not doing at all. This sting causes many to leave Christianity, and many of these end up in something really questionable. I'll call them "groups."

During this transitional period of my life, God never told me to leave traditional Christianity. In spite of everything I knew and saw to be false, He never once told me to cut and run, and I believe it's because of that – staying under that covering, good, bad or indifferent (and trust me, there was a lot of bad) – not leaving Christianity "protected" me from getting involved with any of those other... "groups."

Remember how I mentioned in the last Chapter that this isn't about trading or replacing one goofy thing, traditional Christianity, for another thing, traditional Judaism? His grace and mercy kept me from getting involved with "another goofy thing." Because I was under "covering" and not alone where wolves could prey on me, I was spared. So I stayed within the framework of charismatic Christianity and continued learning and understanding these things (Torah) that were absent from my faith.

I didn't know how to apply them practically into my life, so I trusted Him to teach me that as well.

In Revelation 12:17 and 14:12, it describes Believers as those that keep His commandments, Torah, and have their faith and trust in Jesus. The Christianity the majority of us have been exposed to have their faith and trust in Jesus but don't keep Torah. Judaism, on the other hand, keeps Torah but they don't have their faith and trust in Jesus. I wanted to be that sort of Believer described in Revelation, and I needed to find Believers that were defined by this same balance described in Revelation, Believers that could say what Paul said in Acts 24:14:

> "But this I confess to you, that according to the Way, which they call a sect, I worship the God of our fathers, believing everything laid down by the Law and written in the Prophets..."

Did you know that that was in there? Let me break that down for you:

"But this I confess to you, that according to **the Way***"* – "The Way" is what Christianity was originally called before it was changed to the ever-popular and derogatory term of "Christian." Google it.

"which they call **a sect***"* – Yup. The Way, "Christianity," was considered and called a sect of Judaism. This is *extremely* important to know and understand. The powers that be were making sure that this was never going to happen even before the original disciples were all murdered. Those powers and their agenda are still at it today.

"*I worship the God of our fathers,* **believing everything laid down by the Law** *and written in the Prophets"* – Seriously? You're telling me that Paul, Christianity's Poster Boy for all things anti-Torah, believed and observed *everything* laid out in the Torah and the Prophets? Well, yeah. Why wouldn't he? If he didn't, he would have been a false Apostle and Prophet. But I digress... yet again...

Where was I? Oh yeah, so I stayed in traditional Christianity, went to and served in church every Sunday, as well as weekly home churches, and continued learning and understanding these things that were absent from my faith (Torah) outside of the "walls of the church." I didn't know how to apply them practically into my life, so I didn't do anything about them and simply trusted in God to teach me that as well. I knew that Believers were defined by their keeping of the commandments and having their faith and trust in Jesus, so I needed to do the same and hopefully find others that did too.

I knew that the obvious options and/or groups available out there – not all of them "bad" but plenty of them with cultish offerings that preyed on the untrained and the less discriminant – weren't necessarily the answer. So after roughly 18 years (yeah, *18 years*), He directed our steps to a certain church, and lo and behold, some of the leadership of this church were modeling, to a certain extent, this "having your faith and trust in Jesus and keeping the commandments" thing I had been looking for. I'd been studying it for so long that it was obvious when I saw it. There was no way I was going to miss it! Finally, someone to model for us this balance of Jesus and keeping His commandments, and, just as it is with so many, as many of you will attest to, one of the first things modeled to us was Shabbat,

As a husband and a father, I told Bill that I wish that I had kept Shabbat sooner with my family because of the dynamic it brings to family and because of the dynamic it brought to *my* family. You can say the popular one liners like "Men, be the priest of your home;" "Children, honor your father and mother;" "Wives, respect your husbands;" and "Husbands, give up your life for your wife like Jesus;" etc., all day long, but what are the practical applications and expressions of those life-altering instructions? I would say that a majority of pastors wouldn't know the answer to that question either. As a family, if you're not actually applying those instructions to your lives, chances are there is a lack of practical application of other biblical instructions in your lives as well. Too bold of a statement? Look at the percentage of divorce and broken homes within the church. That's bold... Well, with Shabbat, you're actually *functioning* weekly in those Christian bookstore one-liners just mentioned. In its rawest form, Shabbat is foundational for life and foundational to living life in God's cycle of blessing:

- He made Shabbat holy at creation (Gen. 2:3)
- He instructs us to keep Shabbat holy (Exod. 20:8)
- Keeping Shabbat is His sign between and *for us to know* that He sanctifies us (Exod. 31:13), and
- He made Shabbat holy *for* us (Exod. 31:14)

It's His holy rest on our behalf, and Shabbat is His covenant sign with us. Keeping Shabbat is the sign that we attest to His creation of our reality in six days; keeping Shabbat is the sign that we are in covenant with and in Him in exactly the same way that keeping His commandments is the sign that we love His son Jesus. It's also a great way to begin applying Deuteronomy 6 into your family dynamic:

> "Now this is the commandment, the statutes and the rules that the LORD your God commanded me to teach you, that you may do them in the land to which you are going over, to possess it, that you may fear the LORD your God, you and your son and your son's son, by keeping all his statutes and his commandments, which I command you, all the days of your life, and that your days may be long.
>
> Hear therefore, O Israel, and be careful to do them, that it may go well with you, and that you may multiply greatly, as the LORD, the God of your fathers, has promised you, in a land flowing with milk and honey. And these words that I command you today shall be on your heart.
>
> You shall teach them diligently to your children, and shall talk of them when you sit in your house, and when you walk by the way, and when you lie down, and when you rise. When your son asks you in time to come, 'What is the meaning of the testimonies and the statutes and the rules that the LORD our God has commanded you?' then you shall say to your son, 'We were Pharaoh's slaves in Egypt. And the LORD brought us out of Egypt with a mighty hand.
>
> And the LORD showed signs and wonders, great and grievous, against Egypt and against Pharaoh and all his household, before our eyes. And he brought us out from there, that he might bring us in and give us the land that he swore to give to our fathers. And the LORD commanded us to do all these statutes, to fear the LORD our God, for our good always, that he might preserve us alive, as we are this day. And it will be righteousness for us, if we are careful to do all this commandment before the LORD our God, as he has commanded us.'"
>
> Deuteronomy 6:1-3, 6-7, 20-25

Shabbat Simplified

Establishing a weekly cycle of this blessing and holiness in your life, home, and family is foundational for your blessing and success. That is why I told Bill that I wish that I had done this sooner with my family; Shabbat is a family affair. I tell people all the time that if every American Christian family would do Shabbat, it would singlehandedly change our country. Here's the practical breakdown of what I mean:

- You're having dinner as a family around the table once a week - every week

Apparently this is more of a big deal than I had realized. When I teach Shabbat to people, that is the most novel of ideas to them: *regularly-scheduled family dinners around the table*. Since the beginning of our little family, we have had dinner at the table Monday through Friday consistently. So having dinner as a family around the table "once a week - every week" wasn't much of a stretch for us. Since it apparently is for many, this alone is going to change your family dynamic for the better.

- Mom (or the lady of the house) lights the Shabbat candles and ushers in the Sabbath rest / peace: Shabbat shalom

This first step sets the tone for the evening. If families aren't accustomed to eating dinner around the table, are the children accustomed to seeing and hearing mom pray blessing and peace over them and their house?

- Dad blesses the children

The dad is now functioning as the High Priest of his home. By modeling Jesus in blessing his children, both mom and the children are being blessed, even if they don't realize it. Think of how "atmosphere changing" this is to the home.

- Dad and the children bless mom from Proverbs 31

This is huge. Now the children see and hear dad not only affirm his wife and their mother, they also see dad humbling himself before the entire family and declaring 17 scriptural verses over mom as he lays his hands on her. The children, prompted by their father, now lay hands on their mother as they declare four verses over her. How would you like that, moms?

- Dad blesses Israel

Putting things into perspective by blessing God's Land and His people, a people that you've been grafted into, as a family is putting things into proper alignment. This is something you want your children to know and understand.

- Dad leads the family in communion

This is the biggest thing. I'm amazed at how many dads have never led their families in communion in the privacy of their own home. The results of this are life altering if you do and if you don't. This is Priesthood, men.

Shabbat Guide

Opening Prayer: Mom

Baruch atah Adonai Eloheinu melekh ha'olam, asher kid'shanu b'dam Yeshua. V'tzi'vanu l'hiyot or l'olam.

Blessed are You, Adonai, our Elohim, King of the universe, who sanctified us by the blood of Yeshua and commands us to be a light to the nations.

The Blessing Over the Children:

Sons:
Y'seem-cha Elohim k'Efraim v'chee-me-nasheh

May Elohim make you, my sons, like Ephraim and Manasseh.

Daughters:
Y'seem-aych Elohim k'Sarah, Rivkah, Ra-chel, v'Leah

May Elohim make you, my daughters, like Sarah, Rebekah, Rachel, and Leah.

Blessings Over the Wife: Proverbs 31 (NIV)

A wife of noble character who can find?
She is worth far more than rubies.
Her husband has full confidence in her
and lacks nothing of value.
She brings him good, not harm, all the days of her life.
She selects wool and flax and works with eager hands.
She is like the merchant ships,
bringing her food from afar.
She gets up while it is still night;
she provides food for her family
and portions for her female servants.

She considers a field and buys it;
out of her earnings she plants a vineyard.
She sets about her work vigorously;
her arms are strong for her tasks.
She sees that her trading is profitable,
and her lamp does not go out at night.
In her hand she holds the distaff
and grasps the spindle with her fingers.
She opens her arms to the poor
and extends her hands to the needy.
When it snows, she has no fear for her household;
for all of them are clothed in scarlet.
She makes coverings for her bed;
she is clothed in fine linen and purple.

Her husband is respected at the city gate,
where he takes his seat among the elders of the land.

She makes linen garments and sells them,
and supplies the merchants with sashes.
She is clothed with strength and dignity;
she can laugh at the days to come.
She speaks with wisdom,
and faithful instruction is on her tongue.

She watches over the affairs of her household
and does not eat the bread of idleness.

Her children arise and call her blessed;
her husband also, and he praises her:

(Children)
"Many women do noble things, but you surpass them all."
Charm is deceptive, and beauty is fleeting;
but a woman who fears the LORD is to be praised.
Honor her for all that her hands have done,
and let her works bring her praise at the city gate.

Aaronic Benediction:

Y'va-rech'cha Adonai, v'yeesh-ma reh-cha
Y'ayr Adonai panahv ey-lecha vee-choo-neh-cha
Y'sa Adonai panahv ey-lecha v'yah-sem l'cha
Shalom

May Adonai bless you and keep you
May Adonai make His face shine upon you
and be gracious to you
May Adonai lift up His countenance upon you
and give you peace.
(Numbers 6: 23-24)

Sh'ma:

This is a scripturally based traditional prayer spoken daily by Jewish people worldwide. A declaration of faith for believers in Yeshua has been added.
(Deuteronomy 6:4)

Sh'ma Yisrael, Adonai Elohaynoo, Adonai Echad
Baruch Shem k'vod malchooto l'olam va'ed
Yeshua hu ha-Mashiach hu Adon ha-kol

Hear O Israel, Adonai our Elohim, Adonai is One.
Blessed be the name of His Glorious Kingdom
forever and ever
Yeshua, He is the Messiah, He is Adonai of all.

Blessing Over the Wine:

As we drink the wine, we remember the blood of Messiah that was poured out for us.

Baruch Atah Adonai Eloheynoo Melech ha-olam boray pre hagafen. Amen.

Blessed are You, Adonai, our Elohim, King of the universe Who creates the fruit of the vine. Amen

Blessing Over the Bread:

As we remember the provision of God in our lives, we also remember that Yeshua said to pray in this manner "...Give us this day our daily bread." We know that Yeshua is our bread, our double portion, whose Body was broken on our behalf.

Baruch Atah Adonai Eloheynoo Melech ha-olam ha-motzi lec em mein ha'aretz. Amen.

Blessed are You, Adonai, our Elohim, King of the universe Who brings forth bread from the earth. Amen

Songs:

Shabbat Shalom

Shabbat Shalom, Shabbat Shalom, Shabbat Shabbat Shabbat Shabbat Shalom (2x)
Shabbat Shabbat Shabbat Shabbat Shalom (2x)
Shabbat Shalom, Shabbat Shalom, Shabbat Shabbat Shabbat Shabbat Shalom

(Sabbath peace)

O'seh shalom

O'seh shalom bim'romav
Hu ya'aseh shalom aleiynu
V'al kol Yisrael
Vimru, imru amen (2x)
Ya'aseh shalom
Ya'aseh shalom
Shalom aleiynu v'al kol Yisrael (2x)

*(He who makes peace in His high places
He shall make peace upon us and upon all of Israel and say amen)*

Download our Shabbat Guide to assist you in keeping Shabbat with your own family in your home: http://chameleonchurch.com/pdf/shabbatGuide.pdf

That "Jewish Stuff"

Bill knew where we had come from. He saw that, in spite of being in music professionally, our marriage, our family *and* our faith had somehow survived the rigors of Rock and Roll and we beat the percentages. He saw the Godly fruit in our lives and wanted to ensure the same in his family. He also knew that traditional Christianity didn't have the formula for that success.

I tell people all the time that if every American Christian family would do Shabbat, it would singlehandedly change our country. But they won't do it.

"That's 'Jewish' stuff," is the most popular reason why they won't, and, "we're not 'under the Law,'" they explain, without actually knowing what it is they're talking about.

Funny thing about that "Jewish stuff." In Chapter 2, I discussed the Seven Rabbinic Mitzvahs (commands) not mandated in scripture and how we participate in four of them, "Shabbat Candles" being one of the traditional things that we do and it's the second bullet item in that list.

As you can imagine, there is a huge and exhaustive Rabbinical procedure to this "ritual." I am only going to touch on some main traditional sections of the candle lighting and the contrasts found in how we approach this.

Traditionally, the lady of the house will light the two candles. After the candles are lit, the woman stretches her hands out towards the candles, and moves them inwards in a circular motion – ushering in a special guest, the Shabbat Queen – three times. After the third time, the woman covers her eyes with her hands and recites the following blessing... Let's stop there.

Obviously we're not going to be "ushering in" any "special guests" no matter what your name is and especially if your name is "Shabbat Queen" while two candles are functioning as oracles!

I need to address those who would yell "foul" right about now, and rightfully so!

"Allan, we know your stance on the pagan origins of some of Christianity's rituals (notice that this is also an admittance of paganism in Christianity that they nonchalantly ignore), and you've said that we can't observe them and that they're not redeemable. How can you possibly do *this*?" and they would be completely correct except for the fact that this wasn't a pagan ritual that was "Christianized" – or rather "Judaized."

This is a scriptural observance that has had additional extracurricular activities and manmade traditions incorporated into it – not a perverted observance that has been "sanctified." We keep the scriptural observance and remove the questionable additions that originate from tradition, which is an entirely different thing than what the Romanized Western Church is known for doing. The Romanized Western Church has historically taken a perversion, modified it to some extent – sometimes not at all – then added it to an already non-scriptural manmade observance and stamped "Holy" on it. Now they have their "tradition."

Here's how we remove the questionable traditions: Traditionally, the lady of the house will light the two candles. After the candles are lit she recites the blessing. There's no questionable stretching out of the hands towards the candles; no moving of the hands inwards in a circular motion; no ushering in of a "special guest," no doing this "three times" when after the third time, "the woman covers her eyes with her hands" ...

Then there's the blessing. Here's the traditional prayer:

Blessed are you, ADONAI our Elohim, King of the universe, who has sanctified us with His commandments, and commanded us to kindle the light of the Holy Shabbat.

Because of Messiah, we're sanctified by His blood, not the commandments, and we were never commanded to kindle / light the candles of Shabbat. Remember, this is one of the seven "commands" *added* to the Torah.

Here's the prayer *we* recite:

Blessed are You, ADONAI, our Elohim, King of the universe, who sanctified us by the blood of Yeshua, and commanded us to be a light to the nations.

Before I address naysayers on some of the obvious business above, I want to mention something that I debated sharing regarding aspects of the Shabbat "ceremony." Non-Christians that find themselves at our Shabbat table are the most moved by the Holy Spirit during the "ceremony:" the candle lighting, the communal prayers, the taking of communion, the communal songs and dinner. Non-Christians have been moved to tears of gratitude for being invited to something they say is so beautiful, so uplifting and so moving. In contrast, some Christians have been known to literally manifest demons right from the very start of the service. Sad, I know, but true.

Your House Is On Fire...

With that, I want to clarify that I am in no way, shape or form a "hater" of the Romanized Western Church, Christians or Christianity. I know what some of my comments about the Mainstream Western and Romanized Church and Christians in general might sound like, but my tone is passion, not anger or contempt, and it's only because I care. Your house is on fire!

Would you like for me to walk by, notice that your house is on fire, go home, eat dinner, have dessert, watch a little TV, take a shower and prepare for bed and then remember to send you a polite little email? I think not. Your house is on fire! I'm going to rush the front door, pound on it, try to break it down, throw huge rocks through windows, scream, yell – anything I can do to get your attention and to get you and your family out safely. You may not appreciate the damage to your house and my upsetting the wife and kids and all, and that's totally ok with me. You'll get over it, because you survived the house fire!

I could easily quote the passages about the Watchman on the Wall who, if he doesn't warn another of their sin, their blood is on him, but the blood of the person he does warn, their blood is on their own head, but that would be too easy...

For example: a woman, an old friend that I've known for quite some time, and I recently reconnected after many years. We talked a couple two or three times in the last three or four years but without any real reunion. I decided that she wasn't interested because of how different our spiritual paths have been since the early 1990's. I had tried reaching out on occasion but had given up. So when she asked if we could meet, I was more than happy to do so.

It was great to catch up, but her story was sad and filled with regret, divorce, betrayal, children that had rejected the Lord; quite frankly, the usual. These reunions, as excited as I am to have them, always end up bumming me out because, in the meantime, I'm not sad and filled with regret. Anything I say only magnifies their defeats, their failures and their crises of faith. It's no fun at all. I'm still married to the same woman, and we've raised our children in the Lord who, in turn, are raising their children in the Lord. We have lived exciting and fruitful lives; our tent pegs span the globe with deep and powerful partnerships and relationships with ministries and individuals.

At some point in our conversation, I said something she considered inappropriate or coarse. I actually can't remember what I said, but I do remember what *she* said.

She said, "That's what I mean. How do you do that?"

I was genuinely confused.

"How can you be such a man of God and have language like that? That's why I've stayed away. That's why I haven't reached out. I can't let a man that speaks like that lead me and my children."

She added that maybe I needed to consider the type of people my language was going to attract; and were those the type of people I wanted to lead? I should reconsider the type of "congregation" my language was going to afford me, especially if I wanted to lead a proper church.

Well, that stung. I sat there for a minute, choosing my words and response carefully. I didn't want to say anything that sounded like an excuse. There was a huge lesson here for the both of us. Mind you, she had no real idea what my life had been like the last 22 years. All she really knew was what I had told her about my family. She had no idea of the who's, the what's or the where's, but what she did know was that I was "a man of God."

I apologized. I said something about how I didn't realize that I had said something to her that she considered offensive. Then a true story that my pastor in Dallas had told me about himself came to mind.

My pastor and his wife had recently spent three years in Belgium where they had pastored and led a House of Prayer. In that time, he had made quite a reputation for himself and was known as the "Potty Mouth Pastor." That's right; my extremely conservative pastor was a potty mouth. Apparently, you can say the "S.H." word in Belgium but, boy oh boy, if you're a "man of the cloth," you better never, ever say "crap!" And from the pulpit?!?

I told my friend about my having to apologize to a little old grandma a few years back for the language that had come out of my mouth in front of her while telling her grandson about Jesus. She told me not to even think of it. She told me that over five years prior, her grandson had left the family and the church for a life of heroin, and this was the first time he had come home. Now because of me (and my language), he had given his life back to Jesus.

I told my friend that I was very aware of the audience my language afforded me. I also told my friend that that audience consisted of entrepreneurs, clergy, drug addicts and grandmothers; how that audience spans generations; and how my language wasn't always "coarse." I knew how to watch my tongue, and I had nothing to consider or reconsider. I was a fly fisherman, and my language "matched the hatch" of my audience. If one particular fly wasn't appropriate, then I would change flies just to win some.

What I didn't tell her was that my language ostracized the religious. I also didn't tell her that she should be more concerned with the outcome of her life and how demonically broken her daughter was. And I especially didn't tell her that her concern for my language as being the primary reason for why she "couldn't let me lead her and her family" was only going to continue to keep her where she presently was.

Don't bring me the healing prophet that can tell me all that my life has been; that can heal me from sickness and unclean spirits; who can deliver my daughter from demonic torment. Don't bring that man to me, because he might say...

Your house is on fire. While I was walking by, I noticed that your house was on fire. I got home, ate my dinner, had dessert, watched a little TV, and took a shower. I was preparing for bed when I remembered that your house was on fire. I'm considering a polite little email, but first I must ensure I get the words and tone right... But I digress... yet again and again...

Traditions Continued...

I know, I know... The blessing.

The traditional prayer goes like this:

Blessed are you, ADONAI our Elohim, King of the universe, who has sanctified us with His commandments, and commanded us to kindle the light of the Holy Shabbat.

Because of Messiah, we're sanctified by His blood, not the commandments, and we were never commanded to kindle / light, the candles of Shabbat. Remember, this is one of the seven "commands" *added* to the Torah.

Here's the prayer we recite:

Blessed are You, ADONAI, our Elohim, King of the universe, who sanctified us by the blood of Yeshua and commanded us to be a light to the nations.

Here some people would incorrectly (mis)quote me by saying that changing the questionable aspects of the ritual and traditional prayer doesn't change anything. I would then remind them that we're not changing something "pagan" into something "holy" – we're taking something Holy and purging the questionable traditional additions out of it. I would also give them two examples of Jesus "doing the same:"

1. Keeping the Sabbath, and
2. Calling Himself "Living Water"

(Don't worry, they don't know what I'm referring to either. Heh)

Jesus and Keeping the Sabbath

In Mt. 12; Mark 2; Luke 6; 13; 14; and John 5; 7; 9, Jesus is accused of breaking what the scribes, the Torah-teachers, the Pharisees and the Sadducees considered to be the Sabbath – based on their manmade traditions that they taught as doctrine (recall Chapter 2). By being a "Sabbath breaker," Jesus could be deemed "not from God," a "false prophet," and certainly not "the Messiah." Deuteronomy 13 states that a real prophet from God does not and would not break Torah, thus a false prophet could never be Messiah. Jesus' critics were evoking Deuteronomy 13, as they should have been, in testing His credibility. Unfortunately, their tests were done through their traditionally tainted glasses and not on the actual commandments of God.

In Mt. 12, the disciples plucked heads of grain and ate on the Sabbath, and the Pharisees cried foul. In their defense, Jesus cited what David did when he was hungry, how he entered the Temple and ate the bread of the Presence (the Showbread) that was unlawful for David to eat and strictly for the priests. Jesus then tells them that something greater than the temple was there (Him), and if they understood "I desire mercy, and not sacrifice," (Hosea 6:6) they wouldn't have judged the innocent disciples. Then to really seal the deal, He tells them that "the Son of Man is Lord of the Sabbath." That was a mic drop...

In Mark's version of the same account, Jesus is recorded as saying, "The Sabbath was made for man, not man for the Sabbath." (Mk. 2:27) In case you're still not getting the gist, Mark 3:1-6 might help:

Jesus goes into a synagogue where there was a man with a withered hand. The Pharisees are watching to see if Jesus is going to heal him or not. That's how desensitized they had become to Jesus and His Supernatural Power of creative miracles. They wanted to see if Jesus was going to heal this guy on the Sabbath so that they could accuse Him of breaking the Sabbath, even though there is no actual instruction against "healing on the Sabbath." Knowing this, Jesus says to the guy with the withered hand, "Come here." It's on.

He says to the Pharisees in verse 4, "Is it lawful on the Sabbath to do good or to do harm, to save life or to kill?" They said nothing. Jesus is angry as he looks around the room at them, grieved at their hardness of heart, and says to the man, "Stretch out your hand." The man stretches it out, and it's not a withered hand that he shows them. The

Pharisees leave, find some other factionalists that agree with them, and they start devising a plan to destroy Jesus... for healing a man on the Sabbath. I personally think it was because they knew He was Messiah and there was no seat for them at His table; the table they were dead set on keeping for themselves.

There was an established religious order; an old and traditional established religious order that everyone adhered to and never questioned. It was "based" on God's established order, but it wasn't actually God's established order, and Jesus knew that. In the same exact way, Jesus also knows that *our* "old and traditional established religious order that everyone adheres to and never questions – that was 'based' on God's established order but isn't actually God's established order" is exactly like the Pharisees established religious order.

Their established form of observing Shabbat was marred with manmade traditions taught as doctrine – the Romanized Western Church's established form of observing the Sabbath is marred with manmade traditions taught as doctrine.

Shabbat was / is oppressive, burdensome and riddled with rules, and Jesus was upsetting their legalistic and religious cart. The Sabbath is a day of celebration, a day of blessing and of God's goodness. It's a day given to us by God as a gift and as a sign! (Ezekiel 20:12) Nothing could have been further from the truth of what they had turned it into, and that's why Jesus was so angry with them; angry with their hardness of heart that bred their religious legalism. Their house was on fire! With that, I'm going with Jesus' example and definition of Shabbat, not Judaism's *or* Christianity's.

Unfortunately, many today have been "taught" that Jesus did indeed break the Sabbath as a model of His "doing away with" God's commandments, the Torah – a "New Covenant." They cite Jesus' "breaking of the Sabbath" as "proof text" for why Torah is no longer applicable to Believers. Chalk up another one for Biblical illiteracy. This couldn't be further from the truth...

Jesus Calls Himself "Living Water"

In John 7, we see that it's the Feast of Tabernacles / Booths, Sukkot. Jesus was avoiding Judea, because they were looking to kill Him there, so He was in the Galilee where even his own family rebuked Him out of their unbelief of Him.

Sukkot is the last of the seven Feasts and falls in our Gregorian calendar in September / October. It is also the third of the Three Pilgrimage Festivals (Hebrew *"shalosh regalim"*) where every Jewish male must present himself before God in Jerusalem. This will clarify the dialog in verses 3-8. Jesus *had* to go to Jerusalem. And He does.

By the time Jesus came to walk the earth, an extracurricular ritual had been added to the Feast of Sukkot that we didn't read about in Leviticus 23 back in Chapter 1 (because it isn't in there): The Water Libation Ceremony.

The water libation ritual was popular because of the accompanying ceremony of the water drawing. Each day for seven consecutive days a priest poured a jug full of water into a bowl that drained into the altar. Levite's played lyres, trumpets, harps, cymbals, and other instruments, while other Levite's sang. Three golden candlesticks roughly 75 feet high were lit by young boys on tall ladders. The light of these candles was seen throughout Jerusalem. Men of faith danced and sang in front of these candlesticks while carrying burning torches. As the ceremony progressed through the night, priests blew shofars three times. Rabbis would perform acrobats and juggle flaming touches [sic] as part of the festivities.
(Source:http://www.jewishroots.net/library/holiday-articles/water_libation_ceremony.html)

Because this water libation ceremony had been "added to" the original Torah instruction on how to observe Sukkot, it wasn't permissible. It wasn't technically "lawful," and Jesus knew this. My reason for sharing this is because Jesus didn't condemn this obvious infraction but instead, on the last day of the feast, another High Sabbath, at the climax of the celebration:

> *Jesus stood up and cried out, "If anyone thirsts, let him come to me and drink. Whoever believes in me, as the Scripture has said, 'Out of his heart will flow rivers of living water.'"*
John 7:37-38

Dang...

Instead of condemning a religious manmade tradition on a High Sabbath, Jesus basically takes advantage of the situation and, in reference to this water ritual, announces *Himself* to be that "Living Water," essentially declaring to all of Israel that *He is* indeed Messiah (verses 40-43), and most definitely proclaiming that:

> *"I am the reality that the water in this ceremony symbolizes – the true life giver through whom the Holy Spirit is also given."*

(Source: Jewish Voice Today, September/October 2005 by Guest author Mitch Glaser, President of Chosen People Ministries)

These examples are why I think it's permissible for us to take an actual scriptural Holy Day – *established at creation* (!), Shabbat, that has been mired with tradition and paganism, the candle lighting, remove the traditional errors and the paganism and correct it. Again, this is not the same as "Lent," "Christ's mass" or "Easter;" none of those actually *being* scriptural holy days but merely manmade traditions devised to *replace* actual scriptural observances. Fact: Jesus was born during Sukkot. You want to celebrate His birth? Observe the Feast of Tabernacles!

Note: there is no one actual verse in the TaNaKh that says *'Out of his heart will flow rivers of living water'* but there are at least six references that Jesus could be referring to broadly. Might be a good Bible study for ya.

I've explained how keeping Shabbat is a cyclical blessing for your life and how those blessings are found in scripture even for Gentiles that keep Shabbat; the keeping of the Sabbath will be as a monument and an everlasting name for them in the House of God (Is. 56:5; Acts 10:4):

> *Blessed is the man who does this, and the son of man who holds it fast, who keeps the Sabbath, not profaning it, and keeps his hand from doing any evil." For thus says the LORD: "To the eunuchs who keep my Sabbaths, who choose the things that please me and hold fast my covenant [...] And the foreigners who join themselves to the LORD, to minister to him, to love the name of the LORD, and to be his servants, everyone who keeps the Sabbath and does not profane it, and holds fast my covenant..."*
> Isaiah 56:2, 4, 6

> *"If you turn back your foot from the Sabbath [keep the Sabbath], from doing your pleasure on my holy day, and call the Sabbath a delight and the holy day of the LORD honorable; if you honor it, not going your own ways, or seeking your own pleasure, or talking idly; then you shall take delight in the LORD, and I will make you ride on the heights of the earth [...]"*
> Isaiah 58:13-14a

I tell people all the time that if every American Christian family would do Shabbat, I am of the opinion that it would singlehandedly change our country. But they won't do it. "That's 'Jewish' stuff," they say, or "we're not 'under the Law,'" they explain, without actually knowing what it is they're talking about (for the record, the New Testament defines sin as "the breaking of the Law.") So then I tell them,

"Get rid of the 'Jewish stuff' then":

- Have dinner as a family around the table once a week – every week
- Dad, bless the children
- Dad and the children, bless mom from Proverbs 31
- Dad, bless Israel
- Dad, lead the family in communion

"Can you do that," I ask, "Is that acceptable to you?"

They always say yes.

Upon following up, I almost always find out that they maybe did it once but then they haven't done it again. These are the same people, mind you, that are usually complaining about how their lives never seem to be working out financially, relationally, spiritually, healthwise... You think?

Shabbat vs Sunday Church

The Romanized Western Church equates the Sabbath with going to church on Sunday. This has been true at least since the actual scriptural Sabbath was done away with and "officially changed" to Sunday Morning by the Roman Catholic Church (more on this later.) Add the lack of understanding and lack of context regarding "the Lord's Day" and the "First Day of the Week" from standalone verses like Acts 20:7 and

1 Cor. 16:1-2, (don't forget an unhealthy dose of replacement theology,) and you never know whatcha gonna get. Let's look at the verses about the "First Day of the Week:"

We know that scripturally, traditionally and historically, Shabbat is sundown Friday to sundown Saturday, (Lev. 23:32) and is the last day of the week, even if the majority of the Romanized Western Church won't admit it. You also have to remember that God starts the day at sunset, not in the morning. The following will probably be repeated in Chapter 4, the chapter on Passover.

In Mt. 28:1; Mark 16:2, 9; Luke 24:1; and John 20:1 we find the term "first day of the week" and they're all referencing the account of the women going to the tomb at dawn after Jesus' execution (and clearly *after* the weekly Shabbat.) This is why it's believed that Jesus was raised from the dead at sunrise and that's why we go to church on Sunday morning. But here are the problems:

1. This admits that the Sabbath is Friday sunset to Saturday sunset by claiming these verses to substantiate a Sunday morning "sabbath" based on the women going to the tomb at dawn – after Shabbat – only to find an empty tomb... So why change it, ignore it and lie about it?

2. Jesus had to emulate everything that was written in the Torah and the Prophets about Him (as we saw in Luke) in order for Him to be Messiah. This included mirroring the Passover Lamb selection and entering Jerusalem (more in Chapter 4), His execution (Passover Lamb), His burial (Feast of Unleavened Bread) *and His resurrection* (Feast of Firstfruits.) The problem is, Feast of Firstfruits takes place after the weekly Sabbath (Saturday after sunset) making Saturday night the beginning of the "first day of the week." The body of Jesus was long gone by the time the women had arrived at the tomb early that Sunday morning.

Remember, God starts the day at sunset, not in the morning, and this is where all the confusion begins. The following doesn't help either: Our Gregorian time and calendar, the "Christian" solar calendar originated with the Vatican: Catholicism. Remember?

"Christians must not judaize by resting on the Sabbath, but must work on that day, rather honouring the Lord's Day; and, if they can, resting then as Christians. But if any shall be found to be judaizers, let them be anathema from Christ."
(Source: Council of Laodicea, Canon XXIX, 363-364 A.D.)

Anyone found "guilty" of "resting on the Sabbath" was labeled a "Judaizer." For the record, almost every online definition of "judaizer" is grotesquely incorrect.

Roman Catholicism originally determined, once and for all, what your faith was going to look like way back in the fourth century. They determined that no trace of Judaism was going to be allowed to spoil or taint the Roman Catholic Church so they outlawed (yes, outlawed, see above quote) Shabbat along with Passover and the eating of unleavened bread with similar canons – under penalty of Hell's fire! They also demonized circumcision as also "not for Christians:"
The Council of Vienne (A.D. 1311); The Council of Florence (A.D. 1438-1445) From Cantate Domino — Papal Bull of Pope Eugene IV.

Back to the Sabbath: the following is from *The Convert's Catechism of Catholic Doctrine (A.D. 1910)*:

Q. Which is the Sabbath day?
A. Saturday is the Sabbath day

Q. Why do we observe Sunday instead of Saturday?
A. We observe Sunday instead of Saturday because the Catholic Church transferred the solemnity from Saturday to Sunday.

Q. Why did the Catholic Church substitute Sunday for Saturday?
A. The Church substituted Sunday for Saturday, because Christ rose from the dead on a Sunday, and the Holy Ghost descended upon the Apostles on a Sunday.

Q. By what authority did the Church substitute Sunday for Saturday?
A. The Church substituted Sunday for Saturday by the plenitude of that divine power which Jesus Christ bestowed upon her.

But then you also have this:

> "We Catholics, then, have precisely the same authority for keeping Sunday holy instead of Saturday as we have for every other article of our creed, namely, the authority of 'the Church...' you who are Protestants have really no authority for it whatever; for there **is** no authority for it in the Bible, and you will not allow that there **can be** authority for it anywhere else."

(Source: *The Clifton Tracts*, by the Brotherhood of St. Vincent of Paul, Sanctioned by the Bishop of Clifton, Cardinal Wiseman, with the Approbation of The Most Rev. John Hughes, D. D., Archbishop of New York (A.D. 1856)) [Emphasis mine]

Externally, as *The Convert's Catechism of Catholic Doctrine* tells us, the average person is taught that *Jesus* gave the church the authority to change God's Sabbath. Internally, as the Archbishop approved, Catholicism admits that their "authority" is without biblical merit.

Roman Catholicism replaced God's holy established Sabbath with man's traditional Sunday Morning and replaced God's mandated holy appointed time of Passover with a pagan-infused "Easter." Furthermore, anyone found observing Shabbat and lighting Shabbat candles on Friday after sunset, and anyone celebrating Passover or eating unleavened bread was anathema. Of course, these rulings were made with your best interests in mind: they didn't want us doing any of these things so that no one would mistake us for being Jews. Yes, they also demonized Jewishness. Simply put, since Evangelical Christianity, Protestantism, is nothing more than re-formed Catholicism, they basically just quietly fell into step. (shrug...)

I highly discourage anyone from looking online about things regarding Torah observance (pro or con) simply because the majority of the information out there is disinformation, and I highly discourage the same regarding the truth concerning Roman Catholicism (pro or con) on The Google. No, it's not also disinformation. You can go to official Catholic sites and find this information, but I also want to avoid talking about Catholicism as much as I can for two reasons:

1. A lot has been labeled Catholic Conspiracy Theories, even though much of this information is available at official Catholic websites, and
2. I'm not here to shame anyone, nor is that the purpose

of this book

Unfortunately, it's impossible to discuss these things without referencing Roman Catholicism's part in the deception we were all taught. So to stay in context, we only go to church on Sunday because of Roman Catholicism, since Evangelical Christianity, Protestantism, is simply re-formed Catholicism. This is why this information impacts us and our faith. I don't bring it up just to "bash" another denomination. That would be dishonorable and irresponsible.

This is why Protestant Christianity, the Romanized Western Church, observes the Roman Catholic "sabbath" of Sunday. This is why Protestant Christianity, the Romanized Western Church, observes the Mass of Christ (ChristMass). This is why Protestant Christianity, the Romanized Western Church, observes the Roman Catholic replacement of Passover, "Easter." This is why some of Protestant Christianity, the Romanized Western Church, were taught the Roman Catholic replacement of the Omer Count / Feast of Weeks observance of Lent, and so on and so forth...

This is why we were never taught that the Seven Feasts, Shabbat, the New Moon and the Counting of the Omer were God's Feasts for God's people. Instead, we were taught that they were Jewish Holidays for Jews, and Jesus did away with Judaism; He did away with "Jewish ways," and they have no part in God's true religion, Roman Catholicism – or the re-formation of Catholicism, Protestantism, i.e. Evangelical Christianity, the Romanized Western Church.

FATHER!!

All of this is very upsetting to me. It's upsetting to me, because I take no pleasure in speaking ill of anyone or any one religion. But unless we understand why we believe what we believe, we can't understand that our belief system is flawed and unsound scripturally and that it needs to change. Our house is on fire!!!

On the first day of the week, when we were gathered together to break bread, Paul talked with them, intending to depart on the next day, and he prolonged his speech until midnight.
Acts 20:7

Because the day begins after the sun sets and not in the morning, and because Paul prolonged his talk until midnight (some five or six hours later), Acts 20:7 more than likely took place on Saturday night, technically Sunday, the first day of the week. This also doesn't necessarily imply that it was an official "Sunday-esque church service." It also doesn't imply that it wasn't; they could have been having dinner or a "home church" meeting. Either way, this assumption that the disciples met for "church services on Sunday morning" along with Jesus' presumed resurrection on a Sunday morning are hardly legitimate reasons to usurp God's authority and change His Sabbath.

We're talking about Shabbat vs Sunday Church:

- Shabbat doesn't have to be a "church service"
- Shabbat doesn't *not* have to be a church service
- Meeting Saturday night – after Shabbat – doesn't have to be a church service
- Meeting Saturday night – after Shabbat – doesn't *not* have to be a church service
- Meeting Sunday morning doesn't have to be a church service, and
- Meeting Sunday morning doesn't *not* have to be a church service

What *does* have to happen though is you most definitely have to obey the scriptural fourth commandment and remember the Sabbath and keep it holy! And that means Friday sunset to Saturday sunset. There's no wiggle room there. Not even an erroneous misquoting of Romans 14 and Colossians 2 – to disprove the keeping of Shabbat – can replace or negate this fact.

Presently, we meet on Monday nights for worship and prayer, and we meet on Shabbat. After dinner, Shabbat can be a game night, it can be a sit around the table with coffee and reason the Word night, and it can also be an actual worship and teaching night.

We're praying for a public meeting place where we can at least have a worship night, a weekly Bible study and a dedicated weekly teaching time (church service), along with our weekly Shabbat gathering, a monthly city-wide Shabbat and our monthly Rosh Chodesh celebration. This public meeting place would also facilitate the celebration of the Feast gatherings.

Speaking of gathering; we know that in Acts 15 it stated that the Gentiles would receive Torah instruction in the synagogue (church) on Shabbat. We also know that a contextual reading and understanding of Acts tells us that Paul's ministry was teaching the Torah and the Prophets on Shabbat in the synagogues to Jews and Gentiles. These are two strong arguments for Shabbat to be your church service. Stronger than the erroneous, out-of-context assumption of "the first day of the week" argument.

Me? I could care less either way what day people meet for church. I'm excited just knowing that people are actually in fellowship in this day and age!

I *do* want to be perfectly clear in regard to what I am and what I am not saying in regards to Sabbath versus Sunday Church:

1. Yes, in Revelation 1:10 we find the term "the Lord's day," but it does not indicate what day of the week that day actually was. Creating doctrines or theologies from a single solitary stand-alone verse is incredibly irresponsible, dangerous and really bad exegesis.

2. Yes, in Acts 20:7 it says that they gathered to break bread "on the first day of the week" (Saturday night to Sunday night) but what it doesn't say or insinuate is that they gathered regularly on this day or what time they did gather. It is more probable, based on this (again) stand-alone verse, that this gathering was on Saturday night instead of on a Sunday morning.

3. Because of the position held by Roman Catholicism, that Jesus rose from the dead on a Sunday morning, *they* determined that Sunday was "the Lord's day" without any Biblical merit to that claim. Since Protestant Christianity is re-formed Catholicism, Evangelical Christianity followed suit.

4. I do not believe or teach that you should not meet on "the first day of the week," be it Saturday night or Sunday. Feel free to meet after the Sabbath on Saturday night or anytime on Sunday.

5. What I *do* believe and teach is that you can't claim

that "the first day of the week," Saturday night to Sunday night, is the Sabbath. It's not. "Sunday sabbath" is based on the accounts of the women at the tomb, and all those accounts clearly state that they visited the tomb *after* the weekly Sabbath.

6. What I do believe and teach is that "the first day of the week" did *not* replace the scriptural Sabbath of Friday sunset to Saturday sunset nor is it the "Christian Sabbath." This is not substantiated Biblically by God, Jesus, Holy Spirit or rainbow-colored unicorns. Don't believe it or teach it.

7. What I don't believe or teach is that the disciples met regularly "on the Lord's day" / Sunday, because it doesn't say that.

8. I also don't believe or teach that the disciples stopped observing the scriptural Sabbath or replaced the scriptural Sabbath with "the Lord's day" because it also doesn't say that. In fact, it says the opposite; that they *did* keep the scriptural Sabbath.

9. What I do believe and teach is that regardless of what day you decide to go to church, you best be remembering the Sabbath, Friday sunset to Saturday sunset, and keeping it holy.

Wanna go to church on Sunday? Knock yourself out, but don't say that it's the Sabbath, or that it's the "Christian Sabbath," or that it replaced the Sabbath. Not observing Shabbat on God's designated time of Friday sunset to Saturday sunset is a very bad idea indeed.

Pretty simple, isn't it…?

How Do You Spell S.H.A.B.B.A.T?

Understandably, I'm frequently asked how I observe Shabbat and what constitutes "holy" and "unholy." There's actually no list to go by except for the clearly stated "you shall not do any (ordinary) work," and it is widely held that "ordinary" constitutes the work you do for gainful employment. Traditional Judaism would tell you otherwise, but like I already clarified, I don't subscribe to traditional Judaism's version of Shabbat. I

can tell you two things though:
1. I don't wake up in the morning and say "How can I break the Sabbath today?" and
2. It has nothing to do with legalism

I do believe that we must keep what we learned above regarding Jesus and observing Shabbat as holy when making these decisions for ourselves, our families and our communities. With that said,

Leviticus 23:25 tells us to enjoy Shabbat by avoiding our regular or customary work. This is going to look different for you than it looks for me. Professional photographer? You should probably avoid taking photos that could become gainful for you. On the other hand, if you're not a pro photog, you could spend the entire day taking pics without breaking Shabbat, because you're a plumber. A farmer shouldn't farm. But you, being a plumber, could spend the entire day in the garden because, well, you're not a farmer, you're a plumber. Heh.

Many Sabbatarians, yeah, that's what they're called, are typically very legalistic about the Sabbath. One example is they believe that you shouldn't go out to restaurants because you're causing someone else to work on your behalf based on Exod. 20:10 and Deut. 5:14 respectively:

"...but the seventh day is a Sabbath to the LORD your God. On it you shall not do any work, you, or your son, or your daughter, your male servant, or your female servant, or your livestock, or the sojourner who is within your gates."

"...but the seventh day is a Sabbath to the LORD your God. On it you shall not do any work, you or your son or your daughter or your male servant or your female servant, or your ox or your donkey or any of your livestock, or the sojourner who is within your gates, that your male servant and your female servant may rest as well as you."

Some cite the servant part while others site the sojourner (generally considered "Gentiles.") I'm of the opinion that neither "technically" apply, but many say that you're temporarily hiring a cook, a waiter or a waitress as a servant to work for you, so we should refrain from eating in restaurants on Shabbat. Either way, I don't make it a habit to eat at a restaurant on Shabbat and with that, I also don't judge those that do or don't.

Any form of buying and/or selling on Shabbat is also widely discourage based on Nehemiah 10:31 & 13:15-17. Now, Nehemiah is long after Exodus and Deuteronomy and you won't find that instruction "specifically" in the original Torah, but then again, there was nowhere for Israel to buy or sell in the desert except among themselves, and that distinction is never mentioned. I personally think some sort of system of bartering or trading occurred internally within their ranks, native or otherwise, but again, there's no mention of that. The idea behind the text in Nehemiah was that it was forcing others to work as well as their animals (Exod. 20:10, Deut. 5:14) on Shabbat. We can say that "technically" buying or selling isn't cited in the Torah (Exodus or Deuteronomy), but the reasoning behind Nehemiah is logically sound. Again, I don't make it a habit to buy and/or sell on Shabbat, and I also don't judge those that do or don't. I want to be obedient to the commandment, but I also don't want to follow tradition as a commandment. What we are absolutely certain of is that we are instructed *not* to do any of our ordinary work on Shabbat.

Cooking food on Shabbat is also something many Sabbatarians frown upon citing Exodus 16:

> And the LORD said to Moses, "I have heard the grumbling of the people of Israel. Say to them, 'At twilight you shall eat meat, and in the morning you shall be filled with bread. Then you shall know that I am the LORD your God.'"
> In the evening quail came up and covered the camp, and in the morning dew lay around the camp. And when the dew had gone up, there was on the face of the wilderness a fine, flake-like thing, fine as frost on the ground. When the people of Israel saw it, they said to one another, "What is it?" For they did not know what it was. And Moses said to them, "It is the bread that the LORD has given you to eat. This is what the LORD has commanded: 'Gather of it, each one of you, as much as he can eat. You shall each take an omer, according to the number of the persons that each of you has in his tent.'"
> And the people of Israel did so. They gathered, some more, some less. But when they measured it with an omer, whoever gathered much had nothing left over, and

> whoever gathered little had no lack. Each of them gathered as much as he could eat. And Moses said to them, "Let no one leave any of it over till the morning." But they did not listen to Moses. Some left part of it till the morning, and it bred worms and stank. And Moses was angry with them. Morning by morning they gathered it, each as much as he could eat; but when the sun grew hot, it melted.
>
> On the sixth day they gathered twice as much bread, two omers each. And when all the leaders of the congregation came and told Moses, he said to them, "This is what ADONAI has commanded: 'Tomorrow is a day of solemn rest, a holy Sabbath to the LORD; bake what you will bake and boil what you will boil, and all that is left over lay aside to be kept till the morning.'" So they laid it aside till the morning, as Moses commanded them, and it did not stink, and there were no worms in it. Moses said, "Eat it today, for today is a Sabbath to the LORD; today you will not find it in the field. Six days you shall gather it, but on the seventh day, which is a Sabbath, there will be none." On the seventh day some of the people went out to gather, but they found none. And the LORD said to Moses, "How long will you refuse to keep my commandments and my laws? See! The LORD has given you the Sabbath; therefore on the sixth day he gives you bread for two days. Remain each of you in his place; let no one go out of his place on the seventh day." So the people rested on the seventh day. Exodus 16:11-30

I opted to go with the whole account for context but the verses used to support no cooking on Shabbat are verses 22-24:

> On the sixth day they gathered twice as much bread, two omers each. And when all the leaders of the congregation came and told Moses, he said to them, "This is what the LORD has commanded: 'Tomorrow is a day of solemn rest, a holy Sabbath to the LORD; bake what you will bake and boil what you will boil, and all that is left over lay aside to be kept till the morning.'" So they laid it aside till the morning, as Moses commanded them, and it did not stink, and there were no worms in it.

Israel is to gather twice as much manna on Friday because it was unlawful for them to gather any manna on Shabbat. Besides, there wasn't any to gather on Saturday morning anyways... Gathering was considered work and this would be a better argument for abstaining from purchasing food or eating out on Shabbat, in my opinion. Verse 23:

> "...'Tomorrow is a day of solemn rest, a holy Sabbath to the LORD; bake what you will bake and boil what you will boil, and all that is left over lay aside to be kept till the morning.'"

Israel is to bake and boil on Friday. This is why many do not cook on Shabbat. Let's keep reading verse 23:

> "and all that is left over lay aside to be kept till the morning."

So we see here that not everything was baked or boiled on Friday and it also didn't rot in the morning (verse 24). Are we to assume that what wasn't previously baked or boiled on Friday that was laid aside until morning wasn't baked or boiled later that day during Shabbat?

Side note: Look at how many times Israel disobeyed or pushed the boundaries of this simple instruction, like naughty children, in verse 12 (grumbling), verse 20 (left some until morning), and verse 27 (went out to gather on Shabbat.) Just like we do.

Then there's this passage from Torah regarding the first and seventh days of the Feast of Unleavened Bread, which are High Sabbath days:

> On the first day you shall hold a holy assembly, and on the seventh day a holy assembly. No work shall be done on those days. But what everyone needs to eat, that alone may be prepared by you.
> Exodus 12:16

If it is permissible to prepare (cook?) on the High Holy days, which are High Sabbaths, is it then permissible to prepare (cook?) on the weekly Shabbat?

Have you ever watched Seinfeld? Have you ever seen Season 7 – Episode 6: *The Soup Nazi*? In this episode, a new soup restaurant opens up and they sell the best soup man has ever tasted. Ever. But in order for you to get the soup, you have to present yourself exactly in a way that is acceptable and determined by the owner/chef while you're in line, at the counter, how you order and how you receive and pay for your order, or, "**No soup for you!!**"

It's easy for humans to become like the Soup Nazi in regards to Shabbat or the Torah in general, and I've had my disagreements with them along the way. They tell me that I'm a Shabbat-Breaker because;

- I occasionally buy and sell on the Sabbath
- I occasionally eat at restaurants on the Sabbath
- I cook on the Sabbath
- I've performed with my worship band on the Sabbath

I try to be as kind and gentle with them as I can and bring up some basic things like,

- Did the mailman deliver your mail today? This one tends to freak some of them out. The very religious determine right then and there, as if I was suggesting it, to stop their mail delivery on Saturday. Oi vey...
- Is the electricity on at your house? Because, there's some guy you'll never know working at the power plant – on your behalf – making sure your power is on.
- Did it snow today? Did you have to travel on roads that were plowed to make it up the mountain to get to church tonight? You drove on roads that someone worked on – on your behalf – on the Sabbath.

See what I mean?

We want to avoid legalism. Keeping the commandments of God cannot become a legalistic observance of those commands. It's counterproductive. And when and where does it stop and who determines that? Here are a couple examples of what traditional Judaism deems proper Sabbath observance:

- If you leave a light on or off, you can't turn it on or off on the Sabbath
- Don't forget to unplug the light in your refrigerator in

case you have to open it on the Sabbath, so the light won't turn on. But since that's based on Exod. 35:3 regarding "You shall kindle no fire..." which is also interpreted as "Thou shall not cook" on the Sabbath, what are you doing opening up the frig?
- Elevators are marked "odd" and "even" in Israel and open on every floor on Shabbat so that you don't have to push your floor button, because that's considered work
- Forget about walking or driving anywhere

This is what Jesus was dealing with in regard to the appropriate observance of Shabbat.

Again, I don't judge those that do or don't turn on or off lights, open or close the refrigerator, push or don't push elevator buttons or travel on the Sabbath.

In Matthew 12:1-8, when Jesus and his disciples were walking through the grain fields on Shabbat and His disciples were seen plucking and eating heads of grain by the Pharisees, the Pharisees cried foul: "Look, your disciples are doing what is not lawful to do on the Sabbath." Jesus reminded them of David and his men eating the showbread from the temple, which was clearly a violation, and Jesus basically told the Pharisees that they were religiously and legalistically in error. He also had this to point out in regards to "profaning the Sabbath" in verse 5:

> *"Or have you not read in the Law how on the Sabbath the priests in the temple profane the Sabbath and are guiltless?"*

Jesus further challenges the Pharisee's understanding of Torah by referencing the fact that the priests clearly did "ordinary work" on Shabbat: They made the fires, killed, flayed, and dressed the sacrifices and all manner of manual labor necessary for the religious services. Besides the continual daily burnt offerings every week, the priests were required, *on Shabbat*, to sacrifice two lambs – doubling their "ordinary work" on the Sabbath day!

Jesus' point is clearly made that the priests performed servile duties in the temple which could be considered a violation of Shabbat by the religious, but that was never the case. It was necessary work for the public worship of God and therefore not considered profane. In other words, observing Shabbat was never meant to be a grueling, heavy-handed, legalistic burden!

Take this sound advice and example from Jesus and correlate it contextually with what we studied in Matthew 5 and Jeremiah 7. The Father's desire regarding keeping and observing His Torah has always been about the intention of the heart. Our actions are to reflect our hearts in right standing before Him. This is the exact opposite of what traditional Judaism advocates and what many in the Western Church falsely believe we do as Torah-observant believers in Jesus. Remember, Christians are the ones freaking out legalistically, because you stopped eating pork! Heh... Now, these "intentions of the heart" are not a license *not* to keep Torah, His commandments, as many like to use as an excuse or as their "Get Out of Torah Free" card while all the while misquoting Jeremiah 31:33. What is it about our need for "loopholes" to qualify our disobedience?!?

Do I always go out to restaurants on Shabbat? No. I also don't go or *not* go to restaurants simply based on it *being* Shabbat. Do I always buy and/or sell on Shabbat? No. I also don't buy and/or sell *or* buy and/or sell based on it *being* Shabbat. Do I always cook on Shabbat? No. I also don't cook *or* cook based on it *being* Shabbat and I also don't judge those that do or don't.

Does the Day We Keep as a Sabbath Really Matter?

It's astonishing how adamant the Western Church is in their belief that the day they keep as a "sabbath" doesn't matter to God and how they're "free" to observe, as their sabbath, any day they choose "because of Jesus," or my favorite, "God knows my heart." (Yes. Yes, He does. And you just incriminated yourself scripturally (Jeremiah 17:9-10.)) It's just as astonishing how Jesus is Christianity's primary excuse for this sort of biblical lawlessness.

I also understand that this is what the Western Church has been told and that this is what the Western Church has been taught, but a basic look into God's Word would show even the most limited student of the Bible that the common narrative and the scriptural record conflict with each other. So does the day we keep as a Sabbath really matter to God? Well of course it does! The language used in the Ten Commandments should be enough for us to come to that conclusion on our own:

"*Remember* the Sabbath day, to keep it holy."

Do you or anyone else you know "remember" things like times, dates, and/or appointments if they're not important to you? Here's the real question: Do you or anyone else you know "remember" things in order to forget or dismiss them? No! You remember to remember!! So then, why does "Jesus" afford us the "liberty" to forget this? Jesus only said what He heard the Father say, and the Father clearly said to remember the Sabbath day, a *specific* day, not just *any* day of your choosing, and then to keep that specific day holy!

In Exodus 19, we see that Moses and all of Israel have assembled before the Living God, per His instructions, at the base of Mount Sinai. This is when and where God established His instructions for those that would call upon His name; His instructions for humans that make the voluntary decision to serve Him; His covenant instructions for those who call themselves "Believers" – the wedding vows, if you will, between the Bridegroom and His Bride – the vows His Bride voluntarily makes covenant with to be known as His. These are the instructions that "set you apart" from the rest, the covenants that make Him your God and you His people, a nation of Kings and Priests (Exodus 24).

We see that Moses and all of Israel have assembled before the Living God at the base of Mount Sinai. Then Moses entered the cloud and went up into the mountain for 40 days and 40 nights. If that doesn't bring shivers down your spine...

For the following 40 days and nights, God downloaded to Moses all of the instructions – all of the covenants that God Himself was making with humankind; how to live, how to live with your fellow man, how to live with and among strangers, how to live with and worship God, etc.

The *last thing* – the *very last instruction* recorded in this meeting – that God gave to Moses before Moses came down from the mountain after 40 days and nights was this:

*"**Above all you shall keep my Sabbaths**, for **this is a sign between me and you throughout your generations, that you may know that I, the LORD, sanctify you**.*

***You shall keep the Sabbath, because it is holy for you**. Everyone who profanes it shall be put to death. Whoever does any work on it, that soul shall be cut off from among his* *people.*

Six days shall work be done, but the seventh day is a Sabbath of solemn rest, holy to the LORD. Whoever does any work on the Sabbath day shall be put to death.

Therefore the people of Israel shall keep the Sabbath, observing the Sabbath throughout their generations, **as a covenant forever.**

It is a sign forever between me and the people of Israel *that in six days the LORD made heaven and earth, and on the seventh day he rested and was refreshed.'"*
Exodus 31:13-17 [Emphasis mine]

After 40 days and 40 nights, alone with God on Mount Sinai, the last thing God instructs Moses is something God had already told Moses. He repeated Himself: *"Above all else you shall keep my Sabbaths..."*

- **This is a sign between Me and you** throughout your generations, that you may know **that I, the LORD, sanctify you**
- Because **it is holy for you**
- Six days shall work be done, but the seventh day is **a Sabbath of solemn rest, holy to the LORD**
- **Keep the Sabbath**, observing the Sabbath throughout your generations, **as a covenant forever**
- **It is a sign forever between me and you** that in six days the LORD made heaven and earth, and on the seventh day he rested and was refreshed

So, you decide for yourself; "Does the day we keep as a Sabbath really matter?" It does to Him...

In Summary

Appointed Time: Shabbat

Significance: The fourth of the Ten Commandments. A Holy day; holy to us and for us on our behalf. A day of remembrance of creation and freedom from Egyptian slavery. Shabbat is a sign between God and man, a sign of our sanctification and creation

Observance: You have a special meal with family and friends.

It's a weekly "reboot" and a day of solemn rest so no ordinary work is done. It's a day for refreshing

Length: 24 hours, Friday sunset to Saturday sunset

As we saw earlier in this Chapter, Shabbat is a holy day that was made holy on our behalf and a day for us to remember creation. It's also a day for us to remember our freedom from Egyptian slavery:

> *Observe the Sabbath day, to keep it holy, as the LORD your God commanded you.*
>
> *Six days you shall labor and do all your work, but the seventh day is a Sabbath to the LORD your God. On it you shall not do any work, you or your son or your daughter or your male servant or your female servant, or your ox or your donkey or any of your livestock, or the sojourner who is within your gates, that your male servant and your female servant may rest as well as you.*
>
> **You shall remember that you were a slave in the land of Egypt**, *and the LORD your God brought you out from there with a mighty hand and an outstretched arm.* **Therefore the LORD your God commanded you to keep the Sabbath day.**
>
> Deuteronomy 5:12-15 [Emphasis mine]

I also stated earlier that Shabbat is a family affair. Here are some ways we can enjoy Shabbat as families, communities or as individuals and couples:

- Go on a drive together and take a picnic lunch
- Kick a soccer ball around or fly a kite
- Read a book, the Torah portions, and/or the Word alone or together
- Playing games, arts and crafts or puzzles are a great way to spend the day
- Go on a hike or walk
- Take a bike ride
- Skype family or friends
- Go to the beach, lake or river
- Fishing is a great time with the Lord
- Take a nap, but most definitely,

- Enjoy Father God and His blessings!

Jesus said that Shabbat was made for man, not man for Shabbat. It serves me, I don't serve it. I keep Shabbat out of obedience, not out of legalistic ritual. Shabbat is life. Covenant life. And covenant life is freedom not bondage. Remember Shabbat and keep it holy. Amen.

Remember a long time ago, in a galaxy far, far away, when I said that the results of observing Shabbat are life-altering for a family if you do and life-altering for a family if you don't? And how leading your family in Shabbat was Priesthood?

I reconnected with a family after having very little to no communication with them for roughly 12 years. They were both active in their local church the last time I remember seeing them which was shortly after their first child was born. By the time we reconnected, they had had two more children, they were no longer active in a local church and it was painfully obvious that something had gone awry. Mom was a fall-down drunk, the kids had no concept of Jesus, and dad was... well, dad just wanted out.

I took him aside and asked him, "What is going on here? What happened to you guys?!" He began to sob. He didn't know how it happened. They had stopped going to church years ago, they hadn't slept in the same bed for years, he secretly prayed and wished that his wife would have an affair so that he could leave her... the story went on and on. "Help me. I don't know what to do..." This was a desperate man.

I, on the other hand, wasn't surprised to hear any of it. I already knew what had happened. It's not rocket science, and I see it all the time. Being in a touring ministry band puts me in certain situations. I see church-pastor-congregant dynamics, and I also see husband-wife-marriage-family life dynamics.

A few years ago, my wife and I took a road trip that put us in half a dozen Christian homes; homes from various denominational backgrounds. These were the homes of people we had known for some time; families that we had deep relationships with; these weren't strangers. I was working on a "Husbands Being the Priest of Their Homes" project, so we decided to take advantage of the situation and do some field work and "rate" these families on the following:

1. Did they pray for / over us upon our arrival?
2. What was the dynamic between mom and dad?
3. What was the dynamic between the kids and dad?
4. What was the dynamic between dad and the fam?
5. Did dad lead his family?
6. Did dad model Jesus to his family?
7. Did they pray for / over us before we left?

The answer to these questions will tell you everything you need to know about a man. And while all these families fared well with our "secret shopper scoring system," there was one family that scored high in all seven areas with flying colors. Since then, they have started observing and keeping God's Word, the commandments, Torah.

Back to my old friend: "Help me... I don't know what to do!"

I did, but there was no quick fix for this train wreck.

He was going to have to repent and actually get saved. He needed a revelation of the person of Jesus for himself before he could help his declining family situation. The question was, could he repent? Could he repent and fall back into love with his wife – no matter how long it took for her to have that same revelation of Jesus for herself – the same revelation before she could help her declining family situation?

Their repentance would cover the children but there were going to be some deep-rooted issues there, issues that only spiritual warfare, with lots of fasting and no small amount of deliverance, could mend. Love covers a multitude of sins, and they desperately needed to mend the lack of healthy, Godly love within them.

I was only in town for a couple days. I wasn't in a position to "fix" them, nor could I fix them. This was something they were going to have to do themselves. Yeah, I was bummed; I was bummed out for finding my friends in this deplorable situation, and I was bummed out because I knew the path they were going to have to take in order for them to be restored; a narrow path that few take because it's a path riddled with resistance (Mt. 7:13-14). And that's what I basically told him.

I told my friend that he needed to get saved. Really saved. I told him that he needed to repent and beg God to spare him for the mess he had made of his marriage and family. It was basically a come to Jesus talk and if he was serious about asking me for my help, there was something I could do but it would be entirely on him to implement.

"I can tell you about and show you how to keep the Sabbath with your family. And if you start there, if you do that, you just might survive this."

So we modeled and taught them as a family how to do Shabbat, and then we continued on our tour and left town. A couple weeks later, I followed up with him and found out that they had done Shabbat the week after we had left but they were no longer going to do it, because they were not "under the law" and not required to do "that Jewish stuff" as Christians. I said okay, and left it at that. It really sucks when the birds eat the seed that is on the path or when the sun scorches the seed without roots that is on rocky ground.

A year later, we were back to visit, and their situation had deteriorated severely. There had been no repentance. There was only tolerance for what their lives had become. I watched as he mocked what I proposed, trampling on what was holy while he turned on me and attacked me. This went on for months afterward. It was horrible. I watched as they got a divorce and as their family was torn apart. I watched as they all left what little remained of their faith and embraced their new church of resentment, anger, bitterness and perverted humanistic reasoning – the demonic. I watched a lifelong friendship vanish before my eyes. I was to blame for his life's woes; if only I had never told him about Jesus...

I wish I could say that this was an isolated case. It isn't, and it wasn't. I've seen this happen with other families, individuals and ministries. All because of that "Jewish stuff..."

"Bill," on the other hand, has been leading his family in Shabbat since the day he asked me that question. Both he and his family continue to grow in the full knowledge of Messiah. I couldn't be prouder of them.

CHAPTER 4

PASSOVER (PESACH) AND THE FEAST OF UNLEAVENED BREAD
Worthy is the Lamb that was slain

"These are the appointed feasts of the LORD, the holy convocations, which you shall proclaim at the time appointed for them. In the first month, on the fourteenth day of the month at twilight, is the LORD's Passover.

And on the fifteenth day of the same month is the Feast of Unleavened Bread to the LORD; for seven days you shall eat unleavened bread. On the first day you shall have a holy convocation [a High Sabbath]; you shall not do any ordinary work. But you shall present a food offering to the LORD for seven days. On the seventh day is a holy convocation [a High Sabbath]; you shall not do any ordinary work."
Leviticus 23:4-8

As I shared in the Introduction, I started writing this book the week that I returned from the Prophetic Conference we attended in Las Vegas in February 2017. With that in mind, the calendar breakdowns in this Chapter will be based on 2017's Spring Feasts which are less than six weeks away! If you're a member of the Chameleon Church Facebook group (https://facebook.com/ChameleonChurch), you've seen this year's breakdown already. We have lots of ground to cover so let's begin!

The History

> *And the LORD, God made for Adam and for his wife garments of skins and clothed them.*
> Genesis 3:21

Adam and Eve had disobeyed the commandment of ADONAI; they had allowed themselves to be seduced by the serpent and had eaten from the Tree of the Knowledge of Good and Evil. In the shame of their nakedness, they had made garments of fig leaves. These garments weren't suitable to Father God, so He made them garments of skins and clothed them. The first recorded blood-atoning sacrifice…

> *For the life of the flesh is in the blood, and I have given it for you on the altar to make atonement for your souls, for it is the blood that makes atonement by the life.*
> Leviticus 17:11

Atonement requires the shedding of blood. This is why ADONAI "made them garments of skins." This rule of atonement has been woven into the fabric of our space-time continuum from the very beginning. Just last week, a popular "Christian" artist came out decrying the penal substitutionary model of atonement. "…that God needed to be appeased with blood is not beautiful. It's horrific," was the exact quote. Sadly, I don't think it's going to adversely affect his record or concert sales.

Cain and Abel were Adam's firstborn sons. Cain was a worker of the ground and Abel was a keeper of sheep. The common thread of Torah – throughout Scripture from the very beginning – is evident here as we see both sons preparing a sacrifice for ADONAI; Cain's sacrifice, an offering of the fruit of the ground, and Abel, who also brought of the firstborn of his flock and of their fat portions (Gen. 4:3b-4).

The account states that ADONAI accepted Abel's sacrifice but that ADONAI didn't accept Cain's. We don't know exactly why. Was it because (according to the language can we presume, suppose, assume maybe, that), Abel's sacrifice was from his "firstfruits", that this was a Firstfruits Offering? *Abel brought the firstborn of his flock and of their fat portions…* We don't know for sure. What we do know is that Cain was very angry, because ADONAI had rejected his offering.

The LORD said to Cain, "Why are you angry, and why has your face fallen? If you do well, will you not be accepted? And if you do not do well, sin is crouching at the door. Its desire is for you, but you must rule over it."
Genesis 4:6-7

The Holman translation says, "...sin is crouching at the door. Its desire is for you, but you must *master* it."

This is vital information. I think ADONAI may have been testing Cain by rejecting his sacrifice. Surely He knew the condition of his heart. Cain was the firstborn, after all, and God had claims to him. I think He may have been testing Cain with a warning, "If you do right you're gonna be ok. But if you decide not to do the right thing, sin is *crouching* at your door and it wants to devour you. But you can master it. You can beat this thing. You *must* rule over it!"

I shared this primarily because it's about sacrifices. It's about offerings unto God, and the offering that was accepted, Abel's, may have been a Firstfruits Offering. Why is that significant? As we continue unlocking the Feasts, you'll see the cadence, the rhythm of God's journey for us, is played out to the beat of firstfruits. Abel's sacrifice was definitely a blood / animal sacrifice and, more importantly, it was a well-received and accepted sacrifice. Later in this Chapter, we'll take a look at God's historical cycle of sacrifices.

Moses / Egyptology and the 18th Dynasty

Jump roughly 2600 years to Egypt, where Israel has been living for approximately 200 years. There's a new Pharaoh in town, and he doesn't know Joseph. It seems that this new Pharaoh also doesn't recognize Joseph's contribution to the Egyptian empire and is more concerned with the size of Israel's population; that their numbers may be more than Egypt can manage or control. What if war broke out, and Israel decided to join Egypt's enemies, fight against them and leave? So Pharaoh decides to deal with Israel shrewdly by distressing, oppressing and tasking them with Egypt's heavy lifting, such as building Pharaoh's store cities. In spite of this, Israel continues to multiply and spread across Egypt.

This only increased Egypt's anxiety and fear towards Israel, so they enslaved them and were ruthless towards them. The Hebrew midwives were instructed to kill all newborn Israeli males, but out of their fear of God, they disobeyed the Pharaoh's instructions so that Israel continued to multiply and strengthen. Pharaoh then instructs Egyptians to carry out the task of murder by throwing all Israeli newborn boys into the Nile.

> Now a man from the house of Levi went and took as his wife a Levite woman. The woman conceived and bore a son, and when she saw that he was a fine child, she hid him three months.
> Exodus 2:1-2

Did you notice that Moses was a Levite? But of course he was! The Hebrew midwives have been instructed to murder males at birth. They fear God over Pharaoh and disobey the Egyptian's edict. Pharaoh then instructs all male Israelites to be thrown into the Nile. This is the climate into which this little Levite boy was born. Moses is put into a basket and into the Nile to hide him:

> Now the daughter of Pharaoh came down to bathe at the river, while her young women walked beside the river. She saw the basket among the reeds and sent her servant woman, and she took it. When she opened it, she saw the child, and behold, the baby was crying. She took pity on him and said, "This is one of the Hebrews' children."
> Exodus 2:5-6

Moses' sister, Miriam, had been watching the basket, and when she saw Pharaoh's daughter take the basket with the crying baby, she asked if she should go and call on a Hebrew nurse to nurse the child for her. With the Egyptian Princess' permission, Miriam goes and gets her mother. They were instructed to take the child and nurse it and were paid to do so. Verse 10:

> When the child grew up, she brought him to Pharaoh's daughter, and he became her son. She named him Moses, "Because," she said, "I drew him out of the water."

Moses' father was Amram the Levite. His mother's name was Jochebed (Exod. 6:20). Moses was of a pure Levitical line, and 80 years before the Exodus, Israel was a great people. They were no longer referred to as a tribe; they were a people.

Moses will be raised in Pharaoh's family and in Egypt's court.

He will have the best education the world has to offer and will lack nothing. He will also have power as a favored Son of Egypt.

1500 years later, a disciple of Jesus, Stephen, will say this about Moses:

> And Moses was instructed in all the wisdom of the Egyptians, and he was mighty in his words and deeds.
> Acts 7:22

It is said that Moses was raised up as a general of Egypt's armies at the suggestion of Egypt's oracles and prophets to counter the strained relations with Ethiopia. Moses is victorious against Ethiopia and becomes a celebrated war hero, turning Egyptian leaders against him out of fear:

- Moses is a foreigner, a Hebrew
- Moses represents Israel, who are numerous
- Moses has become very powerful
- Moses has shown military innovation that might introduce new customs
- Envy and fear turns Egypt against Moses

(Source: Josephus: *Antiquities of the Jews* 2/9:7-10:2)

Then Moses makes a mistake; he kills an Egyptian. If the account of Josephus is true, Pharaoh now has his reason to get rid of Moses. When Pharaoh hears that Moses has murdered a fellow Egyptian, Pharaoh wants Moses dead. Moses flees Egypt through the desert to Midian, where he immediately makes a name for himself by stopping some shepherds that were bullying the seven daughters of the Midian priest:

> When they [the seven daughters] came home to their father Reuel, he said, "How is it that you have come home so soon today?" They said, "An Egyptian delivered us out of the hand of the shepherds and even drew water for us and watered the flock." He said to his daughters, "Then where is he? Why have you left the man? Call him, that he may eat bread."
> Exodus 2:18-20

Two verses later, Moses is married to Reuel's daughter, Zipporah, and they have a son named Gershom.

There's an hypothesis that Moses lived in the 18th Dynasty when two to three Pharaohs ruled regionally at the same time. It suggests that a people called the Hyksos lived in the northern delta region and are described as "shepherd kings" whom the Egyptians considered foreigners. This hypothesis suggests that these are the descendants of Joseph who lived there with royal status because of Joseph's good standing in Egypt during the seven-year famine.

An inscription of Queen Hatshepsut, Pharaoh's daughter, refers to the Hyksos people being driven out of this northern delta. Egyptian records suggest a warrior people (barbarians) that lived in the Northland among these shepherd kings were driven out by Egypt due to a situation that threatened what could be the Hebrews. Because they were shepherds, they were unable to defend themselves. This weakness, though their number was great, was the ideal combination for an Egyptian workforce, thus the slavery of Israel and Egypt's protection of them.

(The Brooklyn Papyrus from the 12th – 13th dynasty is a list of foreigner slaves. It is a business document listing family structures and slave duties. The lists state that some slaves were Semites of Syrian and Israeli background with Semitic / Hebrew slave names.)

In this 18th Dynasty hypothesis, Pharaoh's daughter is possibly the daughter of Pharaoh Thutmosis I, who had no male heir. Her name was Nefure / Hatshepsut. There are several statutes of Nefure holding a male child who is wearing ornaments indicating royalty and/or the heir to the Egyptian throne. Is the child she's holding, named Senmut, the Hebrew Levite, Moses? Did she adopt this Israeli boy, born into slavery, because her father had no heir, positioning herself for future rule? The name Senmut means "mother's brother" meaning that through her, Senmut had the right to inherit the throne, since Nefure bore the right but couldn't become Pharaoh herself. History tells us that she would eventually become Queen. If this Senmut is indeed Moses, what happens to him in Egyptology?

It is probably that Senmut abused his power and that at a particular point in the reign of Hatshepsut he fell into disgrace, as demonstrated by the damage done to most of his monuments.
(Source: F. Tiradritti (1999) *The Cairo Museum Master Pieces of Egyptian Art*, Thames and Hudson, London, England)

This is exactly what happened to Moses:

As heir to the throne, murdering a fellow Egyptian, then escaping Egypt; this would have been a disgrace from an Egyptian perspective. According to Egyptian tradition, everything – monuments, statues, scrolls etc. – would have been destroyed. You would have been erased from history.

Here's a very interesting fact that I never stopped to consider before: History tells us that Thutmosis IV (also known as Amenhotep III), the Pharaoh that succeeded Thutmosis I, was not a firstborn son. Whoever the Pharaoh of the Exodus account was, he survives the Angel of Death during the first Passover. This could be because of the fact that he was not a firstborn son or because the Exodus account states that The Destroyer would begin with Pharaoh's first born. Or does the Exodus account state that The Destroyer would begin with Pharaoh's first born, because Pharaoh himself wasn't a firstborn son?

Regardless, here are some interesting facts about Thutmosis IV / Amenhotep III, the Pharaoh from the 18th Dynasty that could parallel the Pharaoh that Moses was sent to in the Exodus account:

- Thutmosis IV was the second born son of Amenhotep II.
- Thutmosis IV killed his firstborn brother to take the crown
- The Dream Stela of Thutmosis IV, found between the front paws of the Sphinx, was used to legitimize the murder by claiming it was directed by the Sphinx in a dream
- King Tutankamun (yes, *that* King Tut): An inscription on a statue of a lion dedicated by King Tutankhamen to the temple of Soleb, claims Amenhotep III as his *father*
- King Tutankhamen supposedly reigned from the age of 9 until his mysterious death at 18. He was the only heir apparent to the throne (Crowned Prince) that may have co-reigned with his father in his later years (Exod. 11:5: ...*from the firstborn of Pharaoh who sits on his throne...*)
- King Tut's tomb, found in the Valley of the Kings by Howard Carter in 1922, was said to be

a *"cursed"* tomb. His burial looks rushed and in a tomb generally too small and not designed for a reigning pharaoh's burial

(Source: "The Hidden Moses." http://www.aloha.net/~mikesch/moses.htm)

Is Thutmosis IV the Pharaoh that perished with his armies while pursuing Moses into the Sea?

Is King Tutankamun, the firstborn son of Pharaoh Thutmosis IV, the firstborn son of Pharaoh struck dead by the Angel of Death in Exodus 12:29?

> *And the LORD said to Moses in Midian, "Go back to Egypt, for all the men who were seeking your life are dead."*
> Exodus 4:19

Thutmosis III died ca. 1450, and his son, Amenhotep II, ascended the throne. If the chronology proposed in this hypothesis is correct, Moses returned to Egypt around 1446 BC, roughly four years into the reign of Amenhotep II. Again, if this hypothesis has any merit, how were Moses and Aaron able to gain an audience with this new Pharaoh? Moses - Senmut / Thutmosis II, the adopted son of Hatshepsut and living heir to the throne, was Pharaoh Amenhotep II's step-uncle.

> *Moreover, the man Moses was very great in the land of Egypt, in the sight of Pharaoh's servants and in the sight of the people.*
> Exodus 11:3b

> *By faith Moses, when he was born, was hidden for three months by his parents, because they saw that the child was beautiful, and they were not afraid of the king's edict. By faith Moses, when he was grown up, **refused to be called the son of Pharaoh's daughter**, choosing rather to be mistreated with the people of God than to enjoy the fleeting pleasures of sin. He considered the reproach of Christ greater wealth than the treasures of Egypt, for he was looking to the reward. By faith he left Egypt, **not being afraid of the anger of the king** [Pharaoh], for he endured as seeing him who is invisible. By faith he kept the Passover and sprinkled the blood, so that*

> the Destroyer of the firstborn might not touch them [Israel].
> Hebrews 11:23-28 [Emphasis mine]

I included this information, because I want to paint a picture of this man, this Levite, this Prophet that precedes the Messiah Jesus; this Egyptian noble, this warrior, this Nephilim killer... This is the man that delivers Israel from Egypt, that has been given the task to fashion Israel from a people into a nation – a nation of Kings and Priests unto ADONAI. This is who God calls the humblest man that ever walked the face of the earth; the man that God chose to speak to face to face – like you speak to a man; the man that God showed His physical manifestation to and lived to tell about it! The man whose body Lucifer argued over... This is the man, the Levitical priest, who was personally given God's instruction on how you and I are to live – here on this earth – in the Way that proves to everyone that we are truly His.

Moses / Egypt and the Deliverance of Israel

We all should know the story in Exodus Chapter 3 of how after 40 years of tending his father-in-law's sheep on the backside of the mountain, an angel of ADONAI appears to Moses on Mount Horeb in the form of a bush on fire that isn't being consumed by the flames – and this ignited bush speaks to him:

> And Moses said, "I will turn aside to see this great sight, why the bush is not burned." When the LORD saw that he turned aside to see, God called to him out of the bush, "Moses, Moses!" And he said, "Here I am." - "I am the God of your father, the God of Abraham, the God of Isaac, and the God of Jacob." And Moses hid his face, for he was afraid to look at God.
> Exodus 3:3-4, 6

I don't know about you, but that's amazing to me; when you know beyond a shadow of a doubt that He knows you by name, and He calls you by that name.

Moses is told that God has heard the affliction of Israel at the hand of their taskmasters and that He has come down to deliver them and to bring them to the Land promised them through Abraham. Moses is to be sent to Pharaoh, and Moses is to bring the children of Israel out of Egypt.

In Exodus 4, Moses doubts that he will be taken seriously before the people, so God gives him great power through the use of his staff as an oracle. Moses then makes the excuse that he's a horrible public speaker, but God insists. He will be Moses' mouth and teach him what to speak. Moses then asks God to send someone else. This angers God, who then concedes and allows Moses to take his brother Aaron, the Levite, who is a good speaker. Moses will tell Aaron what to speak, God will be with both their mouths and teach both of them what to do:

> "He [Aaron] shall speak for you to the people, and he shall be your mouth, and you shall be as God to him. And take in your hand this staff, with which you shall do the signs."
> Exodus 4:16-17

Moses reunites with his brother, Aaron, and brings him up to speed with the plan. They then return to Egypt and go before the elders of Israel. They tell them the plan and do the signs that God told Moses to do before the people, and they believe the brothers.

In Exodus Chapter 5, Moses and Aaron go before Pharaoh and tell him that ADONAI, the God of Israel, says to let His people go on a three-day journey into the wilderness so that they can have a feast and sacrifice to Him. Pharaoh basically says, "Who is this God? He's not the boss of me. I don't know this guy, and I'm not going to let you go." The brothers explain how God has met them; please let them go on this trip, or God might punish them if they don't.

Pharaoh says, "Dudes, why are you taking the people away from their work?" He then proceeds to instruct the taskmasters not to provide Israel with the straw they need to make bricks. Israel is instructed to gather the straw that they need for bricks themselves, doubling their workload, and they are to make sure that their quota remains the same. According to Pharaoh, they obviously have free time on their hands to ask him for a week-long vacation so that they can go on a spiritual retreat. Pharaoh instructs his taskmasters to make sure Israel works even harder because of their idle laziness.

The Israeli foremen are then beaten for not making their required quota... basically, Moses and Aaron going before Pharaoh didn't go over very well. The people aren't happy with the brothers, and Moses has no idea why he was even sent to Pharaoh in the first place.

In Exodus Chapter 6, God establishes His Word to Moses that Israel will surely be delivered by God's strong hand. The brothers are commanded to continue going before Pharaoh, petitioning him to let Israel go, and to continue displaying their signs and wonders to him. But the heart of Pharaoh is hardened. Chapters 7-10 are the account of the various plagues that were brought down on Egypt because of Pharaoh's hardened heart, and in Chapter 11, we see God's plan to end this standoff once and for all:

> So Moses said, "Thus says the LORD: About midnight I will go out in the midst of Egypt, and every firstborn in the land of Egypt shall die, from the firstborn of Pharaoh who sits on his throne, even to the firstborn of the slave girl who is behind the handmill, and all the firstborn of the cattle."
> Exodus 11:4-5

The Passover: Exodus 12:1-20

> The LORD said to Moses and Aaron in the land of Egypt, "This month shall be for you the beginning of months. It shall be the first month of the year for you. Tell all the congregation of Israel that on the tenth day of this month every man shall take a lamb according to their fathers' houses, a lamb for a household. And if the household is too small for a lamb, then he and his nearest neighbor shall take according to the number of persons; according to what each can eat you shall make your count for the lamb. Your lamb shall be without blemish, a male a year old. You may take it from the sheep or from the goats, and you shall keep it until the fourteenth day of this month, when the whole assembly of the congregation of Israel shall kill their lambs at twilight.
> "Then they shall take some of the blood and put it on the two doorposts and the lintel of the houses in which they eat it. They shall eat the flesh that night, roasted on the fire; with unleavened bread and bitter herbs they shall eat it. Do not eat any of it raw or boiled in water, but roasted, its head with its legs and its inner parts. And you shall let none of it

remain until the morning; anything that remains until the morning you shall burn.

In this manner you shall eat it: with your belt fastened, your sandals on your feet, and your staff in your hand. And you shall eat it in haste. It is the LORD's Passover. For I will pass through the land of Egypt that night, and I will strike all the firstborn in the land of Egypt, both man and beast; and on all the gods of Egypt I will execute judgments: I am the LORD.

The blood shall be a sign for you, on the houses where you are. And when I see the blood, I will pass over you, and no plague will befall you to destroy you, when I strike the land of Egypt. "This day shall be for you a memorial day, and you shall keep it as a feast to the LORD; throughout your generations, as a statute forever, you shall keep it as a feast.

Seven days you shall eat unleavened bread. On the first day you shall remove leaven out of your houses, for if anyone eats what is leavened, from the first day until the seventh day, that person shall be cut off from Israel.

On the first day you shall hold a holy assembly, and on the seventh day a holy assembly. No work shall be done on those days. But what everyone needs to eat, that alone may be prepared by you. And you shall observe the Feast of Unleavened Bread, for on this very day I brought your hosts out of the land of Egypt. Therefore you shall observe this day, throughout your generations, as a statute forever.

In the first month, from the fourteenth day of the month at evening, you shall eat unleavened bread until the twenty-first day of the month at evening. For seven days no leaven is to be found in your houses. If anyone eats what is leavened, that person will be cut off from the congregation of Israel, whether he is a sojourner or a native of the land. You shall eat nothing leavened; in all your dwelling places you shall eat unleavened bread."
Exodus 12:1-20

We're going to break down Exodus 12:1-20 into practical segmented sections with New Testament and real-world examples. The goal of this exercise is to alleviate any seeming contradictions, confusion or frustration and to bring clarity and understanding regarding the Torah instruction of observing Passover and the Feast of Unleavened Bread and to apply tangible and realistic application to the instruction.

Passover / The Feast of Unleavened Bread is the first of the Three Pilgrimage Festivals. Three times a year, every firstborn Israeli male was to present himself before ADONAI in Jerusalem. This was the first appointed time that the men were to present themselves.

God has set things up in such a way that we are required to do the work of determining His ways – with His instructions as our guide – in order for us to follow and obey Him and the commandments. Let me explain. Think of this as a treasure map or a noble quest, and then think of the multiple passages that allude to this proactive journey:

It is the glory of God to conceal things, but the glory of kings is to search things out.
Proverbs 25:2 – See also Proverbs 20:5

And then think of the parables of Jesus regarding what the Kingdom of Heaven is like:

The kingdom of heaven is like treasure hidden in a field, which a man found and covered up. Then in his joy he goes and sells all that he has and buys that field.
Matthew 13:44 – See also the rest of Mt. 13

We're also supposed to knock, seek and ask. It's an incredibly interactive and proactive thing, this walking in the Way. But now we have a problem: The Western Church's fear of "works" and their fear of a "works-based mentality" has made them anemic. They're so in fear of "works unto salvation" that the common theology across the board of denominations is that once you're saved, you don't have to do anything! This convolution is based on an erroneous and unhealthy "interpretation" (it's more a matter of a lack of understanding than "interpretation") of Ephesians 2:8-9: "Salvation is by grace not works..." First of all, of course salvation is by grace, but *we're not talking about salvation!* Nothing that we have discussed thus far – nothing that we are going to discuss from here on out – is about salvation. Remember one of the first things we established early on in this book: Torah observance, also known as "Keeping the Commandments," is for blessing – not salvation. The "works" required to determine His ways; i.e. "work out your own salvation with fear and trembling" we do because we *are* saved! (Phi. 2:12. Yeah, Paul used the "W" word).

Faith Without "Works"

> What does it profit, my brethren, if someone says he has faith but does not have works? Can faith save him? If a brother or sister is naked and destitute of daily food, and one of you says to them, "Depart in peace, be warmed and filled," but you do not give them the things which are needed for the body, what does it profit?
>
> Thus also faith by itself, if it does not have works, is dead. But someone will say, "You have faith, and I have works." Show me your faith without your works, and I will show you my faith by my works. You believe that there is one God. You do well. Even the demons believe – and tremble! But do you want to know, O foolish man, that faith without works is dead?
>
> Was not Abraham our father justified by works when he offered Isaac his son on the altar? Do you see that faith was working together with his works, and by works faith was made perfect? And the Scripture was fulfilled which says, "Abraham believed God, and it was accounted to him for righteousness." And he was called the friend of God.
>
> You see then that a man is justified by works, and not by faith only. Likewise, was not Rahab the harlot also justified by works when she received the messengers and sent them out another way? For as the body without the spirit is dead, so faith without works is dead also.
> James 2:14-26 (NKJV)

I deliberately used the New King James Version for this passage in James so that no one could say that I was using a biased "Torah friendly" version for this example. I also refrained from emphasizing any of it. I also would like to note that James uses two examples from the TaNaKh to make his point.

Using the word "works;" stating that you believe that works are a part of your Christian faith; quoting James verbatim: "that a man is justified by works;" stating that our Christian faith "without works is dead" and that faith alone cannot / does not save, is considered heretical by the majority.

How did this obvious fact of our faith, a fact spoken of as an essential and crucial characteristic of this faith throughout the entire Bible, become so perverted? Well, we can attribute the beginning of this "doctrine of demons" with the outlawing of Torah.

I think James, *the brother of Jesus*, the Apostolic leader of the Church, the Apostle that the Apostle Paul was submitted to, would know what he was talking about!

- He clearly asks the redundant question: Can a man's faith without works save him? Can faith alone save?
- He clearly states that faith without works is dead
- He states that he can show us his faith by his works
- He calls those that don't understand or believe that their faith is dead without works "fools"
- He states that our faith is made perfect by these works
- He clearly states that we are *justified* by works! The Western Church denounces this completely, and
- For the third time in this passage, he states again that our faith without works is dead

This is a clear and absolutely crucial teaching by James.

There are actually those that would say that since the letter we call the Book of James was written specifically to "the twelve tribes in the Dispersion" (Jews), that it doesn't apply to Gentile Believers. These people would also tell you that only Paul "technically" applies to Gentiles. If this is the case, then almost nothing of the Bible applies to Gentiles. With this same reasoning, I propose that that would also include the atonement death of the Jew, Jesus; the Messiah of the Hebrews. Especially since "salvation is of the Jews," as Jesus said. If this is the case, throw this book away, and we can all just call it a day.

But since you brought up Paul...

> *For we are God's fellow **workers**. You are God's field, God's building. According to the grace of God given to me, like a skilled master builder I laid a foundation, and someone else is building upon it.* **Let each one take care how he builds upon it.** *For no one can lay a foundation other than that which is laid, which is Jesus Christ.*
>
> *Now if anyone builds on the foundation with gold, silver, precious stones, wood, hay, straw –* **each one's work will become manifest,** *for the Day will disclose it, because it will be revealed by fire, and* **the fire will test what sort of work each one has done.**
>
> **If the work that anyone has built on the foundation survives, he will receive a reward.** *If anyone's work is burned up, he will suffer loss, though he himself will be saved, but only as through fire.*
>
> 1 Corinthians 3:9-15 [Emphasis mine]

Here is Paul's teaching regarding works for Gentiles (for Believers, actually, we're just gonna go with the ludicrous assumption that only Paul is technically applicable to Gentiles.) You want your works to be gold, silver and precious stones. They can withstand the heat from the fire; whereas, wood, hay and straw cannot. Think on the parables of Jesus regarding reaping 30- or 60- or 80-fold and of the talents and minas. The works of the Believer in Jesus will be judged by God. This is not a judgment of your salvation, but a judgment of what your rewards will be *based on your works*.

Back to James.

In James' first chapter, he states that we must be "doers of the Word (TaNaKh), not just hearers" and that those that only hear and not do are deceived. Sound familiar? See, I told you he knew what he was talking about.

And then you have many, the deceived and foolish ones (using James' language), that pervert what James means by "works." I won't bother with that but instead show you exactly what *James* means by "works:"

> *But if a person looks closely into* **the perfect Torah, which gives freedom,** *and continues, becoming not a forgetful hearer but* **a doer of the work it requires,** *then* **he will be**

blessed *in what he does.*

James 1:25 (CJB) *[Emphasis mine so that you wouldn't miss it]*

"The Christian believer that is a doer of the works required by the perfect Torah will be *blessed* in what they do."

The Western Church throws every scriptural action required of us *after* salvation out the window due to fear, ignorance and Biblical illiteracy in regards to the balance of works (and the Torah in general) within their faith in Jesus. This is something we do with just about everything, and it's a massive problem. One last thing before we unpack Exodus 12: James said that the Christian faith is dead when void of the works of Torah and that Believers are justified by these works. Yes, justified.

The Greek word for justified here is *"dikaioo"* (Strong's #G1344). It means:

1. to render righteous or such he ought to be
2. to show, exhibit, evince, one to be righteous, such as he is and wishes himself to be considered
3. to declare, pronounce, one to be just, righteous, or such as he ought to be

and it's the same word used to declare our justification in, through and by Messiah.

Right about now, someone is screaming foul with a stack full of quotes from Romans and Galatians, but since this book is not the subject of apologetics for "works based on Torah observance," I'm not going to address these "contradictions" but merely say that, if you believe that James, Paul's authority, is teaching something in contradiction to Paul's teaching or that Paul, James' subordinate, is teaching something in contradiction to James' teaching, it's because you really don't understand what Paul is actually teaching, contextually, on the subject.

Peter says as much in 2 Peter 3:15-16. If a contradiction does exist, then the New Testament isn't "inspired by God," and the point is moot. Or Paul isn't contradicting James' authority, and you've got it all wrong (See Ro. 2:13). But if Paul is contradicting James' authority, then Paul is a false Apostle, not under authority, and we must go with James, because James was the brother of Jesus. He walked with Jesus and personally sat under His teaching, and James was the leader of the Church!

Remember again that Paul said the Torah was spiritual (Ro. 7:14), thus, a spiritual revelation is required to understand and comprehend Torah. But I digress... again, and again, and again!

I included this segment on James, because it defines "works" for "New Testament Believers" and how those "works" are crucial to the success and/or failure of our faith (1 John 3:4-10). Understanding the proper biblical teaching on "works" is crucial, because "works" is synonymous with observing the Commandments of God, Torah, and our going forward in unlocking the Feasts. (Just for the record and for clarification: The commandments "Do not steal" or "Honor your father and your mother" are "works of Torah.") Not having this proper and balanced understanding of the works of Torah and how they justify and make our faith alive (Paul teaches this in almost every single one of his letters), will only make the actual observance and keeping of God's Commandments a legalistic endeavor, which is something we must avoid.

The Sighting of the Abib

We're going to break down Exodus 12:1-20 into practical, segmented sections with New Testament and real-world examples. The system that God established for us for the keeping of His Commandments, Torah, requires us to do the "work" of determining that Way based on His instructions. So in Exodus 12 when God says:

"This month shall be for you the beginning of months."

It falls on us to determine *when* – by using His instruction manual / His Treasure Map / Torah – to navigate this, our Noble Quest, and the work of that manual to determine that First Month, which instructs us to be vigilant in looking for the New Moon: Rosh Chodesh. That's how we determine when this First Month begins!

Unfortunately, I have to address something before we can continue. I know, I know... We have to address the sighting of the abib in relation to determining "the first month" – also called the Month of Abib. Abib indicates the developmental stage of the barley crops as newly-ripened grain. Barley, in the state of abib, has three stages in their characteristics (Exod. 9:31-32):

1. The barley is flexible with a dark green coloring

2. The seeds have produced enough dry material that they are a lighter yellowish hue and can be eaten parched

3. The barley has developed enough to be brittle and harvestable within two to three weeks

The simplest explanation is, in order for the month to be "abib," the grain has to be ripe, otherwise it couldn't be the Month of Abib (logical, I know). This determination is made *before* the visible crescent of the New Moon, Rosh Chodesh, to determine if the month to come is Abib or a leap year, making the coming month the 13th month – Adar 2. Let's jump ahead of ourselves approximately a few days *after* Passover to understand what it is we are talking about.

In Chapter 5, we will discuss the Feast of Firstfruits that occurs on the Saturday night immediately following the first weekly Sabbath (Shabbat) after Passover. Agriculturally, we would now be two to three weeks after the beginning of the month when the barley has moved beyond the stage of abib and is ready to be brought to the priest as the "wave-sheaf offering:" The Feast of Firstfruits. The "wave-sheaf offering" is the sacrifice brought from the first stalks cut from the harvest during the Feast of Unleavened Bread as described in Leviticus 23:10-11.

Because we are to bring a sheaf to wave days after Passover, it is clear that the barley, which was abib at the beginning of the month, has become harvest-ready 15-21 days later. Therefore, the month of the Abib cannot begin unless the barley has reached a stage where it will be harvest-ready for the Feast of Firstfruits wave-sheaf offering. In Chapter 5, we'll see that Leviticus 23:15 addresses the seven weeks between Passover and Shavuot / Pentecost and that this wave-sheaf offering kicks off the Counting of the Omer as we also see in Deuteronomy 16:9:

> *"From when the sickle commences on the standing grain you will begin to count seven weeks."*

If the barley is not developed enough for the sickle or the wave-sheaf offering, then the month of the abib cannot begin and we must wait till the following month; a leap year, making the coming month the 13th month – Adar 2. Our lunar-based calendar (Chapter 2) has to consider the solar (sun) cycles for the seasons and the years to ensure that the Lunar months stay aligned with the solar cycle. The addition of a 13th

month (leap year) is necessary in some years, otherwise Passover could fall in the winter after a number of decades. This is where the sighting of the abib comes in. This now introduces some challenges:

1. Not all barley ripens in the Land of Israel at the same time
2. Not everyone examining the abib state of ripened barley agrees on which of the possible stages of abib is actually "scriptural abib," and
3. No universal governing body exists to officially determine the sighting of the "official scriptural stage of abib" for a unified observance

Let me explain.

In Chapter 2, we saw that God's calendar is an agricultural calendar, making this information relevant. If the barley isn't abib after Rosh Chodesh for the First Month, then we would be a month early. But since not all barley ripens in Israel at the same time based on geographical location, what region are we to consider? The region that the barley turns abib first? What stage of abib is actually considered abib scripturally? Who makes the final decision regarding abib or no abib and on what authority? These are some real-world issues regarding the sighting of the abib today as the determining factor as to whether or not the First Month of Abib is actually abib or a 13th month leap year; Month of Adar 2.

Nothing above states that the barley must be abib before the start of the First Month, and there is no scripture that clearly states, "*Thou shalt seek the abib barley.*" What *is* clear is that barley takes, on average, two to three weeks to go from an abib stage to the ripened stage. Since Passover / Feast of Unleavened Bread and Firstfruits are pilgrimage Feasts, an early warning was required for Israel to begin their journey to Jerusalem before the Feasts commenced. Was the First Month actually abib, and can the people begin their journey? In the same way that we discussed in Chapter 2 regarding a governing body was needed to determine "officially" when Rosh Chodesh started, that same governing body officially determined that the Month of Abib had or had not commenced based on the stage of the abib.

The past and current process of determination is the physical sighting of the abib in the land of Israel. That means you would physically need "boots on the ground" in Israel to make that determination. The real-world scenario that takes place today is individual groups, (remember those groups I keep talking about?) be it Messianic, Karaite, Sacred Name, Kabbalist, etc., have a representative and/or representatives to determine, for their individual group, if and when the abib is sighted. This means that if these groups determine that there is no abib prior to the New Moon, their Passover / Feast of Unleavened Bread / Feast of Firstfruits, the Feasts in general, will be observed an entire month later than everybody else (this will occur approximately 45 percent of the time in a 19-year solar cycle.) This can also mean that a sighting of the abib early enough can move their group's calendar an entire month *ahead* of everybody else (I have seen this happen, although this is a rare occasion.) "Everybody else" being those that follow the fixed Jewish Calendar and those that don't factor in the abib in their determination of the First Month.

This also means that, based on *where* the representative(s) is/are geographically located and *when* they're geographically located, will determine whether or not and *when* the potentiality of abib is sighted. This means that the four individual groups listed in our example can have varying calendar dates determining when they will be observing Passover / The Feast of Unleavened Bread / Feast of Firstfruits, etc.

Furthermore, the wave-sheaf offering for the Feast of Firstfruits is brought from the first fields to become harvest-ready. This firstfruits offering brought by individual farmers could have varied in ripeness from "abib parched in fire" to fully ripened grain which was allowed to be brought "crushed" or "coarsely ground" according to Leviticus 2:14.

To summarize the sighting of the abib:

1. You must have someone in the Land to visually determine the stage of the barley prior to the New Moon in order to determine if the following month is truly the First Month of Abib or the leap year Month of Adar 2.
2. Not all barley ripens in the Land of Israel at the same time, so the sighting or non-sighting of the abib can be determined by when and where you are in the Land. If your search is not done in concert, it is possible to miscalculate if and when abib was even sighted. Either way, calculations can, will and have varied

between groups.

3. Since no governing body exists to officially determine if the abib has been sighted or which stage of abib is actually the scripturally determined stage of abib, any and all abib sightings are solely based on an individual group's perceptions and conclusions.

4. Since no actual universal governing body exists to officially determine the stage of abib for a unified and cohesive observance, every group's observance of the Spring Feasts – based on the sighting or non-sighting of the abib – is solely based on their individual perceptions and conclusions.

I, we, do not have "boots on the ground" searching for the abib during the Month of Adar. I, we, have no plans to start sending a representative every year to the Land to determine the agricultural state of the barley. I also have no opinion on which "stage" of abib is considered the "scriptural" stage. Personally, I think a lot of the teaching adhered to by these groups surrounding the abib are Rabbinical / traditionally-based.

So how do we deal with the abib and the potentiality of a leap year? Since we don't actively have "boots on the ground" searching for the abib during the Month of Adar, we take our leap year cue from the Jewish fixed calendar.

A leap year in the fixed Jewish calendar occurs 7 times in a 19-year cycle with years 3, 6, 8, 11, 14, 17, and 19 of the cycle being leap years.

This makes it possible for Jewish time reckoning to approximately stay in sync with the solar year simply by adding a certain amount of full months per Metonic cycle. Since 19 years with 12 months accumulate to 228 months, 7 extra months must be added to arrive at a total of 235 months per cycle.

By employing this system, the Jewish calendar deviates from the solar year by 1 day in 216 years.
(Source:https://www.timeanddate.com/date/jewish-leap-year.html)

The Passover

Now we can break down Exodus 12.

The New Moon conjunction for March 2017 fell on Monday, March 27th making the visible crescent possible between Wednesday, March 29th and Thursday, March 30th. It was safe to say that a visible crescent, Rosh Chodesh, was going to be sighted on Wednesday, March 29th, and it was. This New Moon, as we learned in Chapter 2, was the time to blow the shofar, bring your monthly Firstfruits Offering, and have a festive family celebration. It also marked the beginning of the First Month and the anticipation of the Spring Feasts. In Exodus 13:4, it states that the name of this first month is Abib. The month of Abib is also known by its Babylonian name, Nisan.

Tell all the congregation of Israel that on the tenth day of this month every man shall take a lamb according to their fathers' houses, a lamb for a household.
Exodus 12:3

Keeping to the 2017 example with the visible New Moon crescent, Rosh Chodesh, falling on Wednesday, March 29th, the 10th day of the month when we would select a male lamb without blemish as our Passover Lamb, was then on Saturday, April 8th.

Going forward, I will post the Abib date and our 2017 example date to help you with this exercise:

Six days before the Passover [Abib 8/9 – April 7th], Jesus therefore came to Bethany, where Lazarus was, whom Jesus had raised from the dead. When the large crowd of the Jews learned that Jesus was there, they came, not only on account of him but also to see Lazarus, whom he had raised from the dead.

The next day [Abib 9/10 – April 8th] the large crowd that had come to the feast heard that Jesus was coming to Jerusalem. So they took branches of palm trees and went out to meet him, crying out, "Hosanna! Blessed is he who comes in the name of the Lord, even the King of Israel!" And Jesus found a young donkey and sat on it, just as it is written, "Fear not, daughter of Zion; behold, your king is coming, sitting on a donkey's colt!" [Zechariah 9:9]

John 12:1, 9, 12-15

We see in the account of John 12 that on the same day that the Passover Lamb is being selected and brought to the Temple, as per the instruction in Exodus regarding the 10th day, Jesus is entering Jerusalem and being selected by the people as their Passover Lamb. So on this day, Abib 10 / Saturday, April 8th, we chose Jesus of Nazareth to be our Passover Lamb.

Your lamb shall be without blemish...

It's Abib 10/11 (April 8th/9th), and there are four days allotted for the inspection of the Lamb for blemishes: Mt. 21:23-46; Mt. 22; Mark 11:27-33; 12:1-34; Luke 20:1-8; 19-40

Your lamb shall be without blemish, a male a year old. You may take it from the sheep or from the goats, and you shall keep it until the fourteenth day of this month, when the whole assembly of the congregation of Israel shall kill their lambs at twilight.
Exodus 12:5-6

Keeping to the 2017 example with the visible New Moon crescent, Rosh Chodesh, falling on Wednesday, March 29th, the 14th day of the month, Passover, the first appointed time (mo'ed) in God's cyclical year, was then on Wednesday, April 12th. It's Abib 14 and it's The Day of Preparation – but we have one last inspection:

Pilate then called together the chief priests and the rulers and the people, and said to them, "You brought me this man as one who was misleading the people. And after examining him before you, behold, I did not find this man guilty of any of your charges against him. Neither did Herod, for he sent him back to us. Look, nothing deserving death has been done by him. I will therefore punish and release him."
Luke 23:13-16

The final inspection has been made, and the Lamb has been found without blemish. It's Abib 14, the Lamb is being prepared for the slaughter where *"the whole assembly of the congregation of Israel shall kill their lambs at twilight."*

But they all cried out together, "Away with this man,

and release to us Barabbas" – a man who had been thrown into prison for an insurrection started in the city and for murder. Pilate addressed them once more, desiring to release Jesus, but they kept shouting, "Crucify, crucify him! A third time he said to them, "Why, what evil has he done? I have found in him no guilt deserving death. I will therefore punish and release him." But they were urgent, demanding with loud cries that he should be crucified. And their voices prevailed. So Pilate decided that their demand should be granted. He released the man who had been thrown into prison for insurrection and murder, for whom they asked, but he delivered Jesus over to their will.
Luke 23:18-25

"*Groupthink*" is the practice of thinking or making decisions as a group in a way that discourages creativity or individual responsibility.

And as the story goes… Thank you, Abba, for your Son…

At the first Passover, they took some of the blood and put it on the two doorposts and on the lintel of the house where they were eating the roasted lamb with unleavened bread and bitter herbs. The first Passover was a hasty meal; they ate with their belts fastened, their sandals on their feet and their staffs in their hand. ADONAI was passing through the land that night, and He was striking all the firstborn in the land of Egypt, the firstborn of men and beast; and on all the gods of Egypt, He was executing judgment.

The blood shall be a sign for you, on the houses where you are. And when I see the blood, I will pass over you, and no plague will befall you to destroy you, when I strike the land of Egypt. "This day shall be for you a memorial day, and you shall keep it as a feast to the LORD; throughout your generations, as a statute forever, you shall keep it as a feast.
Exodus 12:13-14

Between the Evenings...

> *[...] the whole assembly of the congregation of Israel shall kill their lambs **at twilight**.*
> Exodus 12:6b

> *[...] you shall offer the Passover sacrifice, **in the evening at sunset**, at the time you came out of Egypt.*
> Deuteronomy 16:6b

> *On the fourteenth day of this month, **at twilight**, you shall keep it at its appointed time;*
> Numbers 9:3a

Remember, scripturally the day starts at sundown, so using our 2017 dates, Passover was on Wednesday April 12th, the 14th day of the Hebrew month. On Tuesday, April 11th when the sun went down, Wednesday began, and roughly 22 hours later, before or around twilight, was Passover – before Wednesday's sunset. This, and because it was between the noon day and sunset, is why it's called "Between the Evenings." Between the evening of Tuesday, April 11th (Abib 13) and between the noon of day and the evening of Wednesday, April 12th (Abib 14), we celebrated Passover.

How do we celebrate Passover? How do we celebrate our deliverance by the blood of the Lamb? I'm glad you asked!

Download our Passover Guide to assist you with celebrating Passover in your own home: http://chameleonchurch.com/pdf/passoverGuide.pdf

> *While the people of Israel were encamped at Gilgal, they kept the Passover on the fourteenth day of the month in the evening on the plains of Jericho. And the day after the Passover, on that very day, they ate of the produce of the land, unleavened cakes and parched grain. And the manna ceased the day after they ate of the produce of the land. And there was no longer manna for the people of Israel, but they ate of the fruit of the land of Canaan that year.*
> Joshua 5:10-12

Imagine how amazing the first Passover in the Land was; A

400-year prophecy fulfilled and the completion of a 40-year exodus from Egypt! On the 15th day of Abib, they ate from the produce of the Land along with unleavened cakes and parched grain, and the manna ceased. Everything they knew had just changed. Amazing!

Passover is the foundation of the covenant relationship made between God and His people. Passover is also a declaration of faith that we have been redeemed by the blood of the Lamb! This "Passover Covenant" bridged the gap between man and God. Remember, this is why God wanted to take Israel out of Egypt:

> Say therefore to the people of Israel, 'I am the LORD, and I will bring you out from under the burdens of the Egyptians, and I will deliver you from slavery to them, and I will redeem you with an outstretched arm and with great acts of judgment. **I will take you to be my people, and I will be your God**, and you shall know that I am the LORD your God, who has brought you out from under the burdens of the Egyptians. **I will bring you into the land that I swore to give to Abraham, to Isaac, and to Jacob. I will give it to you for a possession**. I am the LORD.'"
> Exodus 6:6-8

"I will take you to be my people." He made that oath, that promise, that covenant, through blood; not unlike the preceding covenant that was made with Abraham in Genesis 15. This Passover Covenant also fulfilled the covenant promise that was made with Abraham and his descendants: "I will bring you into the land that I swore to give to Abraham." Without this Passover Covenant, there is no blood atonement; therefore, there is no "people" and there is no "Israel of God." The inhabitants in the land of Egypt died in separation, died in their sin; whereas, Israel was baptized into the Lamb. Isaiah confirms that this covenant with the Passover lamb, *The* Passover Lamb, is the foundation of the covenant relationship between God and His people. And this covenant of redemption, this Passover Lamb, was made and slain before the creation and foundations of the earth.

> ...knowing that you were ransomed from the futile ways inherited from your forefathers, not with perishable things such as silver or gold, but with the precious blood of Christ, like that of a lamb without blemish or spot. He was

> foreknown before the foundation of the world but was made manifest in the last times for the sake of you...
> 1 Peter 1:18-20

> And the LORD said to Moses and Aaron, "This is the statute of the Passover: no foreigner shall eat of it, but every slave that is bought for money may eat of it after you have circumcised him. No foreigner or hired servant may eat of it. It shall be eaten in one house; you shall not take any of the flesh outside the house, and you shall not break any of its bones. All the congregation of Israel shall keep it. If a stranger shall sojourn with you and would keep the Passover to the LORD, let all his males be circumcised. Then he may come near and keep it; he shall be as a native of the land. But no uncircumcised person shall eat of it. There shall be one law for the native and for the stranger who sojourns among you."
> Exodus 12:43-49

I included this, because if I didn't, someone would bring it up. I didn't include it to discuss circumcision but instead to discuss the contextual aspect of circumcision. The instruction states that uncircumcised males are not allowed to partake of the Passover. Since we know that New Testament teaching does suggest that salvation makes a man circumcised of heart, we should apply that to Passover; therefore, it is my understanding that non-believers should not be included in the observance of Passover.

I also want to note that "There shall be one Torah (law) for the native (Israeli) and for the stranger (Gentile) who sojourns among you." Verse 38 of this chapter states that a "mixed multitude" (including Gentiles) also left Egypt with Israel. These are additional scriptural proof texts showing that Torah does indeed apply to Gentiles.

In Numbers 9:6-14, we find two additional instructions in regards to the observance of Passover:

> And there were certain men who were unclean through touching a dead body, so that they could not keep the Passover on that day, and they came before Moses and Aaron on that day. And those men said to him, "We are unclean through touching a dead body. Why are we kept from bringing

the LORD's offering at its appointed time among the people of Israel?" And Moses said to them, "Wait, that I may hear what the LORD will command concerning you." The LORD spoke to Moses, saying, "Speak to the people of Israel, saying, If any one of you or of your descendants is unclean through touching a dead body, or is on a long journey, he shall still keep the Passover to the LORD. In the second month on the fourteenth day at twilight they shall keep it. They shall eat it with unleavened bread and bitter herbs. They shall leave none of it until the morning, nor break any of its bones; according to all the statute for the Passover they shall keep it. But if anyone who is clean and is not on a journey fails to keep the Passover, that person shall be cut off from his people because he did not bring the LORD's offering at its appointed time; that man shall bear his sin. And if a stranger sojourns among you and would keep the Passover to the LORD, according to the statute of the Passover and according to its rule, so shall he do. You shall have one statute, both for the sojourner and for the native."

Day of Preparation / Feast of Unleavened Bread

Passover is the first of the three Spring Feasts: Passover, Feast of Unleavened Bread and Feast of Firstfruits. These three Spring Feasts have been traditionally grouped together and are often referred to as the Feast of Unleavened Bread. Passover is a standalone instruction ("feast") as we have seen, but it is also referred to in the gospels as "the first day of Unleavened Bread" (Mt 26:17; Mark 14:12; Luke 22:1, 7), and also "The Day of Preparation" (Mt. 27:62; Mark 15:42; Luke 23:54; John 19:14, 31, 42). This has caused some confusion, so we're going to clear it up right now.

Remember how Passover is observed at twilight, "between the evenings," right before sunset? Well, during Passover, as soon as the sun goes down, it becomes the 15th day of the month and that begins the First Day of the Feast of Unleavened Bread which is a High Sabbath; a High Shabbat:

> And on the fifteenth day of the same month is the Feast of Unleavened Bread to the LORD; for seven days you

shall eat unleavened bread. On the first day you shall have a holy convocation; you shall not do any ordinary work.
Leviticus 23:6-7

Because Passover and the First Day of the Feast of Unleavened Bread literally overlap and are both typically mentioned in the same contextual passages, Passover is also referred to as the first day of Unleavened Bread. The Passover meal is also eaten with matzah, unleavened bread, adding to the confusion for many.

Using our 2017 dates, Passover was on the evening of Wednesday April 12th (Abib 14/15), before sundown. That night, after sunset, began the 15th day of the month, the High Sabbath of the First Day of the Feast of Unleavened Bread. For your calendar / work day Sabbath arrangements, Thursday, April 13th, was a High Sabbath.

Day of Preparation

The 14th day of the month, Passover, is also referred to as the Day of Preparation in the Gospels:

And when evening had come, since it was the day of Preparation, that is, the day before the Sabbath, Joseph of Arimathea, a respected member of the Council, who was also himself looking for the kingdom of God, took courage and went to Pilate and asked for the body of Jesus.
Mark 15:42-43 – See also Luke 23:50-55; John 19:14, 42

"...it was the day of Preparation, that is, the day before the Sabbath..."

The Sabbath this passage is referring to is the High Sabbath of the First Day of the Feast of Unleavened Bread (Lev. 23:7). Passover is referred to as the Day of Preparation, because that is the day you prepare for Passover and the High Shabbat of the First Day of the Feast of Unleavened Bread. Besides all of the celebration and food prep for this double feast day, you also had to first purge your house of leaven. More on that in a bit.

This is also where Eastern and Oriental Orthodox Christianity and Roman Catholicism get their Great / Good Friday idea. Since the Sabbath was approaching, they had to get the body of Jesus off of the cross and into a tomb – and since the Sabbath is Friday at sundown...

ta-da: "Good Friday." But since Friday evening to Sunday morning isn't three days and three nights in the tomb and we know it's Passover, meaning we also know that immediately following Passover at sundown is the First Day of the Feast of Unleavened Bread, a High Sabbath, the Romanized Western Church as a whole is grotesquely in error. By default, so is Protestant / Evangelical Christianity because of it being rooted in re-formed Catholicism. Thus, the Romanized Western Church admits to two things:

- That God's biblical Sabbath is actually Friday, not Sunday, and
- They either don't actually know what the scriptures say about the first day of the Feast of Unleavened Bread starting at sunset and it being a High Sabbath (i.e. Lev. 23), or they just don't care.

Either way, the Sabbath in this passage in Mark and every single passage in the Gospels regarding the burial of Jesus before the Sabbath begins, *is not* the weekly Friday Shabbat. The Shabbat in question is the First Day of the Feast of Unleavened Bread – High Shabbat.

And then you have this:

> Since it was the day of Preparation, and so that the bodies would not remain on the cross on the Sabbath (for that Sabbath was a high day), the Jews asked Pilate that their legs might be broken and that they might be taken away.
> John 19:31

You can't be clearer than that.

Feast of Unleavened Bread

> Seven days you shall eat unleavened bread. On the first day you shall remove leaven out of your houses, for if anyone eats what is leavened, from the first day until the seventh day, that person shall be cut off from Israel.
> Exodus 12:15

Matzah for seven days. If you've never eaten matzah for seven days, you're probably thinking "what's the big deal?" Well, let me tell ya. It's not like regular bread and it has limited taste, and that's it. You start to get very creative with your matzah sandwiches, I'll tell ya what... But the really interesting thing is the spiritual warfare that starts around day three. People start to lose their minds (figuratively speaking). It's amazing. Eating matzah for seven days, obeying the commandment so as not to be "cut off," is the perfect time for the enemy to attack and is one of the hardest and most challenging things you can do. The covenant is made by the eating of matzah, unleavened bread. (Exod. 13:7-9) Of course the enemy is going to attack! And who wants to be cut off by God?! I don't!

On the first day, the day of preparation, before Passover begins, you need to purge your house of leaven. This is where we probably got "spring cleaning" from. Purging your house of leaven, your "territory," is a simple thing unless, of course, you subscribe to the pages and pages of items traditional Judaism deems as "leaven." We don't.

The following is from a paper my lovely wife put together for our community at large a couple of years ago regarding "removing leaven (*se'or* and *chametz*) out of your houses:"

Removing Leaven Out of Your Houses

We tend to overcomplicate things. I mean "we" as humans. Yes, God requires obedience, but He doesn't make it so difficult to obey as to be impossible. Take for instance removing leaven from our homes in order to prepare for the Feast of Unleavened Bread. Did you know that there are literally yeast spores all around you? In the very air we breathe, there is yeast. So while *chametz* has been translated as yeast, we can't get so frantic about it that we stop breathing! (Joking, people, just breathe.)

> *In the first month, from the fourteenth day of the month at evening, you shall eat unleavened bread [matzah] until the twenty-first day of the month at evening. For seven days no leaven [se'or: a leavening agent(s)] is to be found in your houses. If anyone eats what is leavened [chametz: with leaven], that person will be cut off from the congregation of Israel, whether he is a sojourner or a native of the land. You shall eat nothing leavened [with chametz]; in all your dwelling places you shall eat unleavened bread [matzah]."*
> Exodus 12:18-20

The word *chametz* derives from the root meaning "to be sour, to be leavened." Marcus Jastrow, a renowned Talmudic scholar, claims that perhaps the original meaning was "to be hot," which led to another meaning - the color red.

Other words that derive from the same root include *hometz* (or *chometz*), vinegar, and its derivative *humtza,* acid. One example of hometz in the TaNaKh is in Ruth 2:14, where Boaz tells Ruth to: "dip your bread in the vinegar." This sounds like an unusual dip for bread, and it is suggested that perhaps *hometz* here meant sour milk.

There is another explanation, though, which is the Arabic term for chickpea dip – commonly known in English as hummus – which has the same root as *hometz*. In the Talmud, there is reference to a legume known as *himtza*. So perhaps Boaz was suggesting something a little tastier – bread with hummus. Okay, back on subject. (And go ahead and eat hummus during the Feast of Unleavened Bread!)

So why did God command that we remove all traces of se'or (leavening agents) from our homes? Based on the definitions above, chametz can mean hot or leavened. It's possible a more accurate translation in English could be "baked (hot) bread (leavened)." So where God says to eat nothing with chametz "in it" (Exodus 12:20) – it literally means the material from which the bread is made – the mixture, i.e., se'or! If you have the se'or – get rid of it, and if you have the baked bread (which has chametz in it), get rid of that!

So let's keep it simple. The commandments for the Feast of Unleavened Bread (and Passover in bullet 3):

- We are to remove all se'or from our homes and eat matzah (Exod. 12:19)
- We are not to possess chametz in our house or "territory" during Passover and are supposed to eat matzah (Exod. 12:19-20; 13:7; Deut. 16:4)
- We are not to eat chametz during Passover, instead, eat matzah (Exod. 12:18, 20; 13:6; Deut. 16:3)

What do these three bullet points have in common? Eat matzah.

God didn't command this so that we can scour our houses for se'or or chametz (although I do love the spring cleaning!), but it's so we REMEMBER:

> *"And you shall observe the Feast of Unleavened Bread, for on this very day I brought your hosts out of the land of Egypt. Therefore you shall observe this day, throughout your generations, as a statute forever."*
> Exodus 12:17

By removing all baked breads from our meals, we get to remember His miracle of saving His people. We spend that week constantly being reminded of His salvation.

In my opinion, as long as you have gotten rid of baked bread and don't eat it, you are acting in obedience to Torah. Let's take a look of what baked bread is – besides the obvious, the actual loaf of baked bread, either baked in your kitchen or purchased at the store – it is also the key ingredients ready to be turned into baked bread.

> *"Unleavened bread [matzah] shall be eaten for seven days; no leavened bread [chametz] shall be seen with you, and no leaven [se'or] shall be seen with you in all your territory. You shall tell your son on that day, 'It is because of what the LORD did for me when I came out of Egypt.' And it shall be to you as a sign on your hand and as a memorial between your eyes, that the law of the LORD may be in your mouth. For with a strong hand the LORD has brought you out of Egypt."*
> Exodus 13:7-9

It's pretty clear that these key ingredients qualify as well as they are "leavening agents," although they are not all mixed up into chametz. Cake mixes – prepared and ready to be baked, and other mixes and items that can be mixed to make bread – should be removed as well.

So while it may be impossible to get rid of yeast in our homes – it's in the air, remember? – it's very easy to get rid of baked breads, cake mixes, and baking yeast. If you use baking powder or baking soda to bake with, I'd get rid of that too. BUT if you use baking soda for cleaning or fridge smells, it's okay as long as you don't mix it with flour. (When I'm in the grocery store, I basically look at the ingredients, and if it says "leaven," I don't buy it – as an example, some but not all flour tortillas have leaven.)

Some will argue that there are other "leaven" or "leavening agents" other than what was described above. Fact is that the terms "leaven" and "yeast" are relatively modern terms, so there's lots of room for argument! And, honestly, if you choose to go more extreme in getting rid of stuff, then more power to you. I just don't think it has to be as hard as we tend to make it.

What about wine? I know that some rabbis say no to wine and "Passover" wine is made (although not easy to find!) Yes, both bread-making and wine-making are a fermentation process. But wine is not chametz. The issue is not "fermentation." The issue is "**rising**." Wine has not risen and is not baked.

What makes bread rise? Released gas, which is produced by yeast and then driven out of the dough during baking. When making wine, released gases are disposed of, but nothing rises. Both processes go through fermentation, but with bread, the gas produced is the most important part (to make it rise). With wine, the alcohol is the most important part.

Hopefully this has simplified the process for you. I pray it has not added any confusion!

Thanks, babe!

So on the day of preparation, or, on or before the 14th day of the month of Abib, be sure your house and all of your "territory" is purged of leaven / leavening agents (se'or) and leavened items (chametz).

You'll eat only matzah starting at Passover and for the next seven days. For all intents and purposes, the modern observance of Passover, the traditional Seder, is essentially a Shabbat; the First Day of the Feast of Unleavened Bread High Shabbat.

Using our 2017 dates, Passover was on the evening of Wednesday April 12th (Abib 14/15), before sundown. Immediately after sunset began the 15th day of the month of Abib, the High Sabbath of the First Day of the Feast of Unleavened Bread. For your calendar / work day Sabbath arrangements, Thursday, April 13th, was a High Sabbath.

The Feast of Unleavened Bread was then the night of Wednesday, April 12th (Abib 14/15) through the sunset of Wednesday, April 19th (Abib 21/22) making Tuesday, April 18th (Abib 20/21) at sunset the High Sabbath of the Seventh Day of the Feast of Unleavened Bread. For your calendar / work day Sabbath arrangements, Wednesday, April 19th, was the High Sabbath.

> *On the first day you shall hold a holy assembly [a High Sabbath], and on the seventh day a holy assembly [a High Sabbath]. No work shall be done on those days. But what everyone needs to eat, that alone may be prepared by you. And you shall observe the Feast of Unleavened Bread, for on this very day I brought your hosts out of the land of Egypt. Therefore you shall observe this day, throughout your generations, as a statute forever.*
>
> *In the first month, from the fourteenth day of the month at evening [Passover], you shall eat unleavened bread [matzah] until the twenty-first day of the month at evening. For seven days no leaven [se'or] is to be found in your houses. If anyone eats what is leavened [chametz], that person will be cut off from the congregation of Israel, whether he is a sojourner [Gentile] or a native [Hebrew] of the land. You shall eat nothing leavened [chametz]; in all your dwelling places you shall eat unleavened bread [matzah].*
> Exodus 12:16-20

Here we see that the Torah instruction regarding the Feast of Unleavened Bread also applied / applies to Gentiles. With this understanding / instruction in mind, the Apostle Paul, Rabbi Sha'ul, the Apostle to the Gentiles, wrote this to his predominantly Gentile church in Corinth:

> *Do you not know that a little leaven [Greek: zume – Hebrew: se'or] leavens [Greek: zumoo – Hebrew: chametz] the whole lump? Cleanse out the old leaven [Greek: zume – Hebrew: se'or] that you may be a new lump, as you really are unleavened [matzah]. For Christ, our Passover lamb, has been sacrificed. Let us therefore celebrate the festival, not with the old leaven [Greek: zume – Hebrew: se'or], the leaven [Greek: zume – Hebrew: se'or] of malice and evil, but with the unleavened bread [matzah] of sincerity and truth.*
> 1 Corinthians 5:6b-8

There are those that cite this passage in support of Paul's teaching against the literal instructions of Torah using the actual Feast of Passover and Unleavened Bread as example, as some of you may have been taught. The argument is, since Paul wrote "celebrate Passover with sincerity and truth," there is now no reason for Gentiles to observe anything we just discussed. I, of course, find that position quite the liberal misuse of the passage, especially when you take Paul's body of work and life into context.

The Day That Jesus Died

The "Last Supper" was *not* a Passover Seder.

This can be very confusing even to me, because in Matthew 26:17 it says that it was the first day of Unleavened Bread and the disciples ask Jesus where He would like for them to prepare for the Passover. Verse 20 says "when it was evening." This would "logically" have to be the evening of the 14th day since in verse 17 it says that it was already the first day of Unleavened Bread, the Day of Preparation, Passover, making verse 20 the actual evening of Passover.

If verse 20 is the evening of the 14th of Abib, the first day of Unleavened Bread, the Day of Preparation, the actual Passover, then the supper that Jesus is about to eat with His disciples, known as The Last Supper, is, as considered by almost everyone, the Passover meal. But that begs the following questions:

1. How can you be reclining, eating the Passover meal with your buddies, when you're supposed to be dying *as* the Passover Lamb – not *eating* the Passover lamb?

2. Why no mention of a "High Sabbath"? If the Last Supper is the Passover, this would mean that after verse 20, everything is happening on the First Day of the Feast of Unleavened Bread, a High Sabbath: praying in the garden, being arrested, taken to the Sanhedrin, going before Herod and Pilate, being crucified and taken off the cross... all of this occurred on Abib 15, the High Sabbath, the day after the Day of Preparation, the First Day of the Feast of Unleavened Bread – not on the actual Passover day of the 14th of Abib?

There is no mention of it being the High Sabbath of the First Day of the Feast of Unleavened Bread in Matthew's account or in any of the Gospel accounts.

There's another problem: Mt. 27:62, some 36-plus hours later, it says that it's the "next day, that is, *after* the Day of Preparation," making verse 62 *Abib 15*, except for the fact that we just saw that Mt. 26:17-20 allegedly took place on Abib 14, some 36-plus hours prior: the first day of Unleavened Bread, the Day of Preparation, Passover and placing Mt. 26:21 - Mt. 27:1-61 on Abib 15: The First Day of the Feast of Unleavened Bread – a High Sabbath – the day after the Day of Preparation. We just lost 24 hours:

Verse	Day	Activity
Mt. 26:17, 20	Abib 14 "First Day of Unleavened Bread" "Day of Preparation" Passover	"Last Supper" Passover Meal
Mt. 26:21-75 – Mt. 27:1-61	Abib 15 First Day of the Feast of Unleavened Bread High Shabbat The "Day After the Day of Preparation"	Garden prayer Arrested Sanhedrin trial Before Pilate Crucifixion Death Burial
Mt. 62	Abib 16 After the Day of Preparation	Guards are placed at tomb the morning after his death and burial

Let's take a look at Mark's account: Mark 14:12 is more specific by stating "And on the first day of Unleavened Bread, *when they sacrificed the Passover lamb...*" This is undoubtedly Abib 14, right?

The narrative is basically the same as Matthew's; verse 17 says "when it was evening," and so on. Everything is happening on Abib 15, after the sunset following the evening in verse 17: dinner, garden, arrest, the Sanhedrin. It's the High Sabbath of the First Day of the Feast of Unleavened Bread, but again, there's no mention of it being the High Sabbath and no mention of all the Sabbath breaking by literally everything and everybody. Mark 15:1 is the morning of Abib 15 *if* this entire exercise began on Abib 14 before evening as we saw in Mk. 14:12. But now we have a real problem. Joseph of Arimathea is asking for the body of Jesus:

> And when evening had come, since it was the day of Preparation, that is, the day before the Sabbath,
> Mark 15:42

"*And when evening had come*": Based on Mark 14:12 being Abib 14, this is the evening of Abib 15. At sunset it will be Abib 16, the beginning of the *second* Day of the Feast of Unleavened Bread *which isn't a Sabbath*. Again, we lose 24 hours.

"*since it was the day of Preparation, that is, the day before the Sabbath...*" Houston! We have a problem! The Day of Preparation, based on the timeline of both accounts, was yesterday. And this Sabbath was 24 hours ago! And it only gets more confusing if you read this with the Gregorian calendar in mind, because it says "the day before the Sabbath" making this 48 hours off the timeline! See how easily it is to get confused?

What sayeth Luke? Luke 22:7 says that it's "the day of Unleavened Bread, on which the Passover lamb had to be sacrificed." Again, this should literally be Abib 14. Instead of saying that it was evening, verse 14 says "when the hour came." We have to conclude that it is now the High Sabbath of the First Day of the Feast of Unleavened Bread, Abib 15. Now in this account, "when the hour came," Jesus immediately says: "I have earnestly desired to eat this Passover with you before I suffer. For I tell you I will not eat it until it is fulfilled in the kingdom of God" (verses 15-16). Here we can conclude that Jesus *did not* have a Passover meal with His disciples. In the next verse, they take communion. (Note: is there a future Passover coming in the Kingdom of God – post-Jesus' death and resurrection?)

Again the narrative is basically the same as Matthew's and Mark's. Everything is happening on Abib 15: garden, arrest, the Sanhedrin. It's the High Sabbath of the First Day of the Feast of Unleavened Bread, but again, there's no mention of it being the High Sabbath. Verse 66 brings the morning. Luke 23 and Jesus is before Pilate, Herod, then the Crucifixion, again on Abib 15, if the Last Supper was a Passover Seder. Verse 50 begins the account of Joseph of Arimathea asking for the body of Jesus, because it was the Day of Preparation (Abib 14) and the Sabbath was beginning, the High Sabbath of the First Day of the Feast of Unleavened Bread. Again, our timeline is off by 24 hours. Up to verse 54, it was Abib 15 with the sunset starting Abib 16, and now it's

Abib 14 before the High Sabbath of Abib 15!

John?

> Now before the Feast of the Passover, when Jesus knew that his hour had come to depart out of this world to the Father, having loved his own who were in the world, he loved them to the end. During supper, when the devil had already put it into the heart of Judas Iscariot, Simon's son, to betray him, Jesus, knowing that the Father had given all things into his hands, and that he had come from God and was going back to God, rose from supper.
> John 13:1-4a

Now this makes more sense! No mention of it actually *being* Abib 14, the first day of Unleavened Bread, the Day of Preparation, Passover. It's Abib 13, *before* the Feast of Passover! Let's see if the timeline corresponds.

After supper, Jesus washed the disciples' feet. Jesus reveals that He would be betrayed by the one to whom He gives the dipped morsel of bread. He gives it to Judas, then tells him to go, and it was night (Abib 14). We also see another indication that this isn't Passover or the First Day of the Feast of Unleavened Bread – the High Shabbat. Verse 29a:

> Some [of the disciples] thought that, because Judas had the moneybag, Jesus was telling him, "Buy what we need for the feast [...]"

Chapter 18: After some awesome instruction, they go to the garden. It's after sunset, so it's Abib 14: The Day of Preparation, the Passover. Jesus is betrayed, arrested and taken before the Sanhedrin. In the early morning (it's still Abib 14), Jesus goes before Pilate, is crucified and dies. John 19:31a:

> Since it was the day of Preparation, and so that the bodies would not remain on the cross on the Sabbath (for that Sabbath was a high day)

Our timeline now corresponds with the narrative!!

Verse	Day	Activity
Jn. 13:1-4a	**Abib 13**	"Last Supper"
Jn. 18 - 19	**Abib 14** The Day of Preparation Passover	Garden prayer Arrested Sanhedrin trial Before Pilate Crucifixion Death Burial
Jn. 19	**Abib 15** First Day of the Feast of Unleavened Bread High Shabbat The "Day After the Day of Preparation"	Jesus in tomb Guards are placed at tomb the morning after his death and burial

So then what about Matthew, Mark and Luke? Here's my take on it, and it's not very popular:

While I am highly doubtful that the Gospels were originally written in Greek, and we do know that a Hebrew version of Matthew is in circulation, even if the gospels were originally penned in Greek, take into account that those who translated these writings and compiled "the Bible" were not necessarily "Jewish Friendly." In fact, many of them were anti-Semitic, religiously and historically.

And even if their translation and compiling is above reproach, we know that Leviticus 23 and the High Sabbath of the First Day of the Feast of Unleavened Bread was completely disregarded doctrinally and theologically in regard to determining the account of Jesus' death and resurrection, which is why they have "Good Friday" commemorating the death of Jesus. Either the High Sabbath of the First Day of the Feast of Unleavened Bread was a foreign concept to them, and they assumed the Sabbath that was coming that required the Body of Jesus to be taken off the Cross to be the weekly Sabbath, Friday sunset, or…? This brings into question their knowledge of the scriptures and therefore their "authority" and accuracy.

The Biblical narrative isn't incorrect. Our reading of it, based on the tradition that the "Last Supper" is a Passover Seder, makes it "incorrect." I see that the accounts in Matthew, Mark and Luke actually start on the twilight / evening of Abib 13 and at sundown (Abib 14) it was indeed, technically, the first day of Unleavened Bread, the day of Preparation, Passover – but 24 hours prior to the actual Passover twilight prior to the sunset ushering in Abib 15. The only "discrepancy" with dating this account the 13th of the month instead of the 14th of the month is that it makes the tradition of "The Last Supper" *not* an actual Passover Seder but simply a dinner on the night before. This clears up the timeline issues we saw when we held to the tradition that the Last Supper *was* a Passover Seder. It clearly could not be, and I have absolutely no problem with that.

The narrative for three of four gospel accounts makes the Last Supper "look" like a Passover Seder, but an honest and clearer look at it shows that the timeline doesn't agree. The account of John clearly states that the Last Supper is not a Passover Seder, and the timeline agrees.

All four gospel accounts of the Last Supper occur on the evening of the 13th / night of the 14th, the day *of* but not *during* the actual scriptural Passover that actually occurs some 22 hours later.

You also have this "theory:" The Hagigah. *Hagigah* (Hebrew "festival offering", also *chagigah*) was held before the Three Pilgrimage Festivals and consisted of the pilgrimage offerings men were to bring to Jerusalem. Traditionally held between one to three days prior to the Feast, it is suggested that the Last Supper may have been the Hagigah preceding Passover. The Hagigah, also recognized as a "Remembrance Meal," could also be why Jesus instructed His disciples to "do this in remembrance of Me." Based on passages such as Deut. 27:7; Num. 10:10; and 2 Chron. 30:22, the Talmudic Tractate Chagigah, dictate the laws concerning the Three Pilgrimage Festivals pilgrimage offerings. (Source: https://holylanguage.com/mishnah.php - Lesson 30)

The Week That Jesus Died

So then what did this timeline actually look like the week Jesus died? Good question. I'm going to outline it here, but we also have a groovy infographic to help you visualize it:
http://chameleonchurch.com/pdf/passoverWeek.pdf

On the 10th day of the month of Abib, Jesus enters Jerusalem. There was a great celebration for His entering the city and the Temple. He is "chosen" by Israel as their "Passover Lamb."

For the next four days, He is examined and found blameless and without blemish.

On the night of the 13th day of the month, a Tuesday night, Jesus has dinner with his disciples. After sunset, it was now technically the 14th day of the week, Passover. It was also approximately 20-22 hours before the twilight of the 14th day when Passover was instructed to occur. On that Tuesday / Wednesday night, Jesus and His disciples went to the garden; Jesus was arrested; Jesus was taken before the Sanhedrin; Jesus spent His first ever night in Jerusalem in Caiaphas' dungeon.

On the morning of Wednesday, the 14th day of the month, the Passover, the first day of Unleavened Bread, the Day of Preparation, Jesus is taken to Pilate, then to Herod and then back to Pilate for His last examination. Jesus is found to be without fault, but the people and their leaders insist that Pilate turn Jesus over to be crucified. It's now approximately 9:00 am.

At approximately 3:00 pm, Jesus dies. At twilight would be Passover (between the evenings), and His body needs to be removed and entombed before sunset, because that night was the First Day of the Feast of Unleavened Bread, a High Shabbat. It's after sunset, Wednesday night, the 15th of Abib and Jesus has already been entombed:

Wed. sunset to Thurs. sunset: First Day of the Feast of Unleavened Bread a High Shabbat	1st – 24-hour day
Thurs. sunset to Fri. sunset: The "day after" the Day of Preparation The women purchase and prepare spices	2nd – 24-hour day
Fri. sunset to Sat. sunset: the weekly Shabbat	3rd – 24-hour day

Sat. after Shabbat at sunset: Feast of Firstfruits	Jesus rises

Saturday after Shabbat / after the sunset is the Feast of Firstfruits. Jesus rises from the dead with many others, presenting Himself and those that rose with Him as Firstfruits unto the Father.

In Summary

Appointed Time: Passover

Significance: A memorial day commemorating God's passing through the land of Egypt, striking down all the firstborn of both man and beast and executing judgment on all the gods of Egypt. The lamb's blood on Israel's houses was a sign for them, and when God saw the blood, He passed over Israel and no plague destroyed them

Observance: The purging of leaven from your home and territory. A day of preparation for the Passover meal eaten with matzah and the High Sabbath of the First Day of the Feast of Unleavened Bread, also eaten with matzah. A memorial day (Exod. 12:14) in remembrance of when the Angel of Death, the Destroyer, passed over Israel in Egypt and how they were delivered

Length: Originally, a meal eaten in haste. Today, a meal eaten as the High Sabbath of the First Day of the Feast of Unleavened Bread: The Seder

Appointed Time: Feast of Unleavened Bread

Significance: On this very day, God brought Israel out of the land of Egypt. It is to remind us of what ADONAI did for us when we came out of Egypt. It is a sign and a memorial so that the Torah of ADONAI may be in our mouths (Exod. 13:7-9).

Observance: Before the sunset of the 14th day, all leaven is to be removed from your house and territory, and no leaven is to be found in your homes or territory for seven days. Matzah is eaten for seven days. The first and seventh days are High Sabbaths when no ordinary work is to be done

Length: Seven days

We started this Chapter looking at blood sacrifices, and we end this Chapter looking at blood sacrifices:

1. Genesis 3 – An animal is sacrificed, and its blood is shed for a person
2. Exodus 12 – An animal is sacrificed, and its blood is shed for a family
3. Exodus 30 and Leviticus 16:3-34 – An animal is sacrificed and its blood is shed for a nation
4. John 1 – Jesus, the Lamb of God, is sacrificed, and His blood is shed for the world

Leviticus 17:11 tells us that the life of any living thing is in the blood, and God has placed that life's blood on the altar for the atonement of our souls. It is the blood that makes atonement for life.

Passover speaks to our enslaving sin and the sacrifice of blood required for atonement freedom and our deliverance from Egypt, our carnal state. Unleavened Bread speaks to the purging of that sin and bad doctrine / leaven from our lives and homes. Firstfruits: the joy of bringing firstfruits to ADONAI after the redemptive process of deliverance.

Passover is the foundation of the covenant relationship made between God and His people; a declaration of faith that we have been redeemed by the blood of the Lamb! "I will take you to be my people," and He made that oath, that promise, that covenant, through blood.

Without this Passover Covenant, there is no blood atonement for a people; therefore, there would be no "people," and there would be no Israel of God. Egypt died in their sin; whereas, Israel was baptized into the Lamb. This Passover Lamb, *The* Passover Lamb, was prepared and slain before the foundations of the earth.

We eat unleavened bread, matzah, out of obedience to the instruction and to show that we are "unleavened" / without sin or erroneous doctrine before Him while keeping His Torah in our mouths. This covenant is made by the eating of matzah (Exod. 13:7-9).

Passover and the beginning of the High Sabbath of the Feast of Unleavened Bread is also a night of watching kept to ADONAI, just as He watched that night when He brought us out of Egypt (Ex. 12:42).

CHAPTER 5

FEAST OF FIRSTFRUITS / FEAST OF WEEKS (THE OMER COUNT)
Honor Me with the firstfruits of all your increase

And the LORD spoke to Moses, saying, "Speak to the people of Israel and say to them, When you come into the land that I give you and reap its harvest, you shall bring the sheaf of the firstfruits of your harvest to the priest, and he shall wave the sheaf before the LORD, so that you may be accepted [a Firstfruits Offering]. On the day after the Sabbath the priest shall wave it. And on the day when you wave the sheaf, the grain offering shall be of fine flour mixed with oil, a food offering to the LORD with a pleasing aroma, and the drink offering with it shall be of wine. And you shall eat neither bread or grain parched or fresh until this same day, until you have brought the offering of your God: it is a statute forever throughout your generations in all your dwellings.

You shall count seven full weeks from the day after the Sabbath, from the day that you brought the sheaf of the wave offering. You shall count fifty days to the day after the seventh Sabbath."
Leviticus 23:9-16a

Rosh Chodesh was on Wednesday, March 29th, marking the beginning of the First Month and the anticipation of the Spring Feasts. The 14th day of the month od Abib, Passover, was Wednesday, April 12th, before sundown. That night, after sunset, began the 15th day of the month, the High Sabbath of the First Day of the Feast of Unleavened Bread (Thursday April 13th).

On Friday, April 14th (the 16th day of the Hebrew month), after sunset began the weekly Shabbat ending on the sunset of Saturday,

April 15th, the 17th day of the Hebrew month. That Saturday night (after sunset) was the Feast of Firstfruits, the 18th day of Abib: the resurrection of Messiah and Day One of the Omer Count.

Day	Event
Wednesday, April 12th at twilight: 14th of Abib	Passover
Wednesday, April 12th (after sunset) – Thursday, April 13th (at sunset) 15th of Abib	First Day of the Feast of Unleavened Bread High Shabbat
Friday, April 14th (after sunset) – Saturday, April 15th (at sunset) 17th of Abib	Third Day of the Feast of Unleavened Bread Weekly Shabbat
Saturday, April 15th (after sunset) 18th of Abib	Weekly Shabbat ends Feast of Firstfruits begins after sunset Messiah rises Day One of the Omer Count

I want to briefly, briefly address yet another "controversy" (yes, another – can you believe that another exists?) in regard to the correct date to observe the Feast of Firstfruits.

Because the text states "on the day after the Sabbath," and since the First Day of the Feast of Unleavened Bread is a Sabbath, a High Sabbath actually, there are those in both Christianity and Judaism (I hate making that segregation) that suggest that the Feast of Firstfruits and the beginning of the Omer Count occurs and begins after the High Sabbath of the First Day of the Feast of Unleavened Bread, the 16th day of Abib. Then there are those in both Christianity and Judaism that suggest that the Feast of Firstfruits and the beginning of the Omer Count occurs and begins after the *weekly* Sabbath.

Like I said, I want to keep this brief: "The day after the Sabbath" is the same "Sabbath" in verse 3 of Leviticus 23; the seventh day of the week – not "a holy convocation" High Sabbath like we find in verses 7 and 8. Furthermore, the text states that we are to "count for yourselves…

seven Sabbaths" (verse 15) – this would have to be seven *weekly* Sabbaths, not seven "High Sabbaths" considering that there are no seven consecutive High Sabbaths. Furthermore, the instructions specify that:

> "You shall count seven full weeks from the day after the Sabbath, **from the day that you brought the sheaf of the wave offering.** You shall count fifty days to the day after the seventh Sabbath."

[Emphasis mine]

No wave-sheaf offering is made on Passover or on the First Day of the Feast of Unleavened Bread, so the Omer Count couldn't begin following the day after the High Sabbath of the First Day of the Feast of Unleavened Bread. The wave-sheaf offering is made *after* the weekly Sabbath following Passover: *The Feast of Firstfruits*. Because of this, the Feast of Firstfruits will always fall *after* the first weekly Shabbat following Passover – *within* the week of the Feast of Unleavened Bread – and the Counting of the Omer will always commence *after* that same weekly Shabbat, which means that Shavuot / Pentecost will always fall on a Sunday. For an excellent in-depth teaching on this, see "The Wavesheaf Ceremony" by Harold Smith:
http://www.cgfnw.org/downloadlit.php?file=PDF/wavesheaf.pdf

The Feast of Firstfruits

> "...you shall bring the sheaf of the firstfruits of your harvest to the priest, and he shall wave the sheaf before the LORD, so that you may be accepted."

We discussed firstfruits in Chapter 2 and how we give of our monthly firstfruits on Rosh Chodesh to Israel first and then to the House. Israel was to put the first portion of their harvest into a basket and offer it to ADONAI by giving their firstfruits, (Hebrew *"bikkurim"*) referring to the seven species found in the Promised Land: wheat, barley, grapes, figs, pomegranates, olives and dates (Deut. 8:8), to the priest and declaring God's goodness and faithfulness. If they would honor Him in that way, He would bless them incredibly. These monthly firstfruits offerings are an example of the firstfruits brought at the yearly Feast of Firstfruits as we are about to see.

We've seen how firstfruits is significant and how the firstborn male received a double inheritance, and every firstborn male child and male animal were to be consecrated unto ADONAI (Exodus 13:2). Being the first is significant, and honoring the Father with your first, as a sign of your source of blessing, is important to Him and significant to you. Firstfruits and the firstborn are major themes throughout scripture; the choicest and the best.

Israel has been practicing a form of firstfruits throughout their agricultural and spiritual year with their monthly firstfruits offerings and their dedication / consecration of their firstborn of both man and beast. It's a common theme in scripture and in turn, it defines their lifestyle (Exodus 23:16; Leviticus 2:12, 14; 23:20; Numbers 18:12-15, 26; Deuteronomy 18:1-5; 26:2-4, 10; 2 Chronicles 31:5; Nehemiah 10:35-39; Proverbs 3:9; Jeremiah 2:3; Ezekiel 44:30; 48:14).

The yearly pilgrimage of Passover to Jerusalem to present themselves before ADONAI in commemoration of their corporate deliverance, redemption, salvation and provision culminates at the end of the first weekly Shabbat following Passover, during the Feast of Unleavened Bread, with the Feast of Firstfruits.

Israel is to bring a sheaf (omer) of the firstfruits of the harvest of the land (the first barley grain crop to ripen) to the priest. The priest would then wave the sheaf before ADONAI, as a dedication to Him, to be accepted on behalf of the people. A male lamb was then sacrificed as a burnt offering to ADONAI (Lev. 23:12) along with a food offering, a *minchah* (Strong's #H4503: a gift, tribute, an offering), of unleavened bread mixed with oil and a drink offering of wine (Lev. 23:13). The wave offering had to be performed before the crop could be used (Lev. 23:14).

Did you notice the offering that accompanies the wave-sheaf offering?

- A lamb
- Unleavened bread mixed with oil
- Wine

All of the elements that represent Messiah: for the Feast of Firstfruits is when the Anointed Messiah (the Sacrificial Lamb) would rise from the dead (unleavened and oiled) as the accepted offering through the shedding of blood (the wine), to be presented before the Father for His acceptance on behalf of the people (wave-sheaf offering)! Hallelujah!!

A practical way for us to observe the Feast of Firstfruits today is to have communion (with matzah) and worship our risen Messiah while bringing our firstfruits offering before ADONAI.

The week that Jesus died, we saw that He was entombed on Wednesday before sunset, before the High Shabbat of the First Day of the Feast of Unleavened Bread. He is entombed for three days and three nights, just as He prophesied: that the only sign He would show them was the sign of Jonah. Messiah was entombed Wednesday evening through Saturday evening with Saturday – after sunset – ending the weekly Shabbat and ushering in the Feast of Firstfruits, His resurrection.

In order for this Jesus of Nazareth to be Messiah, the Lamb of God that takes away the sins of the world, His death, burial and resurrection had to mimic the pattern established by His Father in the Passover, the Feast of Unleavened Bread and the Feast of Firstfruits as declared by Moses.

Jesus and the others that rose from the dead with Him were those "sheaves of the firstfruits of the harvest" that were being presented to Father God to be accepted.

Jesus, the Firstfruits Offering

Having said this, she turned around and saw Jesus standing, but she did not know that it was Jesus. Jesus said to her, "Woman, why are you weeping? Whom are you seeking?" Supposing him to be the gardener, she said to him, "Sir, if you have carried him away, tell me where you have laid him, and I will take him away." Jesus said to her, "Mary." She turned and said to him in Aramaic, "Rabboni!" Jesus said to her, "Do not cling to me, for I have not yet ascended to the Father; but go to my brothers and say to them, 'I am ascending to my Father and your Father, to my God and your God.'" Mary Magdalene went and announced to the disciples, "I have seen the Lord" – and that he had said these things to her.
John 20:14-18

Mary sees Jesus but doesn't recognize Him. She thinks He's the gardener. Does she think this because Jesus is holding the wave-sheaf offering?

The Feast of Firstfruits is when the first and best sheaves harvested are brought to the Temple as a thanksgiving offering to the Lord of the Harvest. Jesus was the ultimate First and Best of the Harvest, and He was well received by His Father.

When I was in the Garden of Gethsemane several years ago, my dear friend Rami explained how olives were harvested. A sheet of some sort is placed around the base of the olive tree and then the tree is either violently shaken or beaten with a 2x4 to loosen the olives so that they'll fall. Once gathered, the olives are placed on and covered by another softer cloth that is laid over a stone. Heavy stones are then placed on top of the covered olives to squeeze out their juice while the ripe olives yield a blood-red colored juice. The night that Jesus was praying in the Garden of Gethsemane before his crucifixion, *He was being harvested by the Father!*

> To this day I [Paul] have had the help that comes from God, and so I stand here testifying both to small and great, saying nothing but what the prophets and Moses said would come to pass: that the Christ must suffer and that, by being the first to rise from the dead, he would proclaim light both to our people and to the Gentiles."
> Acts 26:22-23

> But in fact Christ has been raised from the dead, the firstfruits of those who have fallen asleep. Christ the firstfruits, then at his coming those who belong to Christ.
> 1 Corinthians 15:20, 23b

In the same way that Israel is the firstfruits of God's harvest of nations (Jeremiah 2:3), Jesus is the Firstfruits of His Father's harvest of the people of those nations. As the Firstborn / Firstfruits of the dead (Col. 1:18) and "...the first of all the fruit of the earth..." (Deut. 26:2), Jesus is also the Firstfruits of the One New Man (Ro. 8:29).

Firstfruits is the Resurrection, *Not* a Sabbath

It has been clearly shown in both the TaNaKh and the New Testament that Firstfruits is the Resurrection of Messiah. Notice also that the instruction for observing the Feast of Firstfruits has no mention of it being a "Holy Convocation: A High Shabbat" or a Shabbat of any form for that matter. In fact, it occurs *after* the weekly Shabbat! To make Messiah's resurrection a "sabbath" for the Romanized Western Church not only undermines the prophetic nature of the Feasts, it also suggests that the TaNaKh is in error for not declaring firstfruits a Sabbath to begin with. In my opinion, this is another form, passive as it might be, of replacement theology.

This prophetic picture of resurrection in the Feast of Firstfruits is seen in His death:

> *Truly, truly, I say to you, unless a grain of wheat falls into the earth and dies, it remains alone; but if it dies, it bears much fruit.*
> John 12:24

The seed of grain, sown into the ground, produces the wave-sheaf and the consequent harvest: a redeemed harvest for ADONAI.

> *For as in Adam all die, so also in Christ shall all be made alive. But each in his own order: Christ the firstfruits, then at his coming those who belong to Christ. Then comes the end, when he delivers the kingdom to God the Father after destroying every rule and every authority and power.*
> 1 Corinthians 15:22-24

And regarding that Kingdom: In Revelation 5, we have the Throne Room scene where John sees a scroll in the right hand of Him Who Sits on the Throne, essentially the "Deed to the Earth," sealed with seven seals. An angel asks what seems a rhetorical question, "Who is worthy to break the seven seals and open the scroll?" No one in heaven and no one in or under the earth is able to open or look at the contents of the scroll, and John begins to weep.

One of the Twenty-Four Elders comforts John and tells him that the victorious and conquering Lion of the Tribe of Judah, the Root of David, is able to break the seven seals and open the scroll. A Lamb, a Lamb with the appearance of having been slaughtered, sacrificed, is standing between the Throne, the Twenty-Four Elders and the Four Living Creatures.

This Lamb that was slain had seven horns and seven eyes – the Seven Spirits of God – that had and have been sent out into all our world. He was found worthy to take the scroll, this deed, break its seals, open it and look at its contents.

When He took the scroll from the right hand of Him Who Sits on the Throne, the Four Living Creatures, along with the Twenty-Four Elders, fell down and worshiped the Lamb, each with a harp and each with golden bowls full of the incense of the prayers of the saints. A new song was / is sung in this Throne Room scene:

> And they sang a new song, saying, "Worthy are you to take the scroll and to open its seals, **for you were slain, and by your blood you ransomed people for God from every tribe and language and people and nation, and you have made them a kingdom and priests to our God, and they shall reign on the earth.**"

Revelation 5:9-10 [Emphasis mine]

"Resurrection Sunday"

So then what about this "Resurrection Sunday" sunrise service stuff? Again, the resurrection, Feast of Firstfruits, is not a Sabbath, nor did it occur on Sunday morning, as we have already explained with the biblical text.

Roman Catholicism, as we have already seen, presumed the authority to change the narrative and taught that Messiah died on a Friday and rose early on a Sunday morn. We have clearly showed the error of that idea, with the actual biblical narratives and timelines. Let me show you who and what *does* observe a "sunrise service" in scripture:

In the Sixth Month, while Ezekiel sat in his house with the elders of Judah (during their Babylonian captivity), Ezekiel states in chapter 8 of his book that the hand of Adonai fell upon him.

A form that appeared as a man stood before him. Below the waist of this form was fire, and above the waist of this form was what looked like bright, gleaming metal. This form reached out with what looked like the form of a hand and grabbed Ezekiel by a lock of his head. The Spirit of God lifted Ezekiel up between heaven and earth, and he describes being taken to Jerusalem by "visions of God."

Ezekiel is taken and shown the north face of the inner courts gateway where the "Image of Jealousy" that "provokes jealousy" was seated. The Glory of God that Ezekiel had previously seen was also there and instructed Ezekiel to look north.

Ezekiel sees the Image of Jealousy at the entrance north of

the altar gate and is asked if he could see what was being done by the House of Israel, the abominations that were taking place and the acts that were driving the Glory of God far away from His very own sanctuary. Ezekiel is then taken to the entrance of the court where he sees a hole in the wall. He is then instructed to dig. Ezekiel begins digging at the hole in the wall, revealing an entrance. Again, Ezekiel is instructed, and he goes in and witnesses the vile abominations taking place and committed there.

Ezekiel obeys, and he sees engraved on all the walls "every form of creeping things" and "loathsome beasts" along with all of Israel's idols. Standing before these demonic engravings are 70 Elders of the House of Israel in incense smoke, smoke that is emitting from the censers they are all holding. The Glory of God askes Ezekiel,

"Son of man, do you see what the Elders of the House of Israel are doing secretly, worshiping each in their 'dark room of images?'"

The Elders were convinced that ADONAI couldn't, wouldn't or didn't see them and that He had forsaken the Land. Ezekiel is taken again but this time to the north gate of the temple where women were "weeping for Tammuz" – worshipping a pagan god. This Sumerian god of food and vegetation, an annual life-death-rebirth deity, has a parallel consort in the goddess Ishtar that is worshiped beginning with the summer solstice with a time of mourning (weeping).

And he brought me into the inner court of the house of the LORD. And behold, at the entrance of the temple of the LORD, between the porch and the altar, were about twenty-five men, with their backs to the temple of the LORD, and their faces toward the east, worshiping the sun toward the east. Then he said to me, "Have you seen this, O son of man? Is it too light a thing for the house of Judah to commit the abominations that they commit here, that they should fill the land with violence and provoke me still further to anger? Behold, they put the branch to their nose. Therefore I will act in wrath. My eye will not spare, nor will I have pity. And though they cry in my ears with a loud voice, I will not hear them."
Ezekiel 8:16-18

In verses three and five of Ezekiel 8, you'll see that in the north entrance of the inner courtyard gate stood "the" – not "an" but "the" – idol that arouses God's jealousy and that provokes His Zealous Indignation. With the exception of the sun and Tammuz, Ezekiel doesn't name these actual objects of worship seen in the Temple. We know that Ahaz, under the influence of the Assyrian king, had removed the brazen altar in the Temple to make room for an idolatrous altar in the Temple itself (2 Kings 16:10-16) and that Manasseh did the same (2 Kings 21:4).

Ezekiel doesn't say that God is jealous of "all the idols of the house of Israel" found in the inner court, Tammuz, or the solar worship (8:10, 14, 16), so why this one?

An interpretation offered by Margaret Odell might be more fitting in the context of Ezekiel. Odell suggests that this is a votive statue and argues that the sacrifices made at the statue are the problem. In her view, the sacrifices most likely to raise the angst of Yahweh are child sacrifices. Odell's argument fits to some extent with Ezekiel's concerns about child sacrifice elsewhere in the text (16:20-36; 20:26,31; 23:37).

Child sacrifice was as repugnant to Ezekiel as it is to us, but Mark S. Smith says, in The Early History of God, page 172, that child sacrifice was Judean practice in the seventh century BCE, and that it was performed in the name of Yahweh as well as other gods.
(Source: Jill Middlemas. *Transformation of the Image*, published in Transforming Visions, page 117)

In the inner court of the Temple, the House of ADONAI, at the entrance, were about twenty-five men *with their backs to the Temple of ADONAI*, and their faces toward the east, *worshiping the sun toward the east*. Further study will show that this sun worship occurred predominantly at sunrise. Here's your sunrise service, and that's a lot of perversion occurring all at the same time in the Temple and its adjacent courts.

You should also know that some scholars believe that the Catholic Church of the Nativity in Bethlehem is built over a cave that was originally a shrine to Tammuz.
(Source: Giuseppe Ricciotti, *Vita di Gesù Cristo*, Tipografia Poliglotta Vaticana (1948) p. 276 n.)

Continuing in Ezekiel 9, we find what happens to these idolaters. Six men with weapons of slaughter in their hands wait for the one clothed in linen with a tattoo machine around his waist to tattoo those in the city that "sigh and groan over all the abominations" that are committed in Jerusalem. As they're being marked by the one clothed in linen, these six men with weapons of slaughter go about striking and killing old men outright, young men and maidens, little children and women, starting at the sanctuary while sparing only those with the mark, tattoo, on their foreheads. They begin the slaughter with the 70 elders found in chapter 8. In chapter 10, the Glory of ADONAI is forced to leave the Temple.

Tragic...

In the same way that these Elders in Ezekiel were convinced that ADONAI couldn't, wouldn't or didn't see them, the Romanized Western Church would have us all believe that because of "Jesus" and this "new covenant," the perversions we have committed and *continue* to commit – against God's Word (Jesus Incarnate) and His commandments (Torah) – as "Christians" – will go unpunished.

Jesus has become our license for lawlessness!

It doesn't work that way, people. Jesus and His covenants only work with our volunteered repentance, and no one is repenting of these perversions. Just. Like. Israel.

The resurrection of my Messiah did not occur on the sunrise of a Sunday morn to be observed with colored eggs that represent the goddess of fertility with an abominable meal of swine (Isaiah 65, 66) on a false sabbath in commemoration of a demonic deity.

The resurrection of my Messiah occurred on the Feast of Firstfruits, the Saturday night after the weekly Sabbath following Passover during the Feast of Unleavened Bread, as instructed by God through Moses and in accordance with the whole council of scripture.

Choose you this day whom you will serve and by whom you'll be represented...

The Principle of Firstfruits

In Chapter 2, I mentioned the cycles. I mentioned how the feasts are synonymous with God's agricultural calendar; the importance of their cyclical order; how we find these cyclical rhythms weekly (Shabbat), monthly (Rosh Chodesh) and yearly (the Feasts). We discussed how these cycles take us from harvest (Passover and Firstfruits) to harvest (Feast of Weeks) toward increase (Shavuot / Pentecost), culminating with the year-end harvest gathering of the Feast of Ingathering – all with an aspect of firstfruits along the way. We could say that firstfruits is the lifestyle indicative to Kingdom Living: "…on earth as it is in heaven."

I also stated that this ever-forward yearly momentum of "further up and further in" speaks to our lifestyle participation. Our growth in understanding the wisdom of applying this "Kingdom Lifestyle" through our worship of giving and the sowing into of firstfruits will reap provision and blessing in our lives. Firstfruits is spiritual in nature, intended to produce a Kingdom mindset in us just as Torah is spiritual in nature: exposing sin, cultivating obedience and, in turn, intended to produce / reap Kingdom blessings / fruit in our lives. This act of honoring God with the first of what you receive is all about His cyclical rhythm of increase birthed out of your obedience to His word:

> *My son, do not forget my teaching, but let your heart keep my commandments, for length of days and years of life and peace they will add to you. Let not steadfast love and faithfulness forsake you; bind them around your neck; write them on the tablet of your heart. So you will find favor and good success in the sight of God and man. Trust in the LORD with all your heart, and do not lean on your own understanding. In all your ways acknowledge him, and he will make straight your paths. Be not wise in your own eyes; fear the LORD, and turn away from evil. It will be healing to your flesh and refreshment to your bones.* **Honor the LORD with your wealth and with the firstfruits of all your produce; then your barns will be filled with plenty, and your vats will be bursting with wine.**
> *Proverbs 3:1-10 [Emphasis mine]*

Did you see the formula?

- Don't forget His teachings (Torah)
- Keep His commandments (Torah)
- Bind and write steadfast love and faithfulness around your neck and on your heart
- Trust in ADONAI with all your heart
- Do not lean on your own understanding
- Acknowledge Him in all your ways
- Don't be wise in your own eyes
- Fear ADONAI

- Turn away from evil
- Honor ADONAI with your wealth and with your firstfruits

This cyclical rhythm from harvest to harvest; this "Firstfruits Lifestyle of Blessing and Provision" continues from the Feast of Firstfruits all the way to our increase with the start of the Counting of the Omer / The Feast of Weeks: the forty-nine-day countdown to the (wheat) harvest festival of Shavuot.

The Counting of the Omer / The Feast of Weeks

You shall count seven full weeks from the day after the Sabbath, from the day that you brought the sheaf of the wave offering. You shall count fifty days to the day after the seventh Sabbath.

Right about now, some of you might be thinking that a 40-some-odd day count around springtime and the Resurrection of Jesus sounds familiar. It should. Many in the Romanized Western Church observe as a "holy time" a similar springtime countdown. This traditional countdown, instead of counting 49 days plus one *from* Passover, does the exact *opposite* from the scriptural instruction of the Omer Count and counts 40 days *toward* Passover's general direction; to a manmade tradition known as "Easter," essentially the Romanized Western Church's official replacement for Passover. This observance, the counting toward "Easter" and "Easter" itself have nothing more than manmade religious traditions to substantiate them. But it does beg the question:

"Why, if we already have a scriptural instruction from God Himself to count 49 days plus one following Passover, would we substitute that with a 40-day count leading up to…?"

You get the idea.

The institution that outlawed the scriptural Sabbath and determined that our faith would observe a manmade day instead; this same institution that outlawed and replaced God's covenant Passover with a manmade tradition, that declared Passover and the eating of unleavened bread anathema; this institution decided to do the exact opposite of the scriptural instruction, and they told everyone that the early church fathers learned this practice they call "Lent" from the original disciples.

> *"The festival, of which we read in Church history, under the name of Easter, in the third and fourth centuries, was quite a different festival from that now observed in the Romish Church, and at that time was not known by any such name as Easter...That festival [Passover] was not idolatrous, and it was preceded by no Lent. 'It ought to be known,' said Cassianus, the monk of Marseilles, writing in the fifth century, and contrasting the primitive [New Testament] Church with the Church of his day, 'that the observance of the forty days had no existence, so long as the perfection of that primitive Church remained inviolate.'"*

(Source: Alexander Hislop *The Two Babylons*, Chapter III, Section II, Easter)

Shrove Tuesday (or Mardi Gras, as it is commonly known) literally means "Fat Tuesday" in French (also known as "Pancake Tuesday" in England) and is associated with the Roman Catholic custom of "Lent," first mentioned in the fifth canon of the Council of Nicaea (A.D. 325). The idea behind Mardi Gras or carnival celebrations is that people overindulge before giving up something for "Lent," which begins the following day with "Ash Wednesday." "Lent" is the 40-day count from "Ash Wednesday" to "Easter." "Lent" is a time of penance, fasting and abstinence. From "Ash Wednesday" to "Easter," many solemnly mark their foreheads with ash, "fasting" or abstaining from certain foods or physical pleasures for 40 days to prepare them for "Easter."

> *"The real aim of Lent is, above all else, to prepare men for the celebration of the death and Resurrection of Christ... the better the preparation the more effective the celebration will be. One can effectively relive the mystery only with purified mind and heart. The purpose of Lent is to provide that purification by weaning men from sin and selfishness through self-denial and prayer, by creating in them the desire to do God's will and to make His kingdom come by making it come first of all in their hearts."*

(Source: Catholic Encyclopedia)

It sounds good. It seems sincere. But it has absolutely nothing to do with anything other than manmade religious tradition and the usurping of scripture. Doesn't basic Christian belief tell us that there's nothing we can do by "works" to "purify" our hearts and minds? That no number of works can wean us from sin? That "acts of self-denial" can't provide us with purification, a desire to do God's will or "make" His Kingdom come? Yeah, they do tell us that....

It begs the other and obvious question:

"Why not actually do what God instructed if you're going to bother at all?"

Well, that answer should be perfectly clear: This "Lent" stuff isn't "Jewish"...

Coming from the Anglo-Saxon Lencten, meaning "spring," "Lent" originated in the ancient Babylonian mystery religion. "The forty days' abstinence of Lent was directly borrowed from the worshippers of the Babylonian goddess...Among the Pagans this Lent seems to have been an indispensable preliminary to the great annual festival in commemoration of the death and resurrection of Tammuz."
(Source: Alexander Hislop *The Two Babylons*, Chapter III, Section II, Easter)

Tammuz. There's that name again. Tammuz was also known as the Babylonian "Messiah." Simply put, this is just another religious counterfeit based on things in which God forbids us to participate. The Feast of Tammuz was usually celebrated in June (also called the "month of Tammuz.") "Lent" was the 40-day count before the feast of "Easter" "celebrated by alternate weeping and rejoicing." So why the embracing of yet another obvious pagan exercise? For the same reasons they did anything;

"To conciliate the Pagans to nominal Christianity, Rome, pursuing its usual policy, took measures to get the Christian and Pagan festivals amalgamated, and, by a complicated but skillful adjustment of the calendar, it was found no difficult matter, in general, to get Paganism and Christianity -- now far sunk in idolatry -- in this as in so many other things, to shake hands"
(Source: ibid.)

Roman Catholicism replaced Passover with "Easter." They moved the pagan Feast of Tammuz to early spring, "Christianizing" it along the way, and "Lent" followed with it.

"This change of the calendar in regard to Easter was attended with momentous consequences. It brought into the Church the grossest corruption and the rankest superstition in connection with the abstinence of Lent."
(Source: ibid.)

"We freethinkers can show that the holidays mean more than just their names by reminding our Christian friends and loved ones to keep Ēostre in Easter.

This is "our" holiday, to signify our Germanic Paganist goddess of fertility Ēostre as we celebrate the Spring Equinox and the bountiful crops with signs of fertility, eggs and rabbits."
(Source: Alex Fierro, Freedom From Religion Foundation Member)

Catholic Tradition	Scripture
Mardi Gras / Fat Tuesday	N/A
Ash Wednesday	N/A
40-day count leading up to "Good Friday" / "Easter"	N/A
"Good Friday"	N/A
"Easter"	N/A
Banned	Passover
Banned	Feast of Unleavened Bread High Sabbath
N/A	Feast of Firstfruits / Resurrection after Weekly Sabbath
N/A	Counting of the Omer / Feast of Weeks 49 Day count (seven Sabbaths) leading up to Shavuot / Pentecost

What did God say about mixing paganism into the worship of Him?

I acquire no element of gratification in speaking so negatively about another religious belief system. But in order to comprehend the reasons behind our forfeiture of the Scriptural Commandments, you must understand the importance of distinguishing the hows, whats and whys of our faith and their developmental influence and history. Our. House. Is. On. Fire. I've said this before: if you want to celebrate the mass of Christ, knock yourself out. If you want to celebrate "Easter," knock yourself out. If you want to celebrate "Lent," knock yourself out. But don't convince yourselves that these practices have biblical merit and are not rooted in paganism. Call it what it is! Again, I don't care if you observe these things, and there's no judgment if you do, but you should *at least* be observing the actual Holy Days that God literally established as covenant signs for His people – not replace them! Don't you think?

Back to the scriptural instruction:

> *You shall count seven full weeks from the day after the Sabbath, from the day that you brought the sheaf of the wave offering. You shall count fifty days to the day after the seventh Sabbath.*

By now you should be able to surmise that God instructed us to count seven Shabbats, 49 days up to 50, because He wanted us to remember what He was about to do: Shavuot, the revelation of Torah – Pentecost, the Indwelling of the Holy Spirit. With Shavuot being the culmination of the deliverance received with Passover, traditionally, some see the Counting of the Omer towards Shavuot as a time of sanctification, personal revelation and repentance – much like the Counting of the Omer's inaccurate religious substitution known as "Lent."

We're going to look at this Counting of the Omer (COTO) / Feast of Weeks (FOW) from four vantage points:

- The Original Exodus
- Post Exodus
- Back in Jesus' Day
- Today

Counting of the Omer (COTO) / Feast of Weeks (FOW): The Original Exodus

The original exodus account starts 72 hours before future Israel would begin the Counting of the Omer and the observance of the Feast of Weeks. Many might ask the question:

"Why did God wait 50 days to give Israel Torah?"

Why *did* God wait? Why didn't He give it to them *before* leaving Egypt? Why didn't He give it to them *during* their trek along the way? There is no concrete or specific answer to this question, but a look at those first seven weeks after leaving Egypt gives us a clue as to why

God may have waited. With three keys in the first verse of the Exodus narrative, here's our first clue:

> When Pharaoh let the people go, God did not lead them by way of the land of the Philistines, although that was near. For God said, "Lest the people change their minds when they see war and return to Egypt." But God led the people around by the way of the wilderness toward the Red Sea. And the people of Israel went up out of the land of Egypt equipped for battle.
> Exodus 13:17-18

1. God led Israel out of Egypt, the long way around, to avoid their future nemeses, the Philistines
2. This longer bypass was to avoid a potential fight and war just in case Israel changed their minds and retreated *back* to Egypt out of fear of a fight, and
3. Regardless of this bypass, Israel left Egypt "equipped for battle"

Israel had just witnessed the most incredible deliverance in human history! They had seen, with their own eyes, one of their own take on the Coptic Priests of Egypt and win with signs and wonders (this is *not* a reference to the Coptic Orthodox Church of Egypt but a reference to the magicians and priests in Pharaoh's court.)

They saw the Nile turn into blood. They saw all the fish in the Nile die, and it stunk. They saw how the Egyptians grew weary of drinking this same water from the Nile. They saw all the waters of Egypt turn to blood; the rivers, their canals, their ponds and all their pools. There was blood even in the vessels of wood and stone.

They saw all of Egypt plagued with frogs. They saw the Nile, the rivers, the canals and pools swarming with frogs. The frogs were in the Egyptians' houses and in their bedrooms and on their beds and in the houses of their servants and of all the people – even in their ovens and kneading bowls. They saw how all the frogs died in the houses, the courtyards and the fields after Moses petitioned God.

They saw how Aaron stretched out his staff and struck the dust of the earth and how the dust became gnats in all the land of Egypt and how there were gnats all over everyone, human and animal.

Israel saw how swarms of flies plagued Pharaoh, his servants and the Egyptian people, how the swarms went into their houses and on the ground. They saw how God set apart the Land of Goshen, where Israel lived, so that no swarms of flies were there. They saw the division between Egypt and themselves and how the land of Egypt was ruined by the swarms of flies.

Israel also saw the hand of ADONAI fall with a severe plague upon Egypt's livestock; the horses, the donkeys, the camels, the herds, and the flocks. They saw how ADONAI made a distinction between the livestock of Israel and the livestock of Egypt so that nothing that belonged to Israel died. They saw all of the livestock of the Egyptians die, but not one of the livestock of Israel died.

They watched Moses take handfuls of soot from the kiln, and throw them in the air in the sight of Pharaoh. The fine dust fell over all of Egypt and became boils breaking out on man and beast.

They watched as Moses rose early in the morning and presented himself before Pharaoh and said to him, "My God will send all His plagues on you, your servants and your people. By now God could have put out His hand and struck you and your people with pestilence, and you would have been cut off from the earth. Tomorrow, God will cause very heavy hail to fall, such as never has been seen in Egypt since the day it was founded until now. Go, get your livestock and all that you have in the field into safe shelter, for every man and beast that is in the field and is not brought home will die when the hail falls on them." Israel watched whoever feared the word of ADONAI among the servants of Pharaoh hurry their slaves and their livestock into the houses, but those that did not pay attention to the word of ADONAI left their slaves and their livestock in the field. They watched Moses stretch out his hand toward heaven as hail fell down on all of Egypt; on man and beast and every plant in the fields. They watched Moses stretch out his staff toward heaven, and ADONAI responded with thunder and hail with fire on all of Egypt. There was fire flashing continually in the midst of the hail, very heavy hail, such as Egypt had never seen since it had become a nation. The hail struck down everything in the fields; both man and beast, every plant and every tree. But in the Land of Goshen, where the people of Israel were, there was no hail.

They watched as Moses stretched out his staff over the land of Egypt yet again, and ADONAI brought an east wind all that day and all that night. When it was morning, the east wind had brought locusts. The locusts came up over all of Egypt and settled on the whole country, filling up the Egyptian houses. Such a dense swarm of locusts had never been seen before nor since. The locusts covered the face of all of Egypt, darkening the land. No one could see the land it was so full of locusts. They ate all the plants and all the fruit from the trees that the hail had left. Not a green thing remained.

Then ADONAI said to Moses, "Stretch out your hand toward heaven, that there may be darkness over the land of Egypt, a darkness to be felt." So Moses stretched out his hand toward heaven, and there was pitch darkness in all of Egypt for three days. The Egyptians couldn't see one another so they stayed indoors all three days. But all of Israel had light where they lived.

> *The LORD said to Moses, "Yet one plague more I will bring upon Pharaoh and upon Egypt. Afterward he will let you go from here. When he lets you go, he will drive you away completely. Speak now in the hearing of the people, that they ask, every man of his neighbor and every woman of her neighbor, for silver and gold jewelry." And the LORD gave the people favor in the sight of the Egyptians. Moreover, the man Moses was very great in the land of Egypt, in the sight of Pharaoh's servants and in the sight of the people. So Moses said, "Thus says the LORD: About midnight I will go out in the midst of Egypt, and every firstborn in the land of Egypt shall die, from the firstborn of Pharaoh who sits on his throne, even to the firstborn of the slave girl who is behind the handmill, and all the firstborn of the cattle. There shall be a great cry throughout all the land of Egypt, such as there has never been, nor ever will be again. But not a dog shall growl against any of the people of Israel, either man or beast, that you may know that the LORD makes a distinction between Egypt and Israel. And all these your servants shall come down to me and bow down to me, saying, 'Get out, you and all the people who follow you.' And after that I will go out." And he went out from Pharaoh in hot anger.*
> *Exodus 11:1-8*

Israel would leave Egypt following that terrible and amazing night, just as Joseph had prophesied so many years before (Exod. 13:19; Heb. 11:22). Even after experiencing the mighty, mighty hand of God in their favor, Israel was still an oppressed people; mentally, emotionally, psychologically and spiritually.

They left Egypt following a Pillar of Smoke by day and a Pillar of Fire by night and were led the long way around to avoid war in case Israel returned to Egypt out of fear. God had them backtrack at the Red Sea to give Pharaoh the impression that they were lost (Exod. 14).

Three days later, Israel was grumbling because the only water available was bitter. God provided, yet again, and made for them a statute, a rule, testing them, saying, "If you will diligently listen to My voice, and do what is right in My eyes, and give ear to My commandments and keep all My statutes, I will put none of the diseases on you that I put on the Egyptians. I am ADONAI, your healer (Jehovah Rapha')." He then leads them to an oasis with twelve springs of water and seventy palm trees and they camped there (Exod. 15).

On the 15th day of the Second month (Ziv), the whole congregation of Israel grumbled again against Moses, wishing they had died by the hand of God in Egypt, where "we sat by the meat pots and ate bread to the full, for you have brought us out into this wilderness to kill this whole assembly with hunger." In response, God provides them with manna – *with instructions* – and quail. But Israel fails to heed the instructions of God or listen to Moses. It was another test, except this test would go on for 40 long years... (Exod. 16)

After that, they moved on to Rephidim, where more quarrelling ensued, again over water: "Why did you bring us up out of Egypt, to kill us and our children and our livestock with thirst?" Israel was first attacked by Amalek at Rephidim but ADONAI gave them the victory.

Jethro, the priest of Midian, Moses' father-in-law, advises Moses to establish judges to help him rule over the people (Exod. 18).

On the third New Moon after leaving Egypt, they entered the wilderness of Sinai. Israel camped before the mountain while Moses went up the mountain to God.

There's a reason why God waited 50 days to give Israel Torah; to make covenant with them. And there's a reason why He didn't give it to them before leaving Egypt.

Fear, Doubt and Unbelief – A "Stiff-Necked" People

This is where we submit to the reality that God is Sovereign. He knew that Israel was full of fear, doubt and unbelief. As we've seen and as we'll continue to see, this same fear, doubt and unbelief would plague them for the next 40 years. Fear, doubt and unbelief, coupled with their stubbornness (they were a stiff-necked people), the cause of their rebellion, would also be the cause of their deaths while wandering the wilderness. This recipe of fear, doubt, unbelief and stubbornness is why they wouldn't be allowed to enter the Promised Land.

Israel lacked the opposite of fear:

- Assurance
- Confidence
- Faith
- Trust
- Bravery
- Courage
- Fearlessness, and
- Heroism

They lacked the opposite of doubt and unbelief:

- Belief
- Certainty
- Confidence, and
- Trust

Yet they were stubborn in their dysfunction. Even after experiencing the mighty hand of God, Israel was a broken and oppressed people; mentally, emotionally, psychologically and spiritually. It's one thing to be dysfunctionally broken; it's another thing to be stubborn in that dysfunction. I think this is why God waited 50 days to give Torah to Israel – to make covenant with them. This is why He didn't, couldn't, give it to them before leaving Egypt. And even then, it would be another 40 years before the Circumcision at Gilgal, where Israel, still trapped within an Egyptian slave mentality, would truly find their identity (Joshua 5).

COTO / FOW: Post Exodus

Year Two: Israel is still in the wilderness of Sinai.

Passover is observed. During the day when Israel was encamped, the Pillar of Cloud covered the tabernacle. In the evening, the Pillar of Fire covered the tabernacle until morning. When the cloud was lifted from over the tabernacle, Israel would set out and follow it to the next place where it would settle down. That's where they would camp. The physical manifestation of God, the Pillar of Cloud and the Pillar of Fire, were in the physical visual sight of Israel for 24 hours a day, 7 days a week, for 40 years (Num. 9).

God instructs Moses to take a census of the people (Num. 1):

> *"Take a census of all the congregation of the people of Israel, by clans, by fathers' houses, according to the number of names, every male, head by head. From twenty years old and upward, all in Israel who are able to go to war, you and Aaron shall list them, company by company. And there shall be with you a man from each tribe, each man being the head of the house of his fathers."*
> *Numbers 1:2-4*

Israel is instructed to camp by individual standards (clans / tribes) under the banners of their fathers' houses facing the tent of meeting on every side (Num. 2).

The Levitical priesthood is established, as is the consecration of firstborn men and beast. A census of the Levites and a census of all firstborns is taken, and the Levites are set aside as belonging to ADONAI, and the firstborn are redeemed (Num. 3).

On the 12th day of the Second month (Ziv), in the second year, the Cloud lifted from over the tabernacle, and Israel set out by stages and left the wilderness of Sinai. This was the first time they mobilized at the command of ADONAI by Moses (Num. 10):

> *And whenever the ark set out, Moses said, "Arise, O LORD , and let your enemies be scattered, and let those who hate you flee before you." And when it rested, he said, "Return, O LORD, to the ten thousand thousands of Israel."*
> *Numbers 10:35-36*

Once again, Israel complained about their misfortunes and the lack of meat in their diet, and when God heard it, He sent fire that consumed some outlying parts of the camp.

> Now the rabble that was among them had a strong craving. And the people of Israel also wept again and said, "Oh that we had meat to eat! We remember the fish we ate in Egypt that cost nothing, the cucumbers, the melons, the leeks, the onions, and the garlic. But now our strength is dried up, and there is nothing at all but this manna to look at." Moses heard the people weeping throughout their clans, everyone at the door of his tent. And the anger of the LORD blazed hotly, and Moses was displeased.
> Numbers 11:4-6, 10

Did you notice that the word "rabble" was used to describe some of them? Moses is a bit overwhelmed by Israel's attitude, so God tells him to establish 70 elders of the people to lighten the administrative burden off of Moses. God also instructs Moses to tell the people to consecrate themselves, because He was going to answer Israel's complaining of wanting to be back in Egypt where they had it so good as oppressed slaves (it's been two years). God was going to send them meat – quail. He was going to send them so much quail, not just for:

> ..."one day, or two days, or five days, or ten days, or twenty days, but a whole month, until it comes out of their nostrils and becomes loathsome to them, because you have rejected ADONAI who is among you and have wept before him, saying, 'Why did we come out of Egypt?'"
>
> While the meat was yet between their teeth, before it was consumed, the anger of the LORD was kindled against the people, and the LORD struck down the people with a very great plague.
> Numbers 11: 19-20, 33

In Joshua 5, we saw that the first Passover in Canaan was observed some 38 years after the above account of the quail and plague. Everyone that had left Egypt with Moses was killed in the wilderness, including Moses. As far as we can be certain, only Joshua and Caleb remained from the multitudes that made the exodus. Joshua 6 starts during the Omer Count when they're about to attack Jericho.

Once again, we see the all-too-common issue of Israel's disobedience, this time in the form of pillaging. Israel was told that everything inside of Jericho belonged to ADONAI; however, Achan the son of

Carmi, son of Zabdi, son of Zerah, of the tribe of Judah, decided to take some of the spoils for himself (Josh. 7).

After the debacle in Joshua 7, Israel is victorious against Ai. Joshua renews the covenant of Torah between Israel, sojourner, native born (verse 33) and God (Josh. 8).

In Joshua 9, we see that the entire Land of Canaan has heard of the fame of Israel and their God and that Israel is to possess all of the Land and destroy all of its inhabitants. Because of this, Joshua and his leaders are deceived into making a pact with the Gibeonites. The conquest of Canaan begins.

Four hundred eighteen years after leaving Egypt, in the fourth year of King Solomon's reign, the building of the First Temple begins in the 2nd month of Ziv (1 Ki. 6; 2 Ch. 3).

In what has become a characteristic trait of Israel, apostasy, Israel returns to God under King Asa in the 3rd month – 60 years after King Solomon (2 Ch. 15).

If you can imagine, around 250 years after King Solomon, about 180 years after King Asa, King Hezekiah re-establishes the Temple service, Shabbat and the Feasts – essentially Torah observance – after approximately five generations of continual lawlessness. King Hezekiah organizes the priests and cuts down the pagan pillars throughout the Land, as well as the Asherim. Israel, in accordance with the newly reestablished observance of Torah, brings their firstfruits offerings and tithes. Amazing! (2 Ch. 29-31)

And the struggle continues. Seventy-five years later, at the age of 16, King Josiah "began to seek the God of his father King David." At the age of 20:

> *[...] in the twelfth year [of his reign] he began to purge Judah and Jerusalem of the high places, the Asherim, and the carved and the metal images. And they chopped down the altars of the Baals in his presence, and he cut down the incense altars that stood above them. And he broke in pieces the Asherim and the carved and the metal images, and he made dust of them and scattered it over the graves of those who had sacrificed to them. He also burned the bones of the priests on their altars and cleansed Judah and Jerusalem. And in the cities of Manasseh, Ephraim, and Simeon, and as far as Naph-*

> tali, in their ruins all around, he broke down the altars and beat the Asherim and the images into powder and cut down all the incense altars throughout all the land of Israel. Then he returned to Jerusalem.
> 2 Chronicles 34:3-7

Wow. How amazing is that?!? It gets even better. At the age of 26, he begins to repair, again, the House of ADONAI (verses 8-13). And while they were repairing the Temple:

> Hilkiah the priest found the Book of the Law of the LORD given through Moses. Then Hilkiah answered and said to Shaphan the secretary, "I have found the Book of the Law in the house of the LORD." And Hilkiah gave the book to Shaphan. Shaphan brought the book to the king [...] Then Shaphan the secretary told the king, "Hilkiah the priest has given me a book." And Shaphan read from it before the king. And when the king heard the words of the Law, he tore his clothes. And the king commanded Hilkiah, Ahikam the son of Shaphan, Abdon the son of Micah, Shaphan the secretary, and Asaiah the king's servant, saying, "Go, inquire of the LORD for me and for those who are left in Israel and in Judah, concerning the words of the book that has been found. For great is the wrath of the LORD that is poured out on us, because our fathers have not kept the word of the LORD, to do according to all that is written in this book."
> 2 Chronicles 34:14b-16a, 18-21

Wowie zowie! This is so amazing to me. You need to stop right here and finish reading the chapter; how Israel's future disaster for not keeping Torah and mixing paganism into the worship of God (sound familiar?) is prophesied; how King Josiah repents with all of Israel for not keeping God's commandments and, once again, covenants with God, as a people, to keep His Torah, and they do, all the days of King Josiah... Thank you, Father...

You might be asking yourself, "What does this have to do with the Counting of the Omer and the Feast of Weeks?" Well, besides being an amazing story, in the next chapter of 2 Chronicles, chapter 35, young, noble and faithful King Josiah observed the Passover, the first step towards observing the Counting of the Omer and the Feast of Weeks.

Now what I'm really hoping is that you're asking yourself the question, "How could Israel be constantly breaking covenant and turning away from these basic truths time and time again?" so that I can tell you how important it is for our need to realize that the Western Church, the Mainstream Romanized Western Church, the majority... Christianity here and now isn't the same Christianity from even just a few years ago. The amount and forms of compromise that have been accepted and embraced by the church today – in the name of "progress," "liberalism," "tolerance," "political correctness" and "inclusion" – are exactly like Israel! And we will see the exact same punishments... and it grieves me... But there is hope! Father, bring us another Josiah!!

Two years after the exiles from Babylon returned to the Land and during the COTO / FOW, Israel started rebuilding the Temple in the Month of Ziv. They encountered resistance from their adversaries, and the rebuilding was put to a stop by King Artaxerxes. The prophets then restarted the work on the Temple in violation of the now-deceased King Artaxerxes' cease-and-desist order, so a new complaint was filed with the new king, Darius, King of Persia, who was reminded of the decree of King Cyrus in regards to the rebuilding of the Temple in Jerusalem. The work was completed on the third day of Adar in the sixth year of the reign of King Darius, just in time for the reinstitution, yet again, of the Passover (Eza. 3 - 6).

Ezra traveled from Babylon back to Jerusalem during this time of the Counting of the Omer / Feasts of Weeks (Eza. 7:9; 8:31-33).

Nehemiah inspected the walls of Jerusalem possibly during this timeframe as noted in chapter 2 of his book.

Ezekiel gets a word about Egypt and Pharaoh (Ezk. 31).

COTO / FOW: In Jesus' Day

On the first day of the Omer, Jesus appears to Mary Magdalene (who thinks Him the gardener), Joanna, Mary the mother of James and the other women with them. The guards set to watch the tomb are bribed for their silence regarding Messiah's resurrection. John and Peter go to the tomb and find it empty. Jesus also appears to two disciples walking into the country on the way to the village of Emmaus.

In John's account, in the evening, Jesus appears to the disciples and breathes on them to receive the Holy Spirit.

In the other gospels, the 11 disciples are rebuked for their unbelief and hardness of heart (fear, doubt and unbelief) when they arrive in the Galilee. They're also:

- Instructed to make disciples of nations
- Instructed to teach those disciples to observe all that Jesus had commanded them (Torah)
- Told what spiritual signs would accompany those believers, and
- Their minds are opened up to the Torah and the Prophets

(Mt. 28; Mk. 16; Luk. 24; Jn. 20)

Eight days later, Jesus appears to the disciples and Thomas (Jn. 20:26).

Jesus causes the miracle of the catching of 153 fish in the Galilee the third time He reveals Himself to them during the COTO / FOW (Jn. 21).

Paul states that Jesus appeared to more than 500 believers at one time during the Omer Count (1 Co. 15:6a).

In Acts 1 Luke writes:

> *He [Messiah] presented himself alive to them after his suffering by many proofs, appearing to them during forty days and speaking about the kingdom of God. And while staying with them he ordered them not to depart from Jerusalem [...]*
> *Acts 1:3-4*

The disciples are given the promise of the Holy Spirit and then Jesus ascends (verses 6-11). The disciples, the women, Mary the mother of Jesus, and His brothers, around 120 of them, are staying in an upper room in Jerusalem. Peter's gift of seeing the scriptures being fulfilled in light of their present-day scenarios starts to kick in, and they nominate Matthias to replace Judas.

COTO / FOW: Present Day

Today, we simply remind ourselves around the dinner table that the Omer Count is in play, what day and week of the Omer Count we're presently on and why we observe the commandment. We also remind ourselves that this Omer Count is leading us to Shavuot / Pentecost:

- When God empowered us through the giving of His Commandments for mankind through His prophetic servant Moses, and
- When God empowered us through the giving and indwelling of His Holy Spirit so that we could *keep* those Commandments

In Summary

Appointed Time: Feast of Firstfruits

Significance: ... "so that you may be accepted" ...

Observance: Bring a Firstfruits Offering to the priest. He shall wave it before ADONAI so that you may be accepted. Offer a food offering with a pleasing aroma to ADONAI, and a drink offering of wine. Additionally, a practical way to observe the Feast is to have communion (with matzah) and worship our risen Messiah while bringing your Firstfruits offering before ADONAI

Length: Hours after the Sabbath following Passover

Appointed Time: Feast of Weeks (Counting of the Omer)

Significance: The counting up to the wheat harvest, Shavuot / Pentecost, in anticipation and in remembrance for what He was about to do; the covenant of Torah and the indwelling of the Holy Spirit

Observance: Every night at dinner during the Omer Count, we say the number of the day and week we are on for seven weeks / seven Shabbats, and on the 50th day it's a High Shabbat

Length: 50 days (49 days / seven Sabbaths +1 day)

Feast of Firstfruits

We see that this cycle of firstfruits giving is a sign of our source of blessing; monthly in the Rosh Chodesh offerings and yearly in the Feast of Firstfruits. This cycle of giving is a sign of our source of blessing.

Israel practices firstfruits throughout their agricultural and spiritual year. It's a common theme in scripture, and in turn, it defines their lifestyle. It needs to begin to define ours.

Israel's yearly pilgrimage of Passover to Jerusalem, to present themselves before ADONAI in commemoration of their corporate deliverance, redemption, salvation and provision, culminates at the end of the first weekly Shabbat following Passover, during the Feast of Unleavened Bread, with the Feast of Firstfruits.

Israel is to bring a Firstfruits Offering to the priest. The priest would then wave the offering before ADONAI, as a dedication to Him to be accepted on behalf of the people. A male lamb was then sacrificed as a burnt offering to ADONAI along with a food offering of unleavened bread mixed with oil and a drink offering of wine (Lev. 23:12-13). All of these elements represent Messiah:

- A lamb
- Unleavened bread mixed with oil
- Wine

Feast of Firstfruits is when the Anointed Messiah (the Sacrificial Lamb) rose from the dead (unleavened and oiled) as the accepted offering through the shedding of blood (the wine), to be presented before the Father for His acceptance on behalf of the people (wave-sheaf offering)! Hallelujah!!

A practical way for us to observe the Feast of Firstfruits today is to have communion (with matzah) and worship while bringing your Firstfruits offering before ADONAI.

The week that Jesus died, He was entombed on a Wednesday before the High Shabbat of the First Day of the Feast of Unleavened Bread. He was entombed for three days and three nights, Wednesday evening through Saturday evening, with Saturday night – after sunset – ending the weekly Shabbat and ushering in the Feast of Firstfruits, His resurrection. This schedule mimicked the pattern established by His Father in the Passover, Feast of Unleavened Bread and the Feast of Firstfruits as declared by Moses.

The Feast of Firstfruits is the Resurrection of Messiah, as has been clearly shown in both the TaNaKh and the New Testament. The instruction for observing the Feast of Firstfruits has no mention of it being a "Holy Convocation: A High Shabbat" or a Sabbath at all. It comes *after* the weekly Sabbath.

The resurrection of Messiah occurred on the Feast of Firstfruits after the weekly Sabbath following Passover during the Feast of Unleavened Bread as instructed by God through Moses and in accordance with the whole council of scripture.

Feast of Weeks / The Omer Count

The Counting of the Omer / The Feast of Weeks is all about us counting up to the wheat harvest – Shavuot / Pentecost – in anticipation and in remembrance for what He was about to do; the covenant of Torah and the indwelling of the Holy Spirit. Every night at dinner during the Omer Count, we say the number of the day and week we are on for seven weeks / seven Shabbats, and on the 50th day, it's a High Shabbat.

I love the way Mark Biltz puts it:

The Counting of the Omer is a countdown to Shavuot / Pentecost, the time of the giving of the Holy Spirit. It is a journey which is begun with Passover, the symbol of our Salvation in Yeshua, and completed at Pentecost, the symbol of our completion through the Spirit. The distance of days between the two events should be a time of spiritual reflection, growth, purification and preparation.
(Source: *The Feasts of the Lord*, http://www.elshaddaiministries.us/pdf/Spring-Festivals.pdf. 12)

The Passover, the exodus from Egypt, the 40-day trek through the wilderness to Mount Sinai; all with one motive behind it all:

*Say therefore to the people of Israel, 'I am the LORD, and I will bring you out from under the burdens of the Egyptians, and I will deliver you from slavery to them, and I will redeem you with an outstretched arm and with great acts of judgment. **I will take you to be my people, and I will be your God**, and you shall know that I am the LORD your God, who has brought you out from under the burdens of the Egyptians.'"*
Exodus 6:6-7 [Emphasis mine]

CHAPTER 6

SHAVUOT (WEEKS) / PENTECOST
I will take you to be My people, and I will be your God

> *"You shall bring from your dwelling places two loaves of bread to be waved. They shall be of fine flour, and they shall be baked with leaven, as firstfruits to the LORD. And the priest shall wave the bread of the firstfruits as a wave offering before the LORD. They shall be holy to the LORD for the priest. And you shall make proclamation on the same day. You shall hold a holy convocation [a High Sabbath]. You shall not do any ordinary work. It is a statute forever in all your dwelling places throughout your generations. And when you reap the harvest of your land, you shall not reap your field right up to its edge, nor shall you gather the gleanings after your harvest. You shall leave them for the poor and for the sojourner: I am the LORD your God."*
> Leviticus 23:17, 20-22

It's Saturday evening June 3, 2017, the 49th day of the Omer Count – the seventh Shabbat is just about to end – when the sun has gone down it will be the 50th day of the Omer Count; Shavuot: a High Shabbat of rejoicing! (Deut. 16:9-12)

In Exodus 19, we see that Moses and all of Israel have assembled before the Living God, per His instructions, at the base of Mount Sinai. This is when and where God established His instructions in written form for those that would call upon His name; His instructions for mankind, for those that make the voluntary decision to serve Him; His covenant instructions for those who call themselves "Believers." In essence, these instructions are the keys of blessing for you, as a Christian / a Believer; the wedding vows, if you will, between the Bridegroom and His Bride – the vows His Bride voluntarily makes covenant with to be known as His. These are the instructions that "set you apart" from the rest. The covenant instructions, the "good works" we were created for in Messiah to do, the works prepared for us in advance (Eph. 2:10). The covenants that make Him your God and you His people, a nation of Kings and Priests (Exodus 24).

Passover; the deliverance and salvation from physical slavery and death and the resulting exodus from Egypt were orchestrated with a single goal in mind: a life-altering, identity-affirming encounter 50 days later with the Living God – Shavuot:

- Deliverance from spiritual slavery
- Forgiveness of sin
- Consecration from paganism to holiness
- Identity as His treasured people, through the
- Revelation of His Covenant: Torah / the Commandments

These all speak of covenant, and they all express the various attributes of Messiah. Shavuot / Pentecost is the bridge that links the Spring and Fall Feasts together, as we're going to see.

Some 3400 years ago, Moses led Israel into the wilderness of Sinai to establish this covenant. Israel would camp in front of Mount Sinai, the very mountain where Moses was first commissioned (Exod. 19:1), while Moses went up the mountain to meet with God.

> *"Thus you shall say to the house of Jacob, and tell the people of Israel: You yourselves have seen what I did to the Egyptians, and how I bore you on eagles' wings and brought you to myself. Now therefore, if you will indeed obey my voice and keep my covenant, you shall be my treasured possession among all peoples, for all the earth is mine; and you shall be to me a kingdom of priests and a holy nation. These are the words that you shall speak to the people of Israel."*
> *Exodus 19:3b-6*

So it begins. The covenant that started with a Gentile named Abram was finally going to be realized with his descendants some 400 years later:

> *"...**if** you will indeed obey my voice **and** keep my covenant, you shall be my treasured possession among all peo-*

> ples, for all the earth is mine; and you shall be to me a kingdom of priests and a holy nation."

This was the reason they had travelled these difficult and endless 40-some-odd days from Egypt to Sinai.

> So Moses came and called the elders of the people and set before them all these words that the LORD had commanded him. All the people answered together and said, "All that the LORD has spoken we will do." And Moses reported the words of the people to the LORD. And the LORD said to Moses, "Behold, I am coming to you in a thick cloud, that the people may hear when I speak with you, and may also believe you forever." When Moses told the words of the people to the LORD, the LORD said to Moses, "Go to the people and consecrate them today and tomorrow, and let them wash their garments and be ready for the third day. For on the third day the LORD will come down on Mount Sinai in the sight of all the people. And you shall set limits for the people all around, saying, 'Take care not to go up into the mountain or touch the edge of it. Whoever touches the mountain shall be put to death. No hand shall touch him, but he shall be stoned or shot; whether beast or man, he shall not live.' When the shofar sounds a long blast, they shall come up to the mountain."
> Exodus 19:7-13

Three days later, there was a blast from a shofar summoning Israel to Mount Sinai where there was smoke, fire and earthquakes while the Shofar's blast grew louder and louder. When God finally spoke, it sounded like thunder. He gave them the Ten Commandments while everyone listened to His thunderous voice in fear.

> Now when all the people saw the thunder and the flashes of lightning and the sound of the shofar and the mountain smoking, the people were afraid and trembled, and they stood far off and said to Moses, "You speak to us, and we will listen; but do not let God speak to us, lest we die." Moses said to the people, "Do not fear, for God has come to test you, that the fear of him may be before you, that you may not sin." The

people stood far off, while Moses drew near to the thick darkness where God was.
Exodus 20:18-21

That long-standing, identifiable fear as a people was now keeping them from the very reason God delivered them from Egypt: Covenant Relationship:

*"...**if you will indeed obey my voice and keep my covenant**, you shall be my treasured possession among all peoples, you shall be to me a kingdom of priests and a holy nation."*

Instead of desiring that personal relationship with ADONAI, the relationship He also desired for them, a relationship that required / requires "obeying His voice" and "keeping His covenants," they balked out of fear and opted for Moses to be their mediator:

*"You speak to us, and we will listen; but **do not let God speak to us**, lest we die."*

This gripping and debilitating fear, their identity, was keeping Israel from wanting to hear His voice, "...lest we die," and it would continue to stand in the way of their relational obedience to God. In addition, this same fear and stubbornness would cause them to reject His prophets as well and, consequently, Messiah.

Moses drew near to the thick darkness where God was manifest as He set out the parameters of the Covenant and His promises of their eventual and successful possession of the Land of Canaan.

In Exodus 24, Moses tells Israel everything ADONAI spoke, including His rules, and to that the entire assembly responded with a resounding, "*Na'aseh v'nishma*" – "All these words and rulings that ADONAI has spoken *'we will do and we will hear / understand."* Then Moses wrote down all that ADONAI had spoken. An altar was built, and twelve pillars representing the twelve tribes were erected. Burnt offerings and peace offerings were made.

Then he took the Book of the Covenant and read it in the hearing of the people. And they said, "All that the LORD has spoken we will do, and we will be obedient." And Moses took the blood and threw it on the people and said, "Behold the blood of the covenant that the LORD has made with you

in accordance with all these words."
Exodus 24:7-8

The Covenant was confirmed. Moses went back up into the mountain for 40 days and nights while God gave him the rest of Torah, the commandments, for their instruction.

Shavuot (Weeks)

"You shall count seven weeks. Begin to count the seven weeks from the time the sickle is first put to the standing grain. Then you shall keep the Feast of Weeks to the LORD your God with the tribute of a freewill offering from your hand, which you shall give as the LORD your God blesses you [firstfruits]. And you shall rejoice before the LORD your God, you and your son and your daughter, your male servant and your female servant, the Levite who is within your towns, the sojourner, the fatherless, and the widow who are among you, at the place that the LORD your God will choose, to make his name dwell there. You shall remember that you were a slave in Egypt; and you shall be careful to observe these statutes."
Deuteronomy 16:9-12

Shavuot (Hebrew "weeks"), the culmination of the seven-week Counting of the Omer, the Feast of Weeks, is the feast of the firstfruits of the wheat harvest (Exod. 34:22). Shavuot is the second of the Three Pilgrimage Festivals on which every first born Israeli male is commanded to present himself before God in Jerusalem (Acts 2; 20:16). Shavuot commemorates the firstfruits of the wheat harvest and the giving of the Torah on Mount Sinai exactly seven weeks after the exodus from Egypt.

It is a High Shabbat. You are to bring a freewill firstfruits offering based on how much God has blessed and prospered you and also offer, as a firstfruits wave offering, a brand new version of a grain / meal offering that had never been offered before: *two* loaves of *baked leavened* bread made of flour that was brought out of your dwelling (baked = fire and two represents the number of testimony / witness, scripturally.) Considering the Torah instruction that all grain offerings are to be made of unburned (no fire) and unleavened bread – matzah, *without* leaven – God was doing something completely new. It is the only time of year the priests were allowed to offer leavened bread.

It is suggested that, because of the exclusion of oil and frankincense and this use of the prohibited leaven (Lev. 2:1-2,11), this new grain / meal offering of these two baked and leavened loaves is a prophetic representation of both Jew and Gentile: The "One New Man" (Eph. 2:13-14). It is also suggested that these two loaves could also represent both covenants or Torah and the Holy Spirit; blessing and curses; and/or His double portion.

The long-standing focus of Shavuot was primarily its agricultural significance with the celebration of ADONAI's provision for His people with the wheat harvest; the bringing of these firstfruits offerings to the temple and the wave-sheaf offering of the two baked leavened loaves. After the destruction of the Second Temple, the focus of Shavuot (from agriculture and its corresponding firstfruits offerings) switched to Mount Sinai and the giving of Torah.

Shavuot: A Marriage Contract and a Bride Betrothed

Alongside the beauty of the prophetic imagery found in the story of Ruth and Boaz, the Kinsman Redeemer, is another beautiful image seen in Shavuot: the marriage between God and Israel as His Bride (Isa. 49:18).

A traditional Jewish marriage consists of two stages: stage one, the betrothal (Hebrew "*erusin.*" "*Ya`ad*" in Exo. 21:8; *charaph*" in Lev. 19:20; "*'aras*" in Deut. 20:7; 22:23), entered into when a betrothal contract is made between two parties. This written contract is known as a "*ketubah*" (fundamentally a Rabbinical replacement of the biblical *mohar*: dowry). The ketubah outlines the rights and responsibilities of the groom in relation to the bride for her protection. Did you catch that? The ketubah outlines the rights and responsibilities of the groom *in relation to the bride for her protection*. Our obedience to His covenants is for our own protection. During the betrothal period, the parties are legally married though they don't physically live with each other. The legally-binding betrothal ketubah can only be dissolved through divorce, called a "*get*" in Hebrew. The second stage is the consummation (Hebrew "*nesu'in*") of the betrothal.

We referenced Jeremiah 2 in Chapter 5 when we discussed how Israel is the firstfruits of God's harvest of nations (Jer. 2:3). In verse 2 of Jeremiah 2 we see that on Mount Sinai Israel was betrothed to and by God Himself:

> "Go and proclaim in the hearing of Jerusalem, Thus says the LORD, 'I remember the devotion of your youth, your love as a bride, how you followed me in the wilderness, in a land not sown.'"

In Exodus 19, when God by the leading of Moses brought the children of Israel to Mount Sinai, God betrothed Himself to Israel. On Mount Sinai, God gave the Torah to Israel (Exod. 20:1-21). At this time, God was making a betrothal contract, a ketubah, with Israel. The ketubah (or written betrothal contract, which is understood to be the Torah) represents "The book of the covenant" (marriage is a covenant) that Moses wrote prior to the revelation at Mount Sinai (Exod. 24:4,7). The Book of the Covenant spelled out mutual obligations of God and Israel just as the ketubah spelled out the obligations between husband and wife. So, God made a marriage contract with Israel in Exod. 19:3-7
(Source: Eddie Chumney - *The Festival of Pentecost (Shavuot)*: http://www.friendsofsabbath.org/Further_Research/Holy%20Days/The-Seven-Festivals-of-the-Messiah.pdf)

> All the people answered together and said, "All that the LORD has spoken we will do." And Moses reported the words of the people to the LORD.
> Exodus 19:8

"*Na'aseh v'nishma*" – "We will do and we will hear / understand." Here, Israel is accepting this covenant. They're effectively accepting God's "marriage proposal."

Another aspect of a traditional Jewish marriage ceremony is the "*chuppah*." A chuppah (also huppah, chipe, chupah, or chuppa) is literally a canopy or covering that the couple stands under during their wedding ceremony.

Brides are likened to the Jewish people who were brought toward Mount Sinai when they received the Torah. Receiving the Torah is a recurring theme of the Jewish wedding ceremony, with the ketubah standing in for the "marriage contract" between God and the Jewish people.

Many commentators liken the giving of the Torah to a wedding between God and the Jewish People. (For instance, the Torah is thought

of as the ketubah and the mountain which was said to have stood as a rooftop over the Jewish people (Rashi, Exodus 19:17) was the chuppah.)
(Source: http://www.jewishcelebrations.com/Wedding/Conservative/Processional.htm)

Note: Rashi, aka Shlomo Yitzchaki, was a medieval French rabbi and author of a comprehensive commentary on the Talmud and the TaNaKh.

In regard to discipleship, I teach that we need the following five points in our lives:

1. An extreme and interactive relationship in and with the Holy Spirit
2. Extreme obedience to God, i.e., His commandments and precepts in our daily life
3. Extreme and excellent stewardship in all areas within our lives, i.e. marriage, family, relationships, business, time, etc.
4. Being the "Friend of the Bridegroom" (John 3:26-30), and then
5. The "Bridal Paradigm" (Rev. 19:7; 21:2, 9; 22:17)

With this in mind, and within a traditional Jewish wedding ceremony setting, we see Moses in Exodus 19:17 "escorting" Israel, the bride, to meet her Bridegroom:

In order for the ketubah, the written contract between the husband and the wife, to be legal in consummating the marriage, it must be signed by the two witnesses, the friends of the bridegroom. Since we can see that Moses was one of the two witnesses, he had to sign the Ketubah (Torah) in order for the full marriage between God and Israel to be consummated.

However, when Moses returned from being with God on Mount Sinai, he did not sign the Ketubah (Torah). Instead he broke the two tablets (ketubah), which were in his right hand (Exodus 32:19), thus not signing the ketubah which God had made with Israel. Therefore, he did not allow Israel to enter into the full marriage.

(Source: Eddie Chumney - *The Festival of Pentecost (Shavuot)*: http://www.friendsofsabbath.org/Further_Research/Holy%20Days/The-Seven-Festivals-of-the-Messiah.pdf)

Israel did not "consummate" (*nesu'in*) the wedding ceremony. This is a great insight and logical conclusion of what transpired at Sinai as we follow Israel's journey to Messiah: man's final hope to *nesu'in* his marriage vows!

In the New Testament, we see how Jesus is the Bridegroom and Believers are betrothed to Him. In traditional Jewish marriage fashion, after the betrothal, Jesus goes back home to prepare a place for His Bride, you and me. We also see the Bridal Paradigm in the Revelation of John:

> *Then I heard what seemed to be the voice of a great multitude, like the roar of many waters and like the sound of mighty peals of thunder, crying out, "Hallelujah! For the Lord our God the Almighty reigns. Let us rejoice and exult and give him the glory, for the marriage of the Lamb has come, and his Bride has made herself ready; it was granted her to clothe herself with fine linen, bright and pure" for the fine linen is the righteous deeds of the saints. And the angel said to me, "Write this: Blessed are those who are invited to the marriage supper of the Lamb." And he said to me, "These are the true words of God."*
> Revelation 19:6-9

> *And I saw the holy city, new Jerusalem, coming down out of heaven from God, prepared as a bride adorned for her husband. And I heard a loud voice from the throne saying, "Behold, the dwelling place of God is with man. He will dwell with them, and they will be his people, and God himself will be with them as their God. Then came one of the seven angels who had the seven bowls full of the seven last plagues and spoke to me, saying, "Come, I will show you the Bride, the wife of the Lamb." And he carried me away in the Spirit to a great, high mountain, and showed me the holy city Jerusalem coming down out of heaven from God.*
> Revelation 21:2-3, 9-10

Did you notice what it said in verse 3?

We discussed in Chapter 4, regarding the Passover and exodus from Egypt, the reason behind bringing Israel out from under the burden of Egypt, the reasons for Israel's deliverance...

We discussed earlier in this Chapter how Passover's deliverance and salvation from physical slavery and death and the resulting exodus from Egypt occurred with one single goal in mind: an encounter 50 days later with the Living God – Shavuot.

We just finished discussing how Shavuot prophetically speaks of the marriage between man and God and how Israel never consummated the marriage vows at Sinai and how Jesus is man's final hope for that consummation; the consummation of "I will take (marry) you (the bride) to be my people (my wife), and I (the Bridegroom) will be your God (our Husband).

We saw this in Exodus 6:7 and we just saw it again, with the New Jerusalem coming out of the sky "as a bride adorned for her husband" in Revelation 21 verse 3!

Here's Exodus 6:7:

> **I will take you to be my people, and I will be your God**, and you shall know that I am the LORD your God, who has brought you out from under the burdens of the Egyptians. *[Emphasis mine]*

And then Revelation 21:3:

> And I heard a loud voice from the throne saying, "Behold, the dwelling place of God is with man. He will dwell with them, **and they will be his people, and God himself will be with them as their God**. *[Emphasis mine]*

This is the gospel unto salvation! *This* is in effect God's "Master Plan" for humanity: The Aleph (Alpha) and the Tav (Omega); "the Wedding Feast of the Passover Lamb that was slain before the foundations of the earth." Our future, as seen in John's Revelation, started all the way back in Egypt!

Now this being the case, how is it possible then for us today to "make ourselves ready" (Rev. 19:7) or "be blessed" and "invited to the Wedding Feast of the Lamb" (Rev. 19:9) if we insist that these same exact contextual Torah Feasts don't apply to us?!? We can't simply repeat the false narrative of "because of Jesus" when even *He* defaults to the Passover-to-Shavuot storyline! Shouldn't we as well?

Pentecost

Acts 2 tells us that it was the "day of Pentecost." Strong's #G4005 *"penthkosthv"*:

Pentecost = "the fiftieth day"

1. the second of the three great Jewish feasts, celebrated at Jerusalem yearly, the seventh week after the Passover, in grateful recognition of the completed harvest

Even the Greek speaks of Shavuot.

It was the 50th Day of the Omer Count, Shavuot, and 120 disciples were waiting in Jerusalem in an upper room as Jesus had instructed them 10 days earlier (Luke 24:49; Acts 1:4). Being the second of the Three Pilgrimage Festivals meant that all firstborn males were in Jerusalem celebrating the completed wheat harvest and the giving of Torah on Mount Sinai. Then the Whirlwind of the Holy Spirit came. With the advent of Pentecost, Shavuot now prophetically pointed to Mount Zion, not just Mount Sinai:

> *For you have not come to what may be touched, a blazing fire and darkness and gloom and a tempest and the sound of a trumpet [the shofar] and a voice whose words made the hearers beg that no further messages be spoken to them [Mount Sinai]. For they could not endure the order that was given, "If even a beast touches the mountain, it shall be stoned." Indeed, so terrifying was the sight that Moses said, "I tremble with fear."*
>
> *But you have come to Mount Zion and to the city of the living God, the heavenly Jerusalem, and to innumerable angels in festal gathering, and to the assembly of the firstborn [pilgrimage festival] who are enrolled in heaven, and to God, the judge of all, and to the spirits of the righteous made perfect, and to Jesus, the mediator of a new covenant, and to the sprinkled blood that speaks a better word than the blood of Abel.*
>
> *See that you do not refuse him who is speaking [Exod. 19:5-6]. For if they did not escape when they refused him who warned them on earth, much less will we escape if*

we reject him who warns from heaven. At that time his voice shook the earth, but now he has promised, "Yet once more I will shake not only the earth but also the heavens." This phrase, "Yet once more," indicates the removal of things that are shaken - that is, things that have been made - in order that the things that cannot be shaken may remain.

Therefore let us be grateful for receiving a kingdom that cannot be shaken, and thus let us offer to God acceptable worship, with reverence and awe, for our God is a consuming fire.
Hebrews 12:18-29

What a perspective from the writer of Hebrews!

Because of the fulfillment of Messiah at Passover (death), the Feast of Unleavened Bread (burial) and the Feast of Firstfruits (resurrection); because of the indwelling of the Holy Spirit at Pentecost, the Covenant made at Sinai, Shavuot, is attainable (Zion)! Torah was given, and the covenant to keep those instructions occurred at Sinai: Shavuot. Messiah rose from the dead, the power of Holy Spirit – the Fire of Sinai – fell as covenant Fire on those in the upper room to keep those instructions for Zion's sake: Pentecost (Acts 2:1-4).

So while all of Jerusalem was reaffirming their covenant with Torah during the second of the Three Pilgrimage Festivals, God was indwelling Israel with His Spirit – repositioning Torah to its original place: the invisible intentions of the heart (as we discussed regarding Mt. 5).

Just as the resurrection of Yeshua represents the Firstfruits of those who have died (1 Cor. 15:20) and fulfills the prophetic ritual of the waving of the omer on the festival of Firstfruits, so the giving of the Holy Spirit to the church fulfills the wave offering of the wheat loaves on the day of Shavuot.
(Source: John J. Parsons - Hebrew for Christians "Shavuot - Revelation and the Fruit of the Spirit": http://www.hebrew4christians.com/Holidays/Spring_Holidays/Shavuot/shavuot.html)

Thus with Shavuot / Pentecost we conclude the Passover season with the Counting of the Omer linking the two Pilgrimage Festivals together.

In Summary

Appointed Time: Shavuot (Weeks)

Significance: The culmination of the Omer Count with the feast of the firstfruits of the wheat harvest. The remembrance of receiving Torah at Mount Sinai and a reminder that we were slaves in Egypt so that we will keep and obey His Torah

Observance: Give a voluntary offering in accordance to the degree in which ADONAI has prospered you. You are also to bake two loaves of bread of fine flour with leaven as firstfruits to ADONAI. The loaves are to be waved by the priest as a wave offering before ADONAI. It is a High Sabbath of rejoicing for the entire family and your community. No ordinary work is to be done

Length: 24 hours, sunset to sunset

Concurrent Celebration: Pentecost

Significance: The baptism and indwelling of the Holy Spirit in the Upper Room in Jerusalem

Observance: Same as Shavuot: Give a voluntary offering in accordance to the degree in which ADONAI has prospered you. You are also to bake two loaves of bread of fine flour with leaven as firstfruits to Adonai. The loaves are to be waved by the priest as a wave offering before ADONAI. It is a High Sabbath of rejoicing for the entire family and your community. No ordinary work is to be done

Length: 24 hours, sunset to sunset

The 50th day of the Omer Count is a High Shabbat of rejoicing. You are to bring a freewill firstfruits offering and also offer, as a firstfruits wave offering, two loaves of baked leavened bread made of flour.

Passover, the deliverance and salvation from physical slavery and death, and the resulting exodus from Egypt was orchestrated with a single goal in mind: an encounter 50 days later with the Living God: Shavuot. It was on this day that Moses and all of Israel assembled before the Living God, per His instructions, at the base of Mount Sinai. This is when and where God established His instructions, Torah, for those that would call upon His name; the keys of blessing as a Believer – the wedding vows, if you will, between the Bridegroom and His Bride – the covenants that "set us apart" from the rest, the covenants that make Him your God and you His people, a nation of Kings and Priests (Exodus 24).

We saw how God betrothed Himself to Israel through the giving of Torah as His marriage contract. Israel failed to consummate the wedding ceremony at Sinai, but a final way for covenant was made in Messiah. We see that Jesus is the Bridegroom and Believers are betrothed to Him. Jesus is man's final hope for that consummation; the consummation of "I will take (marry) you (the bride) to be my people (my wife), and I (the Bridegroom) will be your God (our Husband).

We saw this in Exodus 6:7 and we saw it in Revelation 21:3:

> ***I will take you to be my people, and I will be your God***, *and you shall know that I am the LORD your God, who has brought you out from under the burdens of the Egyptians.* [Emphasis mine]

> *And I heard a loud voice from the throne saying, "Behold, the dwelling place of God is with man. He will dwell with them,* ***and they will be his people, and God himself will be with them as their God****.* [Emphasis mine]

This is the gospel!

This is God's "Master Plan:" The Wedding Feast of the Passover Lamb that was slain before the foundations of the earth. Our future, as seen in John's Revelation, started all the way back in Egypt!

> *I will take you from the nations and gather you from all the countries and bring you into your own land. I will sprinkle clean water on you, and you shall be clean from all your uncleannesses, and from all your idols I will cleanse you. And I will give you a new heart, and a new spirit I will put within you. And I will remove the heart of stone from your flesh and give you a heart of flesh. And I will put my Spirit within you, and cause you to walk in my statutes and be careful to obey my rules. You shall dwell in the land that I gave to your fathers, and you shall be my people, and I will be your God.* Ezekiel 36:24-28

THE FEASTS UNLOCKED | 179

For more about being His people and His being our God, see also: Gen. 17:7-8; Exod. 29:45; Lev. 11:45; 25:38; 26:12; Num. 15:41; Psa. 81:10; Jer. 7:23; 11:4; 30:22; 31:1, 33; 32:38; Ezek. 11:20; 14:11; 34:31; 37:23, 27; Zech. 8:8; 2 Cor. 6:16 (quotes Lev. 26:12; Exod. 6:7; Jer. 31:32; 32:38; Ezek. 37:27); Heb. 8:10 (is a requote of Jer. 31:30-33); Rev. 21:7.

Father God is about to call us with the blast of the Shofar (Yom Teruah / Feast of Trumpets) when we will ready and consecrate ourselves (Yom Kippur / Day of Atonement) as separated and presentable unto Him, for the Feast of Ingathering (Sukkot / Feast of Tabernacles) is upon us!

CHAPTER 7

FEAST OF TRUMPETS (YOM TERUAH) / DAY OF ATONEMENT (YOM KIPPUR)
Shofars and the Cleansing of Iniquities

And the LORD spoke to Moses, saying, "Speak to the people of Israel, saying, In the seventh month, on the first day of the month, you shall observe a day of solemn rest, a memorial proclaimed with blast of trumpets, a holy convocation [a High Sabbath]. You shall not do any ordinary work, and you shall present a food offering to the LORD."

And the LORD spoke to Moses, saying, "Now on the tenth day of this seventh month is the Day of Atonement. It shall be for you a time of holy convocation [a High Sabbath], and you shall afflict [humble] yourselves and present a food offering to the LORD. And you shall not do any work on that very day, for it is a Day of Atonement, to make atonement for you before the LORD your God. For whoever is not afflicted on that very day shall be cut off from his people. And whoever does any work on that very day, that person I will destroy from among his people. You shall not do any work. It is a statute forever throughout your generations in all your dwelling places. It shall be to you a Sabbath of solemn rest, and you shall afflict yourselves. On the ninth day of the month beginning at evening, from evening to evening shall you keep your Sabbath."
Leviticus 23:23-32

It's been 16 weeks since Shavuot (Weeks) / Pentecost. The New Moon / Rosh Chodesh conjunction of September 19th made September 21st the likely date of the visible crescent (and it was) marking the beginning of the seventh month of Ethanim (Tishrei in the Babylonian).

This particular Rosh Chodesh is also a day of solemn rest, a memorial announced with blasts of the shofar and a holy convocation, a High Sabbath. It's the first of the three Fall Feasts: The Feast of Trumpets / Yom Teruah.

Yom Teruah vs Rosh Hashanah

Rosh Hashanah

The Feast of Trumpets / Yom Teruah is widely known by its popular Babylonian derived meaning: "Rosh Hashanah:"

- Literal: "Head of the Year"
- Figuratively: "New Year"

I have said for years that as the enemy has ransacked and perverted the Western Church, the enemy has also ransacked and perverted Judaism. It is also in our enemy's best interest that the two never unite as the One True Way as is God's perfect intended plan through Messiah. Christianity ("Salvation in Jesus") without Judaism (Torah, foundational "root" and "tree") doesn't work so well for a number of biblical reasons. In turn, Judaism without Christianity doesn't work so well for a number of scriptural reasons. Remember, in Acts 24:14 the Apostle Paul defined Christianity, The Way, as a sect of Judaism. With that in mind, the perversion of our conjoined faiths, the renaming of Yom Teruah to "Rosh Hashanah" is the direct result of the influence of Babylonian paganism that started with the adoption of Babylonian month names to the Scriptural calendar:

"The names of the months came up with them from Babylonia."
(Jerusalem Talmud, Rosh Hashanah 1:2 56d)

Another example of this Babylonian influence is the altering of the meaning of Yom Teruah from a memorial of solemn rest with shofar blasts, a holy convocation, a High Shabbat, to a New Year's celebration mimicking the Babylonian New Year of "Akitu" (Sumerian for "barley," "head of the year") that also fell on or around the same time. To keep from the obvious infraction of turning Yom Teruah into a "Jewish Akitu," the rabbis thought it best to simply adopt the name change of "Rosh Hashanah" with its literal and figurative meaning of "Head of the Year" (akitu) and "New Year" respectively. Sound familiar?

The Babylonian Akitu, (literally barley cutting / sowing, head of the year) was observed on the first of Tishrei and the first of Nisan. Judaism simply manufactured their version of a two calendar "New Year's" on the same dates:

- Religious: First of Abib / Nisan, and
- Civil: First of Ethanim / Tishrei (you'll recall this from Chapter 2)

Besides these obvious scriptural problems, we're also talking about a "new year," a *"Head of the Year,"* on the first day of the seventh month – **two weeks before** the Feast of Tabernacles (Sukkot) – described in Exodus 23:16 as the "***End** of the Year*"!

> You shall keep the Feast of Harvest, of the firstfruits of your labor, of what you sow in the field. You shall keep the **Feast of Ingathering at the end of the year**, when you gather in from the field the fruit of your labor.
> [Emphasis mine]

Like I've said before, we are *exactly* like Israel! Oy vey…

Along with altering the purpose of the feast from a memorial High Shabbat with shofar blasts and the name change from Yom Teruah ("day of making a loud noise," "day of shouting") to a Civil New Year's celebration, Rosh Hashanah ("Head of the Year"), traditional Judaism also observes Teshuvah (Hebrew: "repentance," "turning back to God") beginning in the preceding Month of Elul that continues for 40 days, ending with Yom Kippur ("day to cleanse") as an addition to the Feast of Trumpets.

Furthermore, the ten-day period between "Rosh Hashanah" and Yom Kippur, traditionally referred to as the "Days of Awe," or the "High Holy Days," is a time of prayer, self-examination and repentance. "Rosh Hashanah" also traditionally commemorates the creation of the universe by God.

There are, of course, additional traditions associated with the observance of "Rosh Hashanah" such as specific prayers and ritual bathing while the "Ten Days of Awe" is the time to seal your fate in the book of life or death before Yom Kippur.

Yom Teruah is the only Feast Day that falls on a Rosh Chodesh. You'll remember that in Chapter 2 of this book we discussed Israel's knowledge of the lunar conjunction to determine when their Rosh Chodesh feasting should begin and that three days for feasting were set aside for the New Moon observance. We also determined that it wasn't until the visible crescent was seen that Rosh Chodesh was officially started as we looked at the following:

> David said to Jonathan, "Behold, tomorrow is the new moon, and I should not fail to sit at table with the king. But let me go, that I may hide myself in the field till the third day at evening." Then Jonathan said to him, "Tomorrow is the new moon, and you will be missed, because your seat will be empty. On the third day [...]" And when the new moon came, the king sat down to eat food. But on the second day, the day after the new moon, David's place was empty.
> 1 Samuel 20:5, 18-19, 24, 27

They knew when the New Moon was coming but set aside three days for feasting. On seeing the visible crescent, the elders would declare it in order to alert the people that Rosh Chodesh, the beginning of the month, had commenced.

Accordingly, since Yom Teruah falls on a Rosh Chodesh, "Rosh Hashanah" is observed as a two-day holiday to accommodate the determination of Rosh Chodesh. The Torah, on the other hand, ordains only a one-day observance for Yom Teruah: *"on the first of the month," "a day of remembrance."* To further deviate from the instruction, traditionally the first day of "Rosh Hashanah" can only fall on a Monday, Tuesday, Thursday, or a Sabbath. This regulation is an ordinance of the Sages.

> The Talmud Yerushalmi (Eruvin 3:9) notes that our two-day celebration of Rosh Hashanah is an enactment of the early Prophets, who established it for the following reason. During the period of the Prophets, the sanctification of the months was dependent upon hearing the testimony of witnesses who had seen the new moon. On the evening following the twenty-ninth day of Elul, the court would sanctify the day as the first of Tishrei based on the possibility that witnesses might come that day and testify that they had seen the new moon, retroactively establishing Rosh Hashanah on that day. If the witnesses did indeed appear, then that day would be sanctified and the following day would be a regular day - the second of Tishrei. However, if witnesses did not appear, then the following day would be Rosh Hashanah and retroactively, the

previous evening - which the court had sanctified - would turn out to be a regular weekday. So that people would not treat the first day lightly, since its sanctified or weekday status was dependent upon the appearance of witnesses during the course of the day, the early Prophets ordained that Rosh Hashanah be celebrated as a twoday [sic] holiday - with the prohibition of work, the sounding of the shofar, and the order of prayer being observed on both days.

The Rambam (Hilchot Kiddush ha-Chodesh 5:7-8) writes: The Festival of Rosh Hashanah - in the period when they would establish (the calendar) based upon testimony - was celebrated by the majority of the residents of the Land of Israel for two days because they were in doubt [as to when the Festival began], for they did not know when the court had established the new month since the agents of the court did not go out on a Festival. (That is, since Rosh Hashanah is the only Festival celebrated on the first of a month, there was no means of informing those who lived outside of Jerusalem that the court had accepted testimony that the new moon of Tishrei had been sighted. Once the month was established, Rosh Hashanah would begin and the agents of the court would be unable to inform the populace since they could not travel on a Festival.)

What then is the difference between the second day of Rosh Hashanah celebrated when the months were calculated based on testimony, and the second day celebrated nowadays? In the former period, if witnesses did not appear, the first day celebrated would retroactively turn out to be a Rabbinical obligation and the second day would be a Torah obligation. Nowadays, when the calendar is based on fixed calculations, the first day of Rosh Hashanah is a Torah obligation and the second day is a Rabbinical enactment.

(Source: Rabbi Eliyahu Kitov, OBM, *The Book of Our Heritage*)

Yom Teruah

> And the LORD spoke to Moses, saying, "Speak to the people of Israel, saying, In the seventh month, on the first day of the month, you shall observe a day of solemn rest, a memorial proclaimed with blast of trumpets, a holy convocation [a High Sabbath]. You shall not do any ordinary work, and you shall present a food offering to the LORD."
> Leviticus 23:23-25

> *On the first day of the seventh month you shall have a holy convocation [a High Sabbath]. You shall not do any ordinary work. It is a day for you to blow the trumpets [...]*
> Numbers 29:1

Teruah literally means "shout" or "to make a loud noise," so Yom Teruah would translate to "Day of Making a Loud Noise" or the more suitable "Day of Shouting." On the first day of the seventh month of Ethanim, on Rosh Chodesh, we are to keep a solemn High Shabbat: "*you shall observe a day of solemn rest,*" "*a holy convocation.*" It is also a memorial day. "Memorial" here in the Hebrew is Strong's #H2146 "*zikrown*": *memorial, reminder, remembrance*. We're also to mark / announce this memorial day of shouting with shofar blasts (*a memorial proclaimed with blast of trumpets.*) And because it is a High Sabbath, y*ou shall not do any ordinary work, and you shall present a food offering to ADONAI.*

Essentially, the instruction found in Leviticus 23:23-25 is telling us that on this specific Rosh Chodesh, it is to be a High Shabbat of remembrance, a reminder marked or announced with shouts and blasts of the shofar along with a food offering. Sounds simple enough to me. So why the last 4 ½ pages?

> *This day shall be for you a memorial day, and you shall keep it as a feast to the LORD; throughout your generations, as a statute forever, you shall keep it as a feast.*
> Exodus 12:14

It's "interesting" that any amount of research or study on Yom Teruah / Rosh Hashanah / Feast of Trumpets you'll find quite a lot of books, commentaries and articles that suggest that the scriptures say very little about this Feast, as if it were non-consequential. I completely disagree:

"A High Shabbat of remembrance. A solemn reminder announced with blast of shofars."

Most of these writings all ask the same question: "a reminder of what?" Really? Isn't it absolutely clear that this Feast is a reminder of the blowing of a shofar? Contextually, scripturally, what could have possibly been on the minds of all of Israel when they received this instruction? Here's a hint: when was the last time that Israel had heard a significant shofar blast that they should be remembering?

> On the morning of the third day there were thunders and lightnings and a thick cloud on the mountain and **a very loud trumpet** [shofar] **blast**, so that all the people in the camp trembled. Then Moses brought the people out of the camp to meet God, and they took their stand at the foot of the mountain.
>
> Now Mount Sinai was wrapped in smoke because the LORD had descended on it in fire. The smoke of it went up like the smoke of a kiln, and the whole mountain trembled greatly. And as **the sound of the trumpet** [shofar] **grew louder and louder**, Moses spoke, and God answered him in thunder.
>
> Exodus 19:16-19 [Emphasis mine]

Four months previous, Israel was summoned to the base of Mount Sinai by the blast of the shofar where they cowered at the sight and at the audible presence of Elohim, Melech I Ia Olam (God, King of the Universe)!!! Four months ago!!

Four months previous, Israel was summoned to hear the covenants of Torah, and they balked! Want to know why this crucial contextual oversight probably exists? Because Israel balked at the covenants made at Sinai! Who wants to remember that?!? I would also suggest that the same veil of 2 Corinthians 3:13-18 is also at play here. But here's the problem: Yom Teruah isn't God instructing us to remember our failure. Yom Teruah is God instructing us to remember how, when and *why He* approached us with Life-giving precepts!

Don't you remember?

We discussed in Chapter 4 the reason behind bringing Israel out from under the burden of Egypt, the reasons for Israel's deliverance...

We discussed how Passover's deliverance and salvation from physical slavery and death and the resulting exodus from Egypt occurred with one single goal in mind: an encounter 50 days later with the Living God – Shavuot!

We discussed how Shavuot prophetically speaks of the marriage between man and God and how Israel never consummated the marriage vows at Sinai and how Jesus is man's final hope for that consummation; the consummation of "I will take (marry) you (the bride) to be my people (my wife), and I (the Bridegroom) will be your God (our

Husband).

He wants us to remember His Shofar blast of Exodus 6:7!!!

> *I will take you to be my people, and I will be your God, and you shall know that I am the LORD your God, who has brought you out from under the burdens of the Egyptians.* [Emphasis mine]

He wants us to remember that this is the gospel unto salvation; His "Master Plan;" that He loves us, desires us and has taken us as our Bridegroom!

This is what we're supposed to be remembering on Yom Teruah, this holy Rosh Chodesh, this solemn day of remembrance marked with the blasts of shofars, this High Shabbat. Instead, it's about a civil "New Year's celebration," because, once again, we have it all wrong...

> *Blessed are the people who know the festal shout [teruah], who walk, O LORD, in the light of your face...*
> Psalms 89:15

Shofars and Trumpets

We find four words that are used in the TaNaKh for "trumpet:"

1. Strong's #H2689 "*chatsotsĕrah*" (silver trumpet) which occurs 29 times in the KJV
2. Strong's #H3104 "*yobel*" (ram's horn, trumpet) which occurs 27 times in the KJV
3. Strong's #H7782 "*shofar*" (ram's horn) which occurs 72 times in the KJV, and
4. Strong's #H8619 "*taqowa*" (trumpet) which occurs 1 time in the KJV

We find one word that is used in the New Testament for "trumpet:"

1. Strong's #G4536 "*salpigx*" (trumpet) which occurs 11 times in the KJV

The blast of shofars is found all throughout Scripture:

- To Call

- Get Attention
- To Gather / Invite
- To Warn / Announce
- A Call to Battle
- The Announcing of Certain Feasts and Feast Days

The blast of the shofar was significant in Exodus 19:13b (verses 16 and 19 use the word "*shofar*"):

> "When the trumpet [yobel] sounds a long blast, they shall come up to the mountain."

This was a call, an invitation to gather to God, the drawing near.

Leviticus 25:9 uses the shofar to announce the Year of Jubilee on Yom Kippur:

> *Then you shall sound the loud trumpet [shofar] on the tenth day of the seventh month. On the Day of Atonement you shall sound the trumpet [shofar] throughout all your land.*

Numbers 10:1-10 has the instructions regarding the silver trumpets: "*chatsotsĕrah.*" You'll notice in verse 8 that the sons of Aaron, the priests, blew the silver trumpets. You'll also notice in verse 10 that the silver trumpets were blown over the burnt and peace offerings on festival days, appointed feasts and Rosh Chodesh as a reminder for God to remember you.

Shofars were used to overthrow Jericho in Joshua 6.

Shofars were also used as instruments of war with Gideon in Judges 7.

In Joel 2, shofars are used to sound an alarm, to gather the people back to ADONAI, and to consecrate a fast; call a solemn assembly; gather the people and to assemble the elders.

> *God goes up to his throne. There are shouts of joy [teruah] and the blast of trumpets [shofars], as the Lord goes up.*

Psalms 47:5 Good News Translation (GNT)

> *Blow the trumpet [shofar] at the new moon [Rosh Chodesh], at the full moon on our feast day [Pilgrimage Festivals: Passover / Feast of Unleavened Bread and Sukkot].*

Psalms 81:3

Outside of Sinai, where God Himself blasts the shofar, the only two other references of this happening again are in Zechariah 9 and 1 Thessalonians 4 with Messiah, the Bridegroom's return:

> Then the LORD will appear over them, and his arrow will go forth like lightning; the Lord GOD will sound the trumpet and will march forth in the whirlwinds of the south.
> Zechariah 9:14

> For the Lord himself will descend from heaven with a cry of command, with the voice of an archangel, and with the sound of the trumpet of God. And the dead in Christ will rise first.
> 1 Thessalonians 4:16

During Yom Teruah, it is widely accepted that the blast of the shofar is a call to repentance in preparation for the coming Day of Atonement, Yom Kippur. Compare with the fact that Yom Teruah is a day of remembrance, a day of "looking back" and not a time to look forward, the true repentance and atonement of Yom Kippur would come from the remembrance of what occurred at Sinai: the call to covenant with Father God and the disobedience that followed. That would be a day that would be worthy of the instruction to "*afflict yourselves,*" and that would warrant us *"to make atonement before ADONAI"* ...

Yom Teruah, Yom Kippur and the first day of Sukkot all happen in a two-week period. It's essentially one event. Spiritually and practically, we're being instructed to remember Sinai, repent, and be prepared for the ingathering; prepare ourselves through the atonement on and of Yom Kippur for yet *another* opportunity to be gathered – one last time (the "end of the year") – by the blast of the Shofar for Sukkot!

As we're about to see, Yom Kippur, the affliction and atonement of our hearts before ADONAI, is *our* drawing near; whereas, Sukkot is *His* drawing back toward us:

> Then you will call upon me and come and pray to me, and I will hear you. You will seek me and find me, when you seek me with all your heart. I will be found by you, declares the LORD...
> Jeremiah 29:12-14a

> *Draw near to God, and he will draw near to you.*
> James 4:8a

Nehemiah 8 is among the passages cited when studying Yom Teruah, because it takes place on the first day of the Seventh Month (Neh. 7:73; 8:9, 13). Even though there is no mention of the blasting of shofars, there is the instruction to shout, rejoice and feast. Verses 13-17 of chapter 8 would clue us in on why there may not be any mention of shofars since there's also no mention of an observance of Yom Kippur nine days later. What we do see is the tragedy that Sukkot hadn't been observed since "the days of Jeshua (Joshua) the son of Nun."

Nehemiah 8 has also become noteworthy to me during the writing of this book. During this time, it has been suggested prophetically that we as a nation, specifically these United States of America, and we as the people of God globally, are "leaving Babylon," "returning to The Land" and "entering into the days of Ezra." This is significant because of what the Days of Ezra are and what they represent: these were the days when Israel heard God's Torah for the first time since returning from 70 years of Babylonian captivity (2 Chr. 36:21; Jer. 25:11-12; 29:10). These were the days when Israel returned to the study, understanding and application of Torah for the purposes of rebuilding and reestablishing God's house.

If we are entering into a time like the Days of Ezra for the purposes of rebuilding and reestablishing God's house, a time when His church is delivered from their Babylonian captivity; a time when His church will be exposed to His Torah for the first time; a time when His church will return to the study, understanding and practical application of His Torah in their lives; and, out of obedience three months prior, I started writing a resource for that very purpose: *The Feasts Unlocked: A Practical Understanding of God's Holy Days*; Just. Like. The. Days. Of. Ezra… Needless to say, I can't tell you how excited I am!!

In Nehemiah 8, all of Israel is gathered "as one man" at the Water Gate square, and they collectively requested Ezra the Priest to bring with him and to read to them the "Book of the Law of Moses" – the Torah. So Ezra the priest brought with him and read to them the Torah on the first day (Rosh Chodesh) of the Seventh Month, Ethanim: it was Yom Teruah. He read from early morning to midday, and the entire assembly of Israel was attentive to the reading of the Torah.

As Ezra opened the Book of the Torah of Moses, the people stood. Ezra blessed ADONAI, and the people agreed with "Amen. Amen" – hands lifted high and hearts and heads bowed low as they worshipped ADONAI.

The Levites were dispersed throughout the crowd, assisting those in the understanding of the Torah as needed. The Torah was read clearly to all so that all of Israel could understand its meaning.

Ezra, along with Nehemiah and the Levites, instructed the assembly that that specific day was Holy to ADONAI; a day of shouting, rejoicing and feasting, not a day of mourning and weeping. They encouraged all of Israel with these words, because they cried as they listened to the reading of the Torah.

They dispersed the assembly to their own homes instructing them to eat, drink and be merry, for the day was Holy unto God – not to grieve because "the joy of ADONAI was their strength!" The Levites quieted and calmed the assembly as they left to do just that, because they understood the instructions given them.

The next day they reassembled to continue studying the Torah together with Ezra and discovered that they were to dwell in booths, as commanded by God in the Torah through Moses, that very month! They immediately got the word out to all the towns and in Jerusalem that everyone was to gather the materials instructed to build sukkahs. And so they did; on rooftops, in their courts and in the Temple courts. Sukkahs were erected everywhere, even in the squares of the Water and Ephraim gates! Israel hadn't observed the Feast of Booths, Tabernacles, Sukkot, in this magnitude since the days of Joshua of Nun. That's roughly 900 years!

How beautiful is that? Israel responded to the reading of God's Covenant Word of Torah with humility, grieving and sorrow, because they had been estranged for so long from keeping, obeying and following His Word! I say that we need to collectively entertain the great possibility that this needs to be our response today as well.

I love Jason Henderson's sentiment regarding Nehemiah 8:

> *I doubt it is coincidence that this deep call to the heart of Israel took place on the day of the Feast of Trumpets. Like the other Scriptures we have looked at, the focus here again seems to be that God is call-*

ing to hearts. He is getting the attention of those in Israel who gathered before Him as one man.
(Source: *The Feasts of Israel: Israel's Journey in Christ Towards God's Ultimate End*)

Go and read Nehemiah 8 right now, and thank the Lord for His Covenant Word!

> Blessed are the people who know the festal shout [teruah], who walk, O LORD, in the light of your face...
> Psalms 89:15

Yom Kippur / Day of Atonement

> And the LORD spoke to Moses, saying, "Now on the tenth day of this seventh month is the Day of Atonement. It shall be for you a time of holy convocation [a High Sabbath], and you shall afflict [humble] yourselves and present a food offering to the LORD. And you shall not do any work on that very day, for it is a Day of Atonement, to make atonement for you before the LORD your God. For whoever is not afflicted on that very day shall be cut off from his people. And whoever does any work on that very day, that person I will destroy from among his people. You shall not do any work. It is a statute forever throughout your generations in all your dwelling places. It shall be to you a Sabbath of solemn rest, and you shall afflict yourselves. On the ninth day of the month beginning at evening, from evening to evening shall you keep your Sabbath."
> Leviticus 23: 26-32

And How Do We Keep Our Balance? Tradition!

Tevye "Fiddler on the Roof"

By continuing the use of our 2017 date model, the 10th day of the seventh month would have fallen on or around September 30th, and it did. Yom Kippur is considered Judaism's holiest and most solemn day of the year. It is also steeped in tradition, so that is where we'll start.

In traditional Judaism, Yom Kippur is the culmination of the "Days of Awe," the ten-day period of repentance that started with Yom Teruah and the culmination of the Season of Teshuvah, the 40-day period that started on Elul 1 as mentioned earlier.

According to the Jewish sages, seven weeks after the Exodus, on the 6th of Sivan (the fixed date for Shavuot based on the Pharisaical tradition of the Omer Count starting on Abib 16. See Chapters 2 and 6), Moses ascended Sinai to receive the Torah; Shavuot. On the 17th of Tammuz, forty days later, Moses destroyed the tablets with the Ten Commandments that had been written with the Finger of God (Exod. 31:18) out of anger for Israel's sin of idolatry of the golden calf. It is then suggested that Moses interceded on Israel's behalf for an additional forty days until being called back up to Sinai (Exod. 34:1-4) on Elul 1, the start of the Season of Teshuvah. After receiving the new tablets, tradition states that Moses descended Mount Sinai on Tishri 10, Yom Kippur; the zenith of the Season of Teshuvah and the Days of Awe.

Also according to the sages, Yom Teruah is when the righteous are written in the Book of Life and the wicked are written in the Book of Death. During the Days of Awe, however, you have 10 days to atone for your sins and "turn back" to God prior to your fate being sealed on Yom Kippur.

This tradition of the books is based on Moses' conversation with God (Exod. 32:30-33) the day after Israel's sin of idolatry, when Moses offered to be removed from "the Book you have written:"

> The next day Moses said to the people, "You have sinned a great sin. And now I will go up to the LORD; perhaps I can make atonement for your sin." So Moses returned to the LORD and said, "Alas, this people has sinned a great sin. They have made for themselves gods of gold. But now, if you will forgive their sin – but if not, please blot me out of your book that you have written." But the LORD said to Moses, "Whoever has sinned against me, I will blot out of my book."

How amazing is that? Moses was willing to be blotted out of God's Book – as the penalty for sin – on behalf of a stiff-necked people. Remember the profile of Moses from Chapter 4? This Levite, this Egyptian noble, this warrior, this Nephilim killer... this Prophet that precedes the Messiah Jesus just offered himself up on Israel's behalf. This is who

God calls the humblest man that ever walked the face of the earth, and he just gave a mighty prophetic picture of Messiah.

Leviticus 16

To understand the "back story" of Yom Kippur, we need to look at Leviticus 16. Here we'll find the actual instructions for the sacrificial atonement / the cleansing of sins and the commandment to observe Yom Kippur repeated after those instructions. Contextually, chapter 16 starts with chapter 8 when Aaron and his sons are presented to serve ADONAI as priests. Their consecration lasted seven days:

> "Do not leave the entrance to the tent of meeting for seven days, until the days of your ordination are completed, for your ordination will last seven days. What has been done today was commanded by the LORD to make atonement for you. You must stay at the entrance to the tent of meeting day and night for seven days and do what the LORD requires, so you will not die; for that is what I have been commanded." So Aaron and his sons did everything the LORD commanded through Moses.
> *Leviticus 8:33-36 (NIV)*

In chapter 9, Aaron and his sons begin the ministry of priesthood:

> Aaron then brought the offering that was for the people. He took the goat for the people's sin offering and slaughtered it and offered it for a sin offering as he did with the first one. He brought the burnt offering and offered it in the prescribed way.
>
> Moses and Aaron then went into the tent of meeting. When they came out, they blessed the people; and the glory of the LORD appeared to all the people. Fire came out from the presence of the LORD and consumed the burnt offering and the fat portions on the altar. And when all the people saw it, they shouted for joy and fell facedown.
> *Leviticus 9:15-16, 23-24 (NIV)*

Notice in verse 16 that the burnt offering was offered "in the prescribed way." This is important for a number of reasons besides basic obedience. If atonement wasn't made "in the prescribed way," not only would the atonement not "work," it would also be deemed unacceptable and detrimental to the priests. On to chapter 10:

Aaron's two sons, called, instructed and ordained to do the priestly Temple work along with their father, took their censers and, contrary to God's specific instructions, offered "unauthorized fire" with incense to God. Fire then came out from the presence of ADONAI, engulfed them, and they both died right then and there in front of God, Moses and Aaron.

> Moses then said to Aaron, "This is what the LORD spoke of when he said: 'Among those who approach me I will be proved holy; in the sight of all the people I will be honored.' " Aaron remained silent.
> Leviticus 10:3 (NIV)

Moses then instructs the sons of Aaron's uncle to carry out the bodies of their cousins outside the camp.

> Then Moses said to Aaron and his sons Eleazar and Ithamar, "Do not let your hair become unkempt and do not tear your clothes, or you will die and the LORD will be angry with the whole community. But your relatives, all the Israelites, may mourn for those the LORD has destroyed by fire. Do not leave the entrance to the tent of meeting or you will die, because the LORD's anointing oil is on you." So they did as Moses said.
>
> Then the LORD said to Aaron, "You and your sons are not to drink wine or other fermented drink whenever you go into the tent of meeting, or you will die. This is a lasting ordinance for the generations to come, so that you can distinguish between the holy and the common, between the unclean and the clean, and so you can teach the Israelites all the decrees the LORD has given them through Moses."
> Leviticus 10:6-11 (NIV)

This was a harsh lesson to learn and frankly difficult for many to wrap their minds around. How does a "Loving God" do something like that? That's a question asked when this temporal reality is deemed more important or above the reality of God's spiritual Kingdom reality; a question asked by one lacking the spiritual mindset required to fully walk in God's absolute obedience; a question asked out of spiritual ignorance. I'm amazed by Aaron's reaction: *Aaron remained silent.* Here was a man under authority, a man that fully understood the priority of natural physical life in relation to obedience to the King of the Universe.

It was disobedience that drove Adam and Eve out of the Garden. Some also see that as "harsh." A very popular position today is that there is no literal Hell / Lake of Fire. No consequence; that there's no way that a "Loving God" would condemn people to an eternal death.

"I can't believe in a God that would punish people to death. If that's the kind of God He is, then I don't want anything to do with Him" are words I have heard and read out of today's Western Church.

Since their god of love is incapable of doing that or wouldn't do that, they've aligned themselves with a belief of a false god on the premise that because of "love" and "Jesus," this horrible and bloodthirsty "God of the Old Testament" is no longer in play. Unfortunately, they fail to consider the New Testament account in Acts 5 of Ananias and his wife Sapphira being killed by the Holy Spirit for lying about money.

A basic understanding of the epistles and/or the Revelation of John also shows death as the consequence of sin. Altering the narrative doesn't actually change anything. God is still going to judge the living and the dead. It's because of Love that our God must punish disobedience. That's the kind of "love wins" to get behind.

The death of Aaron's two sons is the setting for Leviticus 16. They had approached God with "unauthorized fire contrary to His command." We see a similar example a thousand years later in 2 Kings 18:4 regarding the N'chushtan, the brass or bronze serpent Moses used as an oracle of healing in the desert (Num. 21). By the time King Hezekiah ruled, unauthorized incense was being burned to the graven image.

Leviticus 16 explains that Aaron could not approach ADONAI whenever or however he chose, and the reason was "*so that he will not die.*" "*Drink no wine or strong drink, you or your sons with you, when you go into the tent of meeting, lest you die,*" was another condition when approaching God. There are reasons, rules of engagement, why we are to approach Him in certain ways, at certain times and places; obedience, with death as the consequence of disobedience; presently or eternal. This is how it's always been and always will be.

How many of you are hearing Hebrews 4:16 in your heads right about now? The above doesn't alter or render useless Jesus and His finished work on the cross or the content of Hebrews. The above also doesn't mean that we can't boldly go before the Throne of Grace (He. 4:16). But what we also need to consider is Hebrews 4:1-15, not just the conclusion of verse 16. Context, people…

Contextually, Hebrews 3 sets up the scene with an account of Moses' faithfulness and the warning not to harden your hearts like Israel did in the wilderness (verses 7-11, a quote of Psalm 95:7-11). Verses 16-19 basically summarizes a lot of what we've studied in this book. This is the context for Hebrews 4.

Psalm 95:11 is quoted again, how God's anger made Him swear that Israel would not enter His rest, and then the Sabbath is referenced. We see that even though some received the Good News, that wasn't enough for them to enter into His rest. Then a certain time is established, "today" and a "Shabbat-keeping for God's people" (the final ingathering of Sukkot), a *mo'ed*, an "appointed place," "appointed time," or "appointed meeting;" a fixed time or season, like we learned in Chapter 1. Hebrews 4:11 warns us regarding disobedience, falling short and not entering that rest. We have a great High Priest, Jesus (remember, we're contextually talking about Leviticus 16 and the High Priest Aaron), and then *now*:

- With the foundation of Moses' faithfulness
- With the warning not to harden your hearts just like Israel did in the wilderness
- With the warning of being able to still miss His rest after receiving the Good News
- With the reference of a specific established time and the reference to Shabbat
- With the warning of disobedience and falling short, and
- Because of Our Great High Priest

Now we can *confidently approach the throne from which God gives grace, so that we may receive mercy and find grace in our time of need* – because:

- We're faithful
- Our hearts aren't hardened

- We live the Good News
- We have faith in tomorrow's appointed time and Sabbath
- We're obedient and not falling short, because of
- Our Great High Priest

Conditions. Rules of engagement. You see, Jesus doesn't afford us "freedom" from God's established order of things like so many want to believe. Jesus' teaching wasn't His own – it was His Father's teaching (Jn. 7:16)! Jesus didn't deviate from or alter that pre-established order. God, from the very beginning, made it perfectly clear how, when and where we are to worship Him. And in the same way that Aaron was to approach Father God in a "prescribed way," you and I, in Jesus, are also to approach God in the prescribed way. This book is about some of those ways. Jason Henderson, in his book *The Feasts of Israel: Israel's Journey in Christ Towards God's Ultimate End* calls it "life behind the veil." I love that.

The prescribed way for Aaron to enter the temple included bathing and his priestly garments, a bull for a sin offering for himself and the Levites, two goats taken from the congregation for a sin offering for the people and two rams for burnt offerings on behalf of himself and the people. Atonement. Atonement, or "Kippur," means "to cleanse," and this is what Aaron was doing in Leviticus 16:12-20. Verse 16 says:

> Thus he shall make atonement [kippur] for the Holy Place, because of the uncleannesses of the people of Israel and because of their transgressions, all their sins. And so he shall do for the tent of meeting, which dwells with them in the midst of their uncleannesses.

Aaron is cleansing, "decontaminating" from spiritual and physical impurities, the Holy of Holies, the Tent of Meeting and the Altar (verse 20). Thus, the reason for Yom Kippur is the cleansing of our temples from our sins:

> For on this day shall atonement [kippur] be made for you to cleanse you. You shall be clean before the LORD from all your sins.
> Leviticus 16:30

With the destruction of the Temple in AD 70, observing the sacrifice for the atonement of sin found in Leviticus 16 on Yom Kippur has been challenging to say the least. Various substitutions have been put in place, such as the practice of chickens being used as sacrificial blood atonement in lieu of bulls, goats and rams as well as prayers, fasting and personal suffering.

One's own sufferings are considered to be a substitute, especially the sufferings of the righteous. Orthodox Jews of Eastern Europe used to practise a custom called malkoth, in which they inflicted upon themselves 39 lashes. The apostle Paul was on five occasions subjected to "forty stripes minus one" (2 Cor. 11:24), an ancient Jewish method of corporal punishment for transgressors. Furthermore along this theme, one's own death is also regarded as a substitute for sacrifice, and this mistaken idea is derived from Psalm 116:15: "Precious in the sight of the LORD is the death of His saints." Abraham's sacrifice of his son, Isaac, is also relied upon as a substitutionary sacrifice for atonement, but this act only foreshowed the sacrifice of the Father's son, Jesus. There was no redemptive substance in Abraham's act.

There is still a small segment in the Orthodox community who believe that a substitutionary death is still needed, and they give expression to this belief through the practice of kapparoth. The day before Yom Kippur, a live chicken is obtained and the person confesses his sins over the chicken while circling it over his head. The chicken is eventually killed and thus provide blood atonement for sins.
(Source: *Yom Kippur* by Craig Hartman: http://shalomnyc.org/feasts/yom_kippur.htm)

In spite of Yom Kippur, the day dedicated to atonement, there is no assurance of sins forgiven in Judaism. There is longing, there is hope for forgiveness, but of assurance there is none. This only the Son of God can give to those who come to Him in faith. The Day of Atonement is only a substitute for atonement. Judaism could be best summed up as man's attempt to justify himself by his own effort, without the atonement made by a Saviour. That cannot be done. There can be no substitute for Christ, our Atonement and Propitiator. Judaism has tried hard to find a substitute for Him.
(Source: *The Gospel in the Feasts of Israel* by Victor Buksbazen)

> But when Christ appeared as a high priest of the good things that have come, then through the greater and more perfect tent (not made with hands, that is, not of this creation) he entered once for all into the holy places, not by means of the blood of goats and calves but by means of his own blood, thus securing an eternal redemption.
> Hebrews 9:11-12

Hebrews 9 and 10 are great chapters to study again in light of what we've just learned in regard to Yom Kippur.

Yom Kippur is the Day of Cleansing. It is a High Shabbat; a holy convocation when no ordinary work is done. It is a day of repentance, self-examination and atonement; "At-One-Ment" with the Living God. We are to "afflict" ourselves; busy ourselves with bowed-down humility and present a food offering to ADONAI.

In Summary

Appointed Time: Feast of Trumpets (Yom Teruah)

Significance: A day of solemn remembrance of Mount Sinai (Shavuot)

Observance: A Rosh Chodesh. A High Shabbat of solemn rest; a holy convocation of remembrance when no ordinary work is done. A reminder of Shavuot announced with shouts and blasts of the shofar and a food offering is presented to ADONAI

Length: 24 hours, sunset to sunset

Appointed Time: Day of Atonement (Yom Kippur)

Significance: Day of repentance and cleansing. "At-One-Ment" with God

Observance: A High Shabbat; a holy convocation when no ordinary work is done. It is a day of repentance, self-examination and atonement. We are to "afflict" ourselves; busy ourselves with bowed-down humility and present a food offering to ADONAI

Length: 24 hours, sunset to sunset

Yom Teruah

Yom Teruah is better known by its popular and erroneous Babylonian inspired name, "Rosh Hashanah," and it's meaning of "head of the year / new year."

In reality, Yom Teruah is a Rosh Chodesh; a High Shabbat of solemn rest; a holy convocation of remembrance when no ordinary work is done; a reminder announced with shouts and blasts of the shofar and a food offering presented to ADONAI. On this Day of Remembrance, we are to remember the Shofar Blast of Mount Sinai and the Covenant of Torah that took place at Shavuot.

Yom Teruah is *not* a Rosh Hashanah "New Year's – head of the year" celebration that takes place two weeks before the Feast of Tabernacles (Sukkot) – described in Exodus 23:16 as the *"End* of the Year."

Yom Kippur

Yom Kippur is the Day of Cleansing. It is a High Shabbat; a holy convocation when no ordinary work is done. It is a day of repentance, self-examination and atonement; "At-One-Ment" with the Living God. We are to "afflict" ourselves; busy ourselves with bowed-down humility and present a food offering to ADONAI.

> *Therefore, brothers, since we have confidence to enter the holy places by the blood of Jesus, by the new and living way that he opened for us through the curtain, that is, through his flesh, and since we have a great priest over the house of God, let us draw near with a true heart in full assurance of faith, with our hearts sprinkled clean from an evil conscience and our bodies washed with pure water.*
> *Hebrews 10:19-22*

Father God has called us with the blast of the Shofar (Yom Teruah / Feast of Trumpets). We have readied and consecrated ourselves through His cleansing atonement (Yom Kippur / Day of Cleansing) – separated and presentable unto Him – for the Feast of Ingathering (Sukkot / Feast of Tabernacles) has arrived!

CHAPTER 8

FEAST OF TABERNACLES (SUKKOT)
I have gathered you as My People

And the LORD spoke to Moses, saying, "Speak to the people of Israel, saying, On the fifteenth day of this seventh month and for seven days is the Feast of Booths to the LORD.

On the first day shall be a holy convocation [a High Sabbath]; you shall not do any ordinary work. For seven days you shall present food offerings to the LORD. On the eighth day you shall hold a holy convocation [a High Sabbath] and present a food offering to the LORD. It is a solemn assembly; you shall not do any ordinary work

"On the fifteenth day of the seventh month, when you have gathered in the produce of the land, you shall celebrate the feast of the LORD seven days. On the first day shall be a solemn rest, and on the eighth day shall be a solemn rest. And you shall take on the first day the fruit of splendid trees, branches of palm trees and boughs of leafy trees and willows of the brook, and you shall rejoice before the LORD your God seven days. You shall celebrate it as a feast to the LORD for seven days in the year. It is a statute forever throughout your generations; you shall celebrate it in the seventh month. You shall dwell in booths for seven days. All native Israelites shall dwell in booths, that your generations may know that I made the people of Israel dwell in booths when I brought them out of the land of Egypt: I am the LORD your God."
Leviticus 23:33-36, 39-43

The New Moon / Rosh Chodesh conjunction of September 19th and the visible crescent on September 21st brought us to the beginning of the Feast of Ingathering, the Feast of Tabernacles, Sukkot, on October 5th. We've made it to the end of the year!! (Exod. 23:16)

The Feast of Tabernacles, Sukkot (the plural of "sukkah"), signifies our wandering in the desert wilderness, His provision on our behalf and our dependence on His care all along the way (Deut. 29:5). This Feast, which is also known as "The Feast," reminds us that He had Israel "dwell in booths" after their deliverance from Egypt. These temporary dwelling places, these booths, are individually known as a "sukkah."

Sukkah (Strong's #H5521) is the Hebrew word used in the TaNaKh; whereas, the Greek word equivalent used in the New Testament is "*skēnoō*" (Strong's #G4637). We find this Greek word used as "dwelling" when referring to Jesus' dwelling or tabernacle-ing among us in John 1:14 and in reference to God dwelling among us in Rev 7:15, 12:12, and 13:6. Some translations use this word as "tabernacle" in regard to our physical bodies as seen in 2 Peter 1:13-14 and especially in 2 Corinthians 5:1-10. The theme of "temporary dwelling place" and "temporary physical body" also speaks to our temporary journey through this earth as pilgrims on our way to the final Spiritual Sukkah:

> *Then I saw a new heaven and a new earth, for the first heaven and the first earth had passed away, and the sea was no more. And I saw the holy city, new Jerusalem, coming down out of heaven from God, prepared as a bride adorned for her husband. And I heard a loud voice from the throne saying, "Behold, the dwelling place [tabernacle] of God is with man. He will dwell [Greek: skēnoō. Hebrew: sukkah] with them, and they will be his people, and God himself will be with them as their God."*
> Revelation 21:1-3

Sukkot, to me, is such a fascinating Feast because of all that has occurred to get here (we'll revisit the journey to Sukkot in Chapter 9) and its prophetic significance. Personally, I think Sukkot is also the most challenging of Feasts, whether you believe that only having meals in your sukkah fulfills the observance or whether you believe you're to also sleep inside of it.

The obvious "fulfillment" of the Spring Feasts and Pentecost by

Messiah leaves many to "interpret" the Fall Feasts as being yet "unfulfilled" by Messiah. As much as there are physical, prophetic and spiritual aspects to all of the Feasts, their spiritual significance for humankind are, in my opinion, the end goal of the Father. That said, the physical, prophetic and ultimately spiritual significance to Sukkot would be the ingathering of His people unto Himself – the "dwelling among" – the "being in His Rest" as we just saw in Revelation 21 and as we've seen represented throughout all of the Feasts.

Sukkot brings us from Yom Kippur, the most solemn day of the year to, just five days later, the most festive eight days of the year – from repentance to rejoicing redemption! Because of this, Sukkot is commonly referred to in traditional Jewish prayers and literature as "The Season of our Rejoicing."

Festival of Ingathering

As we have previously discussed, Sukkot is the last of the Three Pilgrimage Festivals (Deut. 16:16-17).

Sukkot carries the dual historical / spiritual and agricultural significance we've seen in the other Pilgrimage Festivals. Sukkot commemorates forty years of wandering in the desert wilderness while living in temporary dwellings. Agriculturally, Sukkot celebrates the gathering of the end of the year harvest known as *Chag ha-Asif*: "of the harvest" – the Festival of Ingathering.

> *You shall keep the Feast of Harvest, of the firstfruits of your labor, of what you sow in the field. You shall keep the Feast of Ingathering at the end of the year, when you gather in from the field the fruit of your labor.*
> Exodus 23:16

Agriculturally, Passover paralleled the planting and harvesting of the barley season and Shavuot the wheat harvest, while Sukkot is the season for harvesting produce. Physically and spiritually, all the crops for the year have been harvested and gathered. God's provision is a time for rejoicing!

This ongoing theme of harvesting, reaping and sowing is one of God's "Love Languages" toward us; the increase of Himself, in and through us, returning to Him as fruit. Just like in the parables of the minas and the talents, He expects a return from our stewardship of His increase. Sukkot, this appointed time of "ingathering," is that reaping of the harvest in and of our lives of His sowing.

> *He calls to the heavens above and to the earth, that he may judge his people: "Gather to me my faithful ones, who made a covenant with me by sacrifice!"*
> *Psalms 50:4-5*

Like we discussed in Chapter 1, God's calendar is an agricultural one, and the Feasts are intricately connected to the land. This is why Jesus used agricultural metaphors as often as He did in the Gospels. Words like planting, seeds and reaping within concepts of sowing, seasons and harvesting, etc.

The first three Spring Feasts are connected to barley, the first crop in Israel's yearly harvest. Seven weeks later (50 days), the assembly is gathered for the wheat harvest and to participate in the receiving of Torah and the baptism of Pentecost on their way to the ingathering of the produce harvest of Booths / Sukkot.

As we've seen, the Feasts are a massive part of Israel's identity; individually, corporately, physically and spiritually. So imagine again the richness these yearly experiences brought to families and individuals. Jesus knew this, so the agricultural symbolism in His discourses rang true to His listeners.

> *"You shall keep the Feast of Booths seven days, when you have gathered in the produce from your threshing floor and your winepress. You shall rejoice in your feast, you and your son and your daughter, your male servant and your female servant, the Levite, the sojourner, the fatherless, and the widow who are within your towns.*
>
> *For seven days you shall keep the feast to the LORD your God at the place that the LORD will choose, because the LORD your God will bless you in all your produce and in all the work of your hands, so that you will be altogether joyful."*
> *Deuteronomy 16:13-15*

Sukkot is Prophetic

Isaiah 4 gives a whopping prophetic look at Sukkot and the sukkah:

> Then the LORD will create over the whole site of Mount Zion and over her assemblies a cloud by day, and smoke and the shining of a flaming fire by night; **for over all the glory there will be a canopy. There will be a booth** for shade by day from the heat, and for a refuge and **a shelter** from the storm and rain. [a sukkah, Sukkot]
> Isaiah 4:5-6 [Emphasis mine]

We see the concept of ingathering used prophetically in Joel 3:12-13, Matthew 13, and Revelation 14:14-20, just to name three.

Zechariah 14 is by far the most popular prophetic account of Sukkot. Verses 1-11 speak of the coming Day of Adonai when He gathers all the nations against Jerusalem for battle: the city is taken and plundered, the women are raped and half of Jerusalem goes into exile. Then He goes out and fights against the enemies of Israel, and in verse 4 we see the mighty picture of Messiah standing on the Mount of Olives:

> On that day his feet shall stand on the Mount of Olives that lies before Jerusalem on the east, and the Mount of Olives shall be split in two from east to west by a very wide valley, so that one half of the Mount shall move northward, and the other half southward.

Verse 8 describes this amazing day:

> On that day living waters shall flow out from Jerusalem, half of them to the eastern sea and half of them to the western sea. It shall continue in summer as in winter.

"On that day living waters shall flow out from Jerusalem..."

Let's go back to Chapter 3 for a minute when we were discussing religious traditions based on paganism versus religious traditions based on scripture. The two examples I gave of Jesus working within those "confines" – the confines of traditions based on the biblical narrative, of course – Jesus would never work with or from a foundation of paganism... I'm referring to when Jesus called Himself "Living Water" during a traditional addition to the Feast of Sukkot:

In John 7, it's the Feast of Tabernacles / Booths, Sukkot. Jesus was avoiding Judea because they were looking to kill Him there, but since Sukkot is the last of the Three Pilgrimage Festivals where every Jewish male presented himself before God in Jerusalem, Jesus *had* to go. An extracurricular ritual had been added to the Feast of Sukkot that isn't found in Torah: The Water Libation Ceremony.

> The water libation ritual was popular because of the accompanying ceremony of the water drawing. Each day for seven consecutive days a priest poured a jug full of water into a bowl that drained into the altar. Levites played lyres, trumpets, harps, cymbals, and other instruments, while other Levites sang. Three golden candlesticks roughly 75 feet high were lit by young boys on tall ladders. The light of these candles was seen throughout Jerusalem. Men of faith danced and sang in front of these candlesticks while carrying burning torches. As the ceremony progressed through the night, priests blew shofars three times. Rabbis would perform acrobats and juggle flaming touches [sic] as part of the festivities.
> (Source:http://www.jewishroots.net/library/holiday-articles/water_libation_ceremony.html)

Because this water libation ceremony had been "added to" the original Torah instruction on how to observe Sukkot, it wasn't technically permissible or "lawful," and Jesus knew this. Jesus didn't condemn this infraction but instead, on the last day of the feast at the climax of the celebration, a High Sabbath:

> Jesus stood up and cried out, "If anyone thirsts, let him come to me and drink. Whoever believes in me, as the Scripture has said, 'Out of his heart will flow rivers of living water.'"
> John 7:37-38

Jesus announces Himself the "Living Water" everyone knew was referenced in Zechariah 14 – declaring Himself to all of Israel that He was indeed Messiah!

We continue in Zechariah:

> And the LORD will be king over all the earth. On that day the LORD will be one and his name one.
> Zechariah 14:9

This is a huge part of His overall plan, a part that is frequently debated by a large cross-section of the Western Church today: God, through the Person of Jesus, becoming "King of all the earth." Many argue that because Jesus told Pilot that "My kingdom is not of this world" in John 18:36, any eschatological reference to a "kingdom on earth" is purely "spiritual" and not literally "physical." God not only isn't interested in nation states, continues this narrative, He especially isn't interested in or on the side of the modern State of Israel (a topic for yet another book), and He isn't coming back to rule the literal physical planet Earth. I obviously have issue with single, stand-alone verses out of context like John 18:36 undermining multiple contextual passages such as Zechariah 8:22; 14:9; Isaiah 2:2-4; Micah 4:1-3; Isaiah 9:6-7; Jeremiah 3:17; Daniel 2:44; etc., just to name seven.

Back to Zechariah 14:12-15 where it tells us what will happen to the nations that waged war against Jerusalem and then we see this:

> Then everyone who survives of all the nations that have come against Jerusalem **shall go up year after year to worship the King, the LORD of hosts, and to keep the Feast of Booths.** And if any of the families of the earth do not go up to Jerusalem to worship the King, the LORD of hosts, there will be no rain on them. And if the family of Egypt does not go up and present themselves, then on them there shall be no rain; there shall be the plague with which the LORD afflicts the nations that do not go up to keep the Feast of Booths. This shall be the punishment to Egypt and the punishment to all the nations that do not go up to keep the Feast of Booths.
> Zechariah 14:16-19 [Emphasis mine]

Wow. The surviving nations that came against Jerusalem along with the families of the earth and Egypt – Gentiles, essentially – will present themselves before ADONAI, in Jerusalem, every year to worship Him and to keep Sukkot. If they don't? They will be plagued and have no rain. Ezekiel 38:15-23 speaks of curses of torrential rains, hailstones, fire and sulfur that will also befall Israel's enemies.

So all the world will be required to travel yearly to Jerusalem to worship Messiah and keep the Feast of Tabernacles / Booths, Sukkot; the Feast of Ingathering. This alone should be enough to convince us that these *mo'edim*, these "appointed times" – these *miqra'ot*, these "holy rehearsals," are something we should be practicing now – rehearsing today, for tomorrow.

> *"The inhabitants of one city shall go to another, saying, 'Let us go at once to entreat the favor of the LORD and to seek the LORD of hosts; I myself am going.'*
>
> *Many peoples and strong nations shall come to seek the LORD of hosts in Jerusalem and to entreat the favor of the LORD. Thus says the LORD of hosts: In those days ten men from the nations of every tongue shall take hold of the robe of a Jew, saying, 'Let us go with you, for we have heard that God is with you.'"*
> Zechariah 8:21-23

The Word Became Flesh and "Tabernacled" with Us

> *In the days of Herod, king of Judea, there was a priest named Zechariah, of the division of Abijah. And he had a wife from the daughters of Aaron, and her name was Elizabeth. And they were both righteous before God, walking blamelessly in all the commandments and statutes of the Lord. But they had no child, because Elizabeth was barren, and both were advanced in years.*
> Luke 1:5-7

Zechariah the priest and his barren wife, Elizabeth, would become the parents of a Nazarite-from-birth known as John the Baptist. It would be interesting to note that they both came from the priestly line of Aaron, making John a full Levitical "Cohen" (Priest) just like his priestly ancestor, Aaron, and his brother, Moses.

> *Now while he [Zechariah] was serving as priest before God when his division was on duty, according to the custom of the priesthood, he was chosen by lot to enter the temple of the Lord and burn incense.*
> Luke 1:8-9

In 1 Chronicles 24, we see David organizing the priests *"according to the appointed duties in their service"* (verse 3b). Verse 4:

> *Since more chief men were found among the sons of Eleazar than among the sons of Ithamar, they organized them under sixteen heads of fathers' houses of the sons of Eleazar, and eight of the sons of Ithamar.*

The priests were divided into 24 *"heads of fathers' houses" /* divisions with Zechariah being in *"the division of Abijah."* 1 Chronicles 24 verses 10 and 19:

> *The first lot fell to [...] the seventh to Hakkoz, the eighth to Abijah [...] These had as their appointed duty in their service to come into the house of the LORD according to the procedure established for them by Aaron their father, as the LORD God of Israel had commanded him.*

The first division began their temple service in the First Month of Abib, which is also known by its Babylonian name, Nisan. This would mean that the eighth division of Abijah would serve during the 10th week of the year in the Third Month, also known by its Babylonian name of Sivan. Luke 1:8-9 tells us that Zechariah's division was serving at the time of his visitation by the angel Gabriel:

> *Then an angel of the Lord appeared to him, standing at the right side of the altar of incense. When Zechariah saw him, he was startled and was gripped with fear. But the angel said to him: "Do not be afraid, Zechariah; your prayer has been heard. Your wife Elizabeth will bear you a son, and you are to call him John.*
>
> *He will be a joy and delight to you, and many will rejoice because of his birth, for he will be great in the sight of the Lord. He is never to take wine or other fermented drink, and he will be filled with the Holy Spirit even before he is born.*
>
> *He will bring back many of the people of Israel to the Lord their God. And he will go on before the Lord, in the spirit and power of Elijah, to turn the hearts of the parents to their children and the disobedient to the wisdom of the righteous — to make ready a people prepared for the Lord."*
> Luke 1:11-17 (NIV)

When Zechariah's time of temple service was completed, he went home and Elizabeth conceived (verses 23-24). In verse 26, during Elizabeth's sixth month, Gabriel visited Elizabeth's cousin, Mary. When Mary was "found with Child," we are in the Ninth Month, known by its Babylonian name of Kislev, when the Feast of Dedication, also known as Hanukkah, occurs (John 10:22).

This timeline places John's birth on or around Passover, the First Month of Abib, and Jesus' birth six months later in the Month of Ethanim, also known by its Babylonian name of Tishri, when the Feast of Tabernacles / Booths, Sukkot, takes place.

The "manger" of Luke 2:12 is more than likely a sukkah when you breakdown the Greek word *phatnē* (Strong's #G5336) that is used here. This word is also translated as "stall" in Luke 13:15. The Hebrew word for stall is *marbeq* (Strongs #H4770). In Genesis 33:17 "Jacob journeyed to Sukkoth and made booths," *sukkah* (Strong's H5521), the plural being sukkot as we saw earlier in this Chapter. The word booth (*sukkah*) was used for Jacob's cattle and the Greek word manger (*phatnē*) is also used for cattle. Sukkot, the Feast of Tabernacles, being the third of the Three Pilgrimage Festivals, would explain the difficulty Mary and Joseph had when it came to finding lodging and why Jesus was born in a sukkah during Sukkot.

John 1:14 states that the Word, Jesus, became flesh and dwelt among us. The word dwelt (*skēnoō*) is the Strong's Greek word #G4637 and its biblical usage being:

- To fix one's tabernacle
- Have one's tabernacle
- Abide (or live) in a tabernacle (or tent)
- Tabernacle

The Strong's definition of the word is:

- To tent or encamp
- To occupy
- To reside as God did in the Tabernacle of old
- A symbol of protection and communion

We can easily see how Sukkot, the Feast of Tabernacles, is synonymous with Messiah's being "among us." So celebrate the birth of Messiah with us during the Feast of Tabernacles!

> *In the beginning was the Word, and the Word was with God, and the Word was God. He was with God in the beginning. Through him all things were made; without him nothing was made that has been made.*
>
> *In him was life, and that life was the light of all mankind. The light shines in the darkness, and the darkness has*

> not overcome it. The true light that gives light to everyone was coming into the world.
>
> He was in the world, and though the world was made through him, the world did not recognize him. He came to that which was his own, but his own did not receive him. Yet to all who did receive him, to those who believed in his name, he gave the right to become children of God – children born not of natural descent, nor of human decision or a husband's will, but born of God.
>
> The Word became flesh and made his dwelling among us. We have seen his glory, the glory of the one and only Son, who came from the Father, full of grace and truth.
> John 1:1-5, 9-14

If there was one way to describe the purposes of God through religion and the biblical text, it would be the theme of God's desire to dwell with man. This theme of "dwelling together" is at the core of our journey from Passover to Tabernacles, from Exodus to Ingathering and at the very heart of everything God has orchestrated on our behalf. It's the reason behind placing Adam in the Garden.

All throughout the scriptures, we see these physical and spiritual "types and shadows" of this desire, the Feast of Sukkot being the end result:

> And let them make me a sanctuary, that I may dwell [sukkah] in their midst.
> Exodus 25:8

The Song of Moses that was sung after the victory at the Red Sea, at the very beginning of this Feast Journey, hints of it:

> You will bring them in and plant them on the mountains of your inheritance. In the place you made your dwelling, your sanctuary, established by your hands.
> Based on Exodus 15:17

We've discussed the purposes of God behind the exodus:

- To lead us to Sinai
- To betroth us unto Himself, and
- To bring us into His rest of Sukkot

God and man tabernacle-ing together, forever, is the practical understanding of God's holy days. So that the nations will know...

> *I will make a covenant of peace with them. It shall be an everlasting covenant with them. And I will set them in their land and multiply them, and will set my sanctuary in their midst forevermore. My dwelling place shall be with them, and I will be their God, and they shall be my people. Then the nations will know that I am the LORD who sanctifies Israel, when my sanctuary is in their midst forevermore."*
> Ezekiel 37:26-28

Observance: Traditional

According to Leviticus 23, Sukkot lasts for a total of seven days plus 1, the eighth day. Traditionally, the two days following the Feast are known as *Shemini Atzeret* ("the eighth (day) of assembly") and *Simchat Torah* ("rejoicing in Torah"), respectively. Though *Simchat Torah* is a separate and additional "holiday" celebrating the end of the Torah reading cycle for the year as Sukkot marks the end of the agricultural year, it is commonly considered a part of Sukkot. Traditionally, you would have about four days from the time Yom Kippur ended to assemble and decorate your sukkah. More on building your sukkah later.

The Four Species – Arba Minim

> *And you shall take on the first day the fruit of splendid trees, branches of palm trees and boughs of leafy trees and willows of the brook, and you shall rejoice before the LORD your God seven days.*
> Leviticus 23:40

Traditionally, the instruction of Leviticus 23:40 is known as *Arba Minim*, the Four Species, or, the *Lulav* and *Etrog*, the palm branches and citron.

The "fruit of splendid trees" is interpreted to be an *etrog*; a citrus fruit native to Israel and similar to a lemon called a citron in English. The "branches of palm trees", "boughs of leafy trees," and "willows of the brook," the *lulav*, are interpreted as palm branches, myrtle, and willows, respectively.

Tradition also states that a single palm branch, three myrtle branches and two willow branches are to be tied together (the *lulav*) and held in one hand while the *etrog* is held in the other. A ritual consisting of blessings and the waving of the four species is also involved to satisfy the scriptural instruction of "rejoicing before ADONAI."

Observance: Scriptural

In Chapter 7, we looked at how Nehemiah 8 brought the restoration of Torah, Yom Teruah and Sukkot back to the Land and Israel as a people in the days of Ezra. They reestablished the remembrance of temporary dwelling places while in the wilderness as instructed in Leviticus 23.

> And they found it written in the Law [Torah] that the LORD had commanded by Moses that the people of Israel should dwell in booths during the feast of the seventh month, and that they should proclaim it and publish it in all their towns and in Jerusalem, "Go out to the hills and bring branches of olive, wild olive, myrtle, palm, and other leafy trees to make booths, as it is written."
>
> So the people went out and brought them and made booths for themselves, each on his roof, and in their courts and in the courts of the house of God, and in the square at the Water Gate and in the square at the Gate of Ephraim. And all the assembly of those who had returned from the captivity made booths and lived in the booths, for from the days of Jeshua the son of Nun to that day the people of Israel had not done so. And there was very great rejoicing.
>
> And day by day, from the first day to the last day, he read from the Book of the Law [Torah] of God. They kept the feast seven days, and on the eighth day there was a solemn assembly, according to the rule.
> Nehemiah 8:14-18

During the Sabbath year, the Shemitah, the Torah was to be read during Sukkot:

> And Moses commanded them, "At the end of every seven years, at the set time in the year of release, at the Feast

of Booths, when all Israel comes to appear before the LORD your God at the place that he will choose, you shall read this law [Torah] before all Israel in their hearing.

Assemble the people, men, women, and little ones, and the sojourner within your towns, that they may hear and learn to fear the LORD your God, and be careful to do all the words of this law, and that their children, who have not known it, may hear and learn to fear the LORD your God, as long as you live in the land that you are going over the Jordan to possess."
Deuteronomy 31:10-13

Sukkot is a seven-day feast plus one additional day.

Day 1:

- Before the evening of the 15th of the month, the start of the High Shabbat when no ordinary work is to be done, your sukkah, your temporary dwelling place, should be assembled and decorated
- Have Shabbat at sunset
- The following morning, the High Shabbat, gather fruit and branches from palm, leafy and willow trees, if possible, based on your geographical location, to celebrate with

Day 1 - 7:

- For seven days we are to dwell in booths
- For seven days we are to have a celebratory atmosphere of rejoicing before God – as a feast *unto* God – using the fruit and branches from palm, leafy and willow trees we have gathered
- For seven days we are to present food offerings to God
- For seven days we are to celebrate. You can
    i. Celebrate by listening to, singing along with, and/or playing festive music
    ii. Celebrate by talking and reasoning about the meaning of Sukkot and the journey that led us here

    iii. Celebrate by praying / worshiping together
    iv. Celebrate by reading the account of Messiah's birth (Mt. 1:18-25; Luke 1; 2:1-38; John 1:1-18)
    v. Celebrate by eating holiday foods, and
    vi. Celebrate just by relaxing inside the sukkah with family and friends. The point is to celebrate!

Day 8:

- On the evening of the 21st day of the Hebrew month, the beginning of the eighth day, is the start of the High Shabbat when no ordinary work is to be done
- Have Shabbat at sunset

Building a Sukkah

"You shall dwell in booths for seven days. All native Israelites shall dwell in booths, that your generations may know that I made the people of Israel dwell in booths when I brought them out of the land of Egypt: I am the LORD your God."
Leviticus 23: 42-43

In remembrance and so that future generations will also know that ADONAI made the people of Israel dwell in booths when He brought them out of the land of Egypt, we are commanded to dwell in temporary shelters for seven days. This temporary dwelling, this booth, is also called a sukkah (think camping.) Assembling a sukkah every year is great for the entire family. It's like building a fort for the kids and the kid in you!

The instruction to "dwell" in a sukkah is interpreted differently by many. Some believe that the commandment is satisfied simply by eating all of your meals in your sukkah. Others believe that eating in and spending as much time as you can in your sukkah is sufficient, while others insist that all of the above, including sleeping in their sukkah – especially sleeping in your sukkah – is the intended instruction of Sukkot.

Traditionally, a sukkah will have at least two and a half walls based on the Hebraic letters in the word "sukkah:" one letter has four sides, one letter has three sides and the other has two and a half sides.

The walls can be solid, canvas, cloth and/or a tarp tied, nailed and/or fastened with zip ties, for example. Any of these methods are acceptable. A sukkah can be of any size but should be large enough for you and your family to "dwell" in it so as to complete the commandment.

Traditionally, the roof of the sukkah is made up of organic materials such as tree branches, bamboo reeds, sticks, or 2x4's placed loosely enough to allow rain to get in and so that the stars can be seen. Traditionally, a water-proof cover can be used when raining but you cannot use that water-proof cover as the sukkah. Traditionally, you would remove this cover to satisfy the instruction of "dwelling in a sukkah."

There are sukkahs of varying materials available for purchase, or you can DIY and build your own. We do. We've built sukkah's using PVC piping for the frame, utilized the wall of the house as the sukkah's back wall and ran tarps for the side walls. We've used purchased rolls of natural reed bamboo garden fencing for the roof, setup a table and chairs and there you have it. The table is usually decorated with a celebratory table cloth, menorah, Shabbat candle holders, flowers and a shofar or two. We run extension cords to power laptops and decorative stringed lights that are strung overhead and on the walls. The table and chairs are easily moved to accommodate cots and sleeping bags.

We also do community campouts in the backyard or at a campground where everyone is "dwelling" in camping tents. That's my favorite. When on tour, every place was a "temporary dwelling place" be it a hotel or the tour bus. Like I've mentioned before, it's not the legalistic observance but the observance from a heart of wanting to be obedient that's important.

Presently and for the last four years, the lower outdoor deck of our home has been our sukkah. The upper deck serves as the roof so the natural reed bamboo garden fencing we used for roofing in years' past are now used as walls along the side railings of our lower deck. Decorative lights are strung and the table is set like we've always have. Whether our sukkah was framed by PVC piping or on our lower deck, assembling and decorating our sukkahs is a family / community event.

What are or have been your sukkah plans? Do you decorate your sukkah by hanging artwork or drawings made by your children? What are some of your family's sukkah traditions?
Let us know: https://facebook.com/ChameleonChurch
(Inspired by Tracey R Rich. Judaism 101: Sukkot: http://jewfaq.org/m/holiday5.htm)

In Summary

Appointed Time: Feast of Tabernacles, Feast of Booths, Feast of Ingathering, Sukkot

Significance: To remember God's provision and protection over Israel while they lived in temporary dwellings in the wilderness after being brought out of Egypt on their way to Canaan. The Fall harvest festival

Observance: The first and eighth days are High Sabbaths. Building and "dwelling" in a booth while offering food offerings in celebration and rejoicing while waving branches and fruit for seven days

Length: Seven days plus one

I am the LORD your God from the land of Egypt; I will again make you dwell in tents, as in the days of the appointed feast.

Hosea 12:9

The Feast of Tabernacles – the Feast of Booths, this Feast of Ingathering, Sukkot – is the culmination and the designed desired end result of the exodus from Egypt.

We've been gathered by Him, for Him and *in* Him. We remember this by dwelling in a temporary physical place that speaks of and calls us to an eternal dwelling place, in and with Him (Rev. 21:1-3).

Sukkot signifies our wandering in the desert wilderness, His provision on our behalf and our dependence on His care all along the way (Deut. 29:5). We've been taken from deliverance and repentance to redemption!

The physical, prophetic and ultimately spiritual significance of Sukkot is this ingathering of His people unto Himself – the "dwelling among" – the "being in His Rest" as we've seen represented throughout all of the Feasts. Sukkot, this appointed time of "ingathering," is the reaping of the harvest in and of our lives of His sowing.

We've seen prophetically how observing or not observing Sukkot will be a determining factor for the Gentiles during Messiah's reign. It would behoove us to be well-versed in this appointed expression of celebratory worship and rejoicing unto our God as we continue ever forward in our earthly sukkah to the spiritual sukkah that awaits us.

For we know that if the tent that is our earthly home is destroyed, we have a building from God, a house not made with hands, eternal in the heavens. For in this tent we groan, longing to put on our heavenly dwelling, if indeed by putting it on we may not be found naked. For while we are still in this tent, we groan, being burdened – not that we would be unclothed, but that we would be further clothed, so that what is mortal may be swallowed up by life.

He who has prepared us for this very thing is God, who has given us the Spirit as a guarantee. So we are always of good courage. We know that while we are at home in the body we are away from the Lord, for we walk by faith, not by sight. Yes, we are of good courage, and we would rather be away from the body and at home with the Lord.

So whether we are at home or away, we make it our aim to please him. For we must all appear before the judgment seat of Christ, so that each one may receive what is due for what he has done in the body, whether good or evil.
2 Corinthians 5:1-10

CHAPTER 9

IN CONCLUSION
The Amazing Journey from Exodus to Ingathering

The LORD said to Moses, "Cut for yourself two tablets of stone like the first, and I will write on the tablets the words that were on the first tablets, which you broke. Be ready by the morning, and come up in the morning to Mount Sinai, and present yourself there to me on the top of the mountain. So Moses cut two tablets of stone like the first. And he rose early in the morning and went up on Mount Sinai, as the LORD had commanded him, and took in his hand two tablets of stone.

And he said, "**Behold, I am making a covenant. Observe what I command you this day.**

You shall keep the Feast of Unleavened Bread. Seven days you shall eat unleavened bread, as I commanded you, at the time appointed in the month Abib, for in the month Abib you came out from Egypt.

Six days you shall work, but on the seventh day you shall rest. In plowing time and in harvest you shall rest.

You shall observe the Feast of Weeks [The Omer Count]**, the firstfruits of wheat harvest** [Shavuot]**, and the Feast of Ingathering** [Feast of Tabernacles] at the year's end. Three times in the year shall all your males appear before the LORD God, the God of Israel.

And the LORD said to Moses, "Write these words, for **in accordance with these words I have made a covenant with you and with Israel.**" So he was there with the LORD forty days and forty nights. He neither ate bread nor drank water. And he wrote on the tablets the words of the covenant, the Ten Commandments.
Exodus 34:1-2, 4, 10a-11a, 18, 21-23, 27-28 [Emphasis mine]

The first pair of tablets with the covenant were written by the very finger of God (Exod. 24; 31:18) but were destroyed by Moses because of the great sin of the people (Exod. 32). This second pair of tablets with the covenant were written by Moses (Exod. 34:28), but it's the content and context of Exodus 34 that I obviously want you to see. But first:

For some internal reason, we have the need to reject absolutes. This "need" goes as far back as the garden. Lucifer seduced the woman by telling her half-truths that "sounded right." God had made the instruction regarding life in the garden very clear:

> And the LORD God commanded the man, saying, "You may surely eat of every tree of the garden, but of the tree of the knowledge of good and evil you shall not eat, for in the day that you eat of it you shall surely die."
> Genesis 2:16-17

Simple enough; "Don't eat from the tree of the knowledge of good and evil..." Here's what the serpent said:

> Now the serpent was more crafty than any of the wild animals the LORD God had made. He said to the woman, "Did God really say, 'You must not eat from **any** tree in the garden'?"
> The woman said to the serpent, "We may eat fruit from the trees in the garden, but God did say, 'You must not eat fruit from the tree that is in the middle of the garden, and you must not touch it, or you will die.'"
> "You will not certainly die," the serpent said to the woman. "For God knows that when you eat from it your eyes will be opened, and you will be like God, knowing good and evil."
> When the woman saw that the fruit of the tree was good for food and pleasing to the eye, and also desirable for gaining wisdom, she took some and ate it. She also gave some to her husband, who was with her, and he ate it.
> Genesis 3:1-6 (NIV) [Emphasis mine]

"Did God actually say...?"

"Does God actually expect you to...," for example, "eat unleavened bread and abstain from pork? You know, the 'other white meat?'"

See how easy that was? Once you question the authority of the text, the authority of His Word...

I so want to believe that Eve's disobedience was due to the confusion brought on by the serpent, but I'm afraid that's just wishful thinking on my part.

Here's another example: Jesus' statement of "if you love Me, you will keep My commandments" (John 14:15). Instead of going with the literal text and accepting that Jesus actually meant "keep My commandments," that internal mechanism of determining what Jesus *really* meant – just like in the garden – once again kicks in, and the commandments He's referring to can't be the literal "commandments" but just "The Two" from Matthew 22:

1. Love the Lord your God with all your heart and with all your soul and with all your mind (Deut. 6:5; Mt. 22:36-37), and

2. You shall love your neighbor as yourself (Lev. 19:18; Mt. 22:39)

Before I continue with the contextual conclusion of Matthew 22, I want to take a quick look at what the Apostle Paul / Rabbi Sha'ul says about this:

> *Owe no one anything, except to love each other, for the one who loves another has fulfilled the law. For the commandments, "You shall not commit adultery, You shall not murder, You shall not steal, You shall not covet," and any other commandment, are summed up in this word: "You shall love your neighbor as yourself."*
> Romans 13:8-9

Take note that the word "fulfilled" in verse eight is the same word used by Jesus in Matthew 5:17 meaning to cause to abound, supply liberally, to cause God's will (as made known in the law) to be obeyed as it should be and God's promises (given through the prophets) to receive fulfilment. It does *not* mean "to do away with." Furthermore, the four commandments Paul uses as an example, as well as "any other commandment" that is "summed up" with "You shall love your neighbor as yourself," have *also* not been "done away with."

So then this begs the question: if *Paul* doesn't eliminate or disregard any of the commandments in Romans 13, why would *Jesus* exclude or eradicate any of the commandments based on Matthew 22, when He clearly states that "*all* the law and the prophets" are hung on, based on, and dependent on Deuteronomy 6:5 and Leviticus 19:18 in verse 40 of Matthew 22?

Well, you see, He didn't. But we have this internal need to reject the absolutes of God's Word with half-truths that sound "good" and "right." Consider additionally these two extremely common examples:

- "Torah doesn't apply to Christians today, especially to Gentile Christians, but the Ten Commandments do"

This "sounds good" and it definitely "sounds right" in the 21st Century except that the Ten Commandments *are* the Torah.

- "Obedience to the Ten Commandments is crucial for one's faith but you can observe any day as "the Lord's Day – the sabbath"

Again, this "sounds good" and it "sounds right" but it completely conflicts with the Fourth Commandment that states otherwise.

When someone tells you that you're religious or legalistic for keeping the Torah, what they're actually saying is that you're religious and legalistic for keeping God's commandments – you're religious and legalistic for obeying God's Word. That sounds like an argument an unbeliever would make, not a "professing Christian."

Call it convenience, call it laziness, or just call it gross negligence and straight up lawlessness, but for some reason, because we have this internal need to reject the absolutes of God's Word with half-truths, doing the absolute very least that we can possibly get away with under the guise of "Freedom in Christ" manifests itself with theologies and doctrines that sound awfully similar to the seductive words spoken by the serpent in the garden...

Here's why I bring this up: Believing that Jesus never taught that we, as Believers, are obligated to obey God as the end result of our salvation is a real thing. Belief in a teaching by Jesus that none of us are expected to keep God's commandments as a result of our salvation is a real thing. The doctrine that Jesus never commanded us to observe and keep Torah is a very real thing.

"Did God actually say…?"

We should also consider the fact that Jesus didn't say "if you love Me, keep My commandments." He said, "if you love Me, *you will* keep My commandments." (John 14:15) I suggest it's an issue of Love or the lack thereof, and then it's an issue of obedience…

So hopefully, by showing you in Romans 13 that Paul believed that the commandments, Torah, were valid for His Gentile church in Rome – by using the same example taught by Jesus in Matthew 22 – I'm hoping that you'll be able to see how in the opening passage of this Chapter from Exodus 34, God's covenant of obedience on our behalf not only included our keeping of the Ten Commandments (Exod. 34:28), but God's covenant of obedience on our behalf *also included* our keeping of His Appointed Feasts and Sabbaths (Exod. 34:1-2, 4, 10a-11a, 18, 21-23, 27).

My little children, these things I write to you, so that you may not sin. And if anyone sins, we have an Advocate with the Father, Jesus Christ the righteous. And He Himself is the propitiation for our sins, and not for ours only but also for the whole world.

Now by this we know that we know Him, if we keep His commandments. He who says, "I know Him," and does not keep His commandments, is a liar, and the truth is not in him. But whoever keeps His word, truly the love of God is perfected in him. By this we know that we are in Him. He who says he abides in Him ought himself also to walk just as He walked.
1 John 2:1-6

Yes, this book has been written with the assumption in mind that you, the reader, have somehow, in some way, and to some extent received the revelation or are in the process of receiving this revelation: that the Scriptures, the TaNaKh, the "Old Testament" – and the information and instructions therein – have not been *"done away with"* or made obsolete, and somehow in some way and to some extent they must apply to you. I'm just reminding you that yes, you are correct to assume all of this. Look at how frequently God had to remind Israel of the same. That internal mechanism that causes us to disregard the actual instruction also causes us to *forget* those same instructions:

> **"Remember** *the Sabbath day, to keep it holy."*
> *Exodus 20:8*

He instructed us to *remember* the Sabbath. Why? So that we wouldn't forget and so that we would keep it holy. We forgot...

Again, this is largely due to our identity crisis – the crisis of identity that we briefly touched upon in Chapter 5 and that will be the topic of my next book that continues where this book leaves off – the continuation of this amazing journey to the Land of Promise that we were delivered from Egypt to possess.

Before we outline and summarize the seven-month journey we just unlocked; a journey of deliverance, repentance and redemption – this Amazing Journey from Exodus to Ingathering – I want to stress, one last time, the importance of the practical understanding of God's holy days:

> *For I want you to know, brothers, that our fathers were all under the cloud, and all passed through the sea, and all were baptized into Moses in the cloud and in the sea, and all ate the same spiritual food, and all drank the same spiritual drink. For they drank from the spiritual Rock that followed them, and the Rock was Christ. Nevertheless, with most of them God was not pleased, for they were overthrown in the wilderness.*
>
> ***Now these things took place as examples for us****, that we might not desire evil as they did. Do not be idolaters as some of them were; as it is written, "The people sat down to eat and drink and rose up to play." We must not indulge in sexual immorality as some of them did, and twenty-three thousand fell in a single day. We must not put Christ to the test, as some of them did and were destroyed by serpents, nor grumble, as some of them did and were destroyed by the Destroyer.*
>
> ***Now these things happened to them as an example, but they were written down for our instruction, on whom the end of the ages has come****. Therefore let anyone who thinks that he stands take heed lest he fall.*
> *1 Corinthians 10: 1-12 [Emphasis mine]*

This alone should squash any imagination that what we have discussed in these pages isn't applicable to Modern Day Christianity...

Paul is telling his "New Testament" Gentile church in Corinth that the time period of scriptural history we just studied in the TaNaKh, the Exodus of Israel in the wilderness, *took place as examples for us.* Examples of what not to do and how not to be!

They were under the sukkah cloud of God; they were led by Moses, the prophet that Jesus Himself was fashioned after (Acts 3:22); they ate and drank spiritually, manna and Messiah respectively. *Nevertheless, with most of them God was not pleased, for they were overthrown in the wilderness.* The Complete Jewish Bible says, "their bodies were strewn across the desert." You do not want to be overthrown by God in the wilderness!

- In 1 Corinthians 10:7, Paul quotes Exodus 32 and the revelry that caused Israel to create the Golden Calf which in turn caused the destruction of the tablets that were written by the very finger of God. They broke the instruction of the Torah
- In 1 Corinthians 10:8, Paul references Numbers 25 when Israel began to whore with the daughters of Moab, sacrificed, ate and bowed to Baal of Peor, *"and twenty-three thousand fell in a single day."* They broke the instruction of the Torah
- And in 1 Corinthians 10:9, Paul references Numbers 21: *"We must not put Christ to the test, as some of them did and were destroyed by serpents"*

From Mount Hor they set out by the way to the Red Sea, to go around the land of Edom. And the people became impatient on the way. And the people spoke against God and against Moses, "Why have you brought us up out of Egypt to die in the wilderness? For there is no food and no water, and we loathe this worthless food." Then the LORD sent fiery serpents among the people, and they bit the people, so that many people of Israel died.

And the people came to Moses and said, "We have sinned, for we have spoken against the LORD and against you. Pray to the LORD, that he take away the serpents from

us." So Moses prayed for the people. And the LORD said to Moses, "Make a fiery serpent and set it on a pole, and everyone who is bitten, when he sees it, shall live." So Moses made a bronze serpent and set it on a pole. And if a serpent bit anyone, he would look at the bronze serpent and live.
Numbers 21: 4-9

> "Now these things happened to them as an example, but **they were written down for our instruction**, on whom the end of the ages has come." [Emphasis mine]

As much as the Church – be it Western, Romanized, Greek, Orthodox, whatever – so badly wants to believe that they're the "New Testament" era church – not the "Old Testament" church – and that the "Old Covenant" teachings don't apply to them, Paul, the Apostle to the Gentiles, is teaching his predominantly Gentile "New Testament" church that yes, the instructions of Torah in the TaNaKh most definitely applies to their "New Testament" instructional and spiritual well-being!

As we've also seen all throughout this exercise, we are *exactly* like Israel. And Israel refused to obey God's commandments, God's Torah, and they paid a heavy price for their disobedience; the entire generation that left Egypt never saw or stepped foot into the Promise Land. They perished in the wilderness! Paul obviously also knew this.

So here we have Paul, Christianity's token poster boy for all things "anti-Torah," telling us that Israel's example in the wilderness and the lessons / instructions… our takeaway: Obedience to Torah applies to us, "the New Testament church," and the penalty of disobedience is death, regardless of "non-Israelite" status:

- Obey God and His covenants and live
- Obey God and His Torah and live
- Obey God and keep His Feasts and live

"If you love me, you will keep my commandments. Whoever has my commandments and keeps them, he it is who loves me. And he who loves me will be loved by my Father, and I will love him and manifest myself to him."
John 14: 15, 21

> For all who have sinned without the law [Torah] will also perish without the law [Torah], and all who have sinned under the law [Torah] will be judged by the law [Torah]. **For it is not the hearers of the law [Torah] who are righteous before God, but the doers of the law [Torah] who will be justified.**
>
> For when Gentiles, who do not have the law, by nature do what the law requires, they are a law to themselves, even though they do not have the law. **They show that the work of the law [Torah] is written on their hearts**, while their conscience also bears witness, and their conflicting thoughts accuse or even excuse them on that day when, according to my gospel, God judges the secrets of men by Christ Jesus. Romans 2:12-16 [Emphasis mine]
>
> Circumcision is nothing, and uncircumcision is nothing; but obeying the commandments of God is everything.
> 1 Corinthians 7:19 (New Revised Standard)

Keeping God's commandments, being obedient to His Word, Torah, is for blessing and a long and good abundant life in the here and now (Exod. 23:25-26; Deut. 7:13-15). Not salvation. It's because of salvation that we choose to obey Him out of love for Him. We love Him because He first loved us, and it's out of that love for us that He invites us on this Amazing Journey from Exodus to Ingathering!

The Amazing Journey from Exodus to Ingathering

As we "unlocked" the Feasts together, we discovered how the first three Spring Feasts were foundational for our deliverance; the fourth feast established our relationship with God as His Bride; and the Fall Feasts represent the relational and eternal purposes of God through our cleansing repentance and redemption of our being gathered to Him. The entire journey points us toward our Bridegroom, Messiah – our Kinsman Redeemer! Each Feast Season speaks to a spiritual exchange between us, the Bride to be, and our Husbandman:

- Passover speaks to our sin and the sacrifice of blood required for atonement and our deliverance from Egypt, our carnal state, while Unleavened

Bread speaks to the purging of sin and bad doctrine / leaven from our lives and homes. Firstfruits: the joy of bringing firstfruits to ADONAI after the redemptive process of deliverance
- The Feast of Weeks' seven-week Count of the Omer keeps our focus on His continued spiritual and physical provision with the anticipation of the wheat harvest, whereas Shavuot (Weeks) itself speaks of the actual wheat harvest of God's physical provision in our lives and the spiritual provision of His Word, Torah, at Mount Sinai. Shavuot also reveals His desire to betroth us as His Bride through the covenant of Torah – His initial "marriage proposal" – along with the giving of His Holy Spirit at Pentecost, completing His richness required for us to live life abundantly
- The Fall Feasts speak of our being called to Him with the blast of the shofar; the consecration of our cleansing through repentance and the redemption given us with the ingathering of His people, His Bride, unto Himself; a people that would become His "tabernacle" in which to dwell in their midst in His Sabbath Rest!

He delivered us from under the yoke of Egyptian slavery to take us as His own people – to bring us to Himself – so as to be our God. This is the purpose for the exodus; the purpose for this amazing, seven-month Feast Journey from Exodus to Ingathering!

- To lead us to Sinai
- To betroth us unto Himself, and
- To bring us into His rest of Sukkot

If we obey Him fully and keep His covenant, He desires to make us His Treasured Possession from all the nations of the earth. We will be for Him a Kingdom of Priests and a Holy Nation, and He will bring us to the Land He swore to give Abraham, Isaac and Jacob as a possession.

Then one of the elders said to me, "Do not weep! See, the Lion of the tribe of Judah, the Root of David, has triumphed. He is able to open the scroll and its seven seals."

> Then I saw a Lamb, looking as if it had been slain, standing at the center of the throne, encircled by the four living creatures and the elders. The Lamb had seven horns and seven eyes, which are the seven spirits of God sent out into all the earth. He went and took the scroll from the right hand of him who sat on the throne.
>
> And when he had taken it, the four living creatures and the twenty-four elders fell down before the Lamb. Each one had a harp and they were holding golden bowls full of incense, which are the prayers of God's people. And they sang a new song, saying: "You are worthy to take the scroll and to open its seals, **because you were slain, and with your blood you purchased for God persons from every tribe and language and people and nation. You have made them to be a kingdom and priests to serve our God, and they will reign on the earth.**"
>
> Then I looked and heard the voice of many angels, numbering thousands upon thousands, and ten thousand times ten thousand. They encircled the throne and the living creatures and the elders. In a loud voice they were saying: "Worthy is the Lamb, who was slain, to receive power and wealth and wisdom and strength and honor and glory and praise!"
>
> Then I heard every creature in heaven and on earth and under the earth and on the sea, and all that is in them, saying: "To him who sits on the throne and to the Lamb be praise and honor and glory and power, for ever and ever!" The four living creatures said, "Amen," and the elders fell down and worshiped.
>
> Revelation 5:5-14 (NIV) [Emphasis mine]

That's the practical understanding of God's holy days: His yearly cycle of transformation into His Treasured Possession – a Kingdom of Holy Priests – God and man tabernacle-ing together forever!

And why? So that the nations will know:

> I will make a covenant of peace with them. It shall be an everlasting covenant with them. And I will set them in their land and multiply them, and will set my sanctuary in their

midst forevermore. My dwelling place shall be with them, and I will be their God, and they shall be my people. Then the nations will know that I am the LORD who sanctifies Israel, when my sanctuary is in their midst forevermore."
Ezekiel 37:26-28

The Feast of Tabernacles – the Feast of Booths, this Feast of Ingathering, Sukkot – is the culmination and the designed, desired end result of the exodus from Egypt. We've been gathered by Him, for Him and *in* Him! So that the nations will know…

Every year, the God of Abraham, Isaac and Jacob invites you on a journey – a journey of deliverance, repentance, and redemption.

This seven-month journey begins in the Spring…

With the deliverance from Egypt through the Passover Lamb – commemorated by the eating of Unleavened Bread – and honored with the Firstfruits Offering.

Across the seven weeks of the wheat harvest into Summer en route to Mount Sinai – the very reason for our deliverance. On Shavuot, He proposes His unending Love to us, His Bride, and indwells us with His Spirit on Mt Zion.

In the Fall, on Yom Teruah, with the blast of the shofar, He reminds us of Sinai where we wavered at His proposal of marriage.

The cleansing repentance of Yom Kippur – our "At-One-ment" – prepares our hearts and spirits for the redemptive ingathering of Tabernacles – Sukkot – where He beckons us into His rest and the Wedding Feast of the Lamb!!

This is the purpose for delivering Israel from Egypt.
This is the purpose for delivering *you* from Egypt.
This is your amazing Journey from Exodus to Ingathering!

Let us rejoice and exult and give him the glory, **for the marriage of the Lamb has come, and his Bride has made herself ready**; *And I saw the holy city, new Jerusalem, coming down out of heaven from God, prepared as a bride adorned for her husband. Then came one of the seven angels who had the seven bowls full of the seven last plagues and spoke to me, saying, "Come, I will show you the Bride, the wife of the Lamb." The Spirit and the Bride say, "Come."*

> And let the one who hears say, "Come." And let the one who is thirsty come; let the one who desires take the water of life without price.
>
> Revelation 19:7; 21:2, 9; 22:17 [Emphasis mine]

The Feasts Summarized

Rosh Chodesh

The Feasts have an important cyclical order to them. You find this cyclical rhythm in the weekly cycle of the Sabbath, in the monthly cycle of the New Moon, and in the yearly cycle of the Feasts themselves. The Feast cycles take us from harvest (Passover and Firstfruits) to harvest (Feast of Weeks), toward increase (Shavuot / Pentecost), and culminating with the year-end harvest gathering of the Feast of Ingathering – all with an aspect of firstfruits along the way.

The New Moon – Rosh Chodesh – determines the beginning of the month and, in turn, the dates for the Feasts Days (Num. 10:10).

> From new moon to new moon, and from Sabbath to Sabbath, all flesh shall come to worship before me, declares the LORD.
>
> Isaiah 66:23

As a family and as a community, Rosh Chodesh is the perfect time for thanksgiving and reflection on the month behind. Celebrate Rosh Chodesh as a festive family celebration with the blowing of the shofar, worship and a meal. The New Moon is also the time to look with anticipation toward all that ADONAI is doing physically, financially, spiritually and prophetically in our lives. Look forward with a teaching on the meaning of the new month. Through prayer and/or inquiring of the prophets like the Shunammite woman had a habit of doing (2 Kings 4:22-23), look forward prophetically for God's revelation for the month to come.

Rosh Chodesh is also the time to bring to ADONAI the first portions of your harvest: Firstfruits. Ask the Father what your monthly firstfruits offering amount should be. It can be a monetary amount from your job, a side venture or a bonus. It can also be actual vegetables and/or fruits from your garden. Your monthly firstfruits is the first of your harvest, be it monetary or otherwise. Honoring the Father with your first and best is the principle behind firstfruits.

Firstfruits is an act of honoring God with the first of what you receive, whereas offerings are an expression of thanksgiving, an act of worship for God's blessings in your life. Both of these, firstfruits and offerings, are given to the priest of the house (your church, your home church, etc.,) and the tithe belongs to the Levites, exclusively. Here are a couple passages regarding the blessings of firstfruits giving:

> *And the first of all the firstfruits of all kinds, and every offering of all kinds from all your offerings, shall belong to the priests. You shall also give to the priests the first of your dough, that a blessing may rest on your house.*
> Ezekiel 44:30

> *Honor the LORD with your wealth and with the firstfruits of all your produce; then your barns will be filled with plenty, and your vats will be bursting with wine.*
> Proverbs 3:9-10

Shabbat

Shabbat is foundational for life and foundational to living life in God's cycles of blessing:

- He made Shabbat holy at creation (Gen. 2:3)
- He instructs us to keep Shabbat holy (Exod. 20:8)
- Keeping Shabbat is His sign between and *for us to know* that He sanctifies us (Exod. 31:13), and
- He made Shabbat holy *for* us (Exod. 31:14)

It's His holy rest on our behalf, and Shabbat is His covenant sign *with* us. Keeping Shabbat is the sign that we are in covenant *with* and *in* Him in exactly the same way that keeping His commandments is the sign that we love His Son Jesus. It's also a great way to begin applying Deuteronomy 6 into your family dynamic.

Establishing a weekly cycle of this blessing and holiness in your life, business, home and family is foundational for your blessing and success. Shabbat is a family affair. I tell people all the time that if every American Christian family would do Shabbat, it would single-handedly change our country. Here's the practical breakdown of what I mean:

- You're having dinner as a family around the table once a week - every week

Apparently, this is more of a big deal than I had realized. When I teach Shabbat to people, that is the most novel of ideas to them: *regularly scheduled family dinners around the table.* Since the beginning of our little family, we have had dinner at the table Monday through Friday, consistently. So having dinner as a family around the table "once a week - every week" wasn't much of a stretch for us. Since it apparently is for many, this alone is going to change your family dynamic for the better.

- Mom (or the lady of the house) lights the Shabbat candles and ushers in the Sabbath rest / peace: Shabbat shalom

This first step sets the tone for the evening. If families aren't accustomed to eating dinner around the table, are the children accustomed to seeing and hearing mom pray blessing and peace over them and their house?

- Dad blesses the children

The dad is now functioning as the High Priest of his home. By modeling Jesus in blessing his children, both mom and the children are being blessed, even if they don't realize it. Think of how "atmosphere-changing" this is to the home.

- Dad and the children bless mom from Proverbs 31

This is huge. Now the children see and hear dad not only affirm his wife and their mother, they also see dad humbling himself before the entire family and declaring 17 verses over mom as he lays his hands on her. The children, prompted by their father, now lay hands on their mother as they declare four verses over her. How would you like that, moms?

- Dad blesses Israel

Putting things into perspective by blessing God's Land and His people, a people that you've been grafted into, as a family, is putting things into proper alignment. This is something you want your children to know and understand.

- Dad leads the family in communion

This is the biggest thing. I'm amazed at how many dads have never led their families in communion in the privacy of their own home. The results of this are life-altering if you do and if you don't. This is Priesthood, men.

If you're still not convinced, re-read Exodus 31:13-17

Jesus said that Shabbat was made for man, not man for Shabbat. It serves us, we don't serve it. We keep Shabbat out of obedience, not out of legalistic ritual. Shabbat is life. Covenant life. And covenant life is freedom, not bondage. Remember Shabbat, and keep it holy. Amen.

Passover / Feast of Unleavened Bread

Passover is the foundation of the covenant relationship made between God and His people. Passover is also a declaration of faith that we have been redeemed by the blood of the Lamb! This "Passover Covenant" bridged the gap between man and God. Remember why God wanted to take Israel out of Egypt:

> *Say therefore to the people of Israel, 'I am ADONAI, and I will bring you out from under the burdens of the Egyptians, and I will deliver you from slavery to them, and I will redeem you with an outstretched arm and with great acts of judgment.* **I will take you to be my people, and I will be your God**, *and you shall know that I am ADONAI your God, who has brought you out from under the burdens of the Egyptians.* **I will bring you into the land that I swore to give to Abraham, to Isaac, and to Jacob. I will give it to you for a possession.** *I am ADONAI.'"*
>
> Exodus 6:6-8 [Emphasis mine]

"I will take you to be my people." He made that oath, that promise, that covenant, through blood. Without this Passover Covenant, there is no blood atonement, therefore there is no "people," and likewise, there would be no "Israel of God." The inhabitants in the land of Egypt died in separation, died in their sin; whereas, Israel was baptized into the Lamb. Isaiah confirms that this covenant with the Passover lamb, *The* Passover Lamb, is the foundation of the covenant relationship between God and His people (Is. 42:1-9). And this covenant of redemption, this Passover

Lamb, was made and slain before the foundations of the earth:

> For you know that it was not with perishable things such as silver or gold that you were redeemed from the empty way of life handed down to you from your ancestors, but with the precious blood of Christ, a lamb without blemish or defect. He was chosen before the creation of the world, but was revealed in these last times for your sake.
> 1 Peter 1:18-20 (NIV)

Passover speaks of our sin and the sacrifice of blood required for atonement. Unleavened Bread speaks of the purging of sin and bad doctrine / leaven from our lives and homes. Firstfruits: the joy of bringing firstfruits to ADONAI after the redemptive process of deliverance.

We eat unleavened bread, matzah, out of obedience to the instruction and to show that we are "unleavened" / without sin and erroneous doctrine before Him. This covenant is made by the eating of matzah (Exod. 13:7-9).

Feast of Firstfruits / The Omer Count

Israel was to put the first portion of their harvest into a basket and offer it to ADONAI by giving their firstfruits to the priest thus declaring God's goodness and faithfulness. If they would honor Him in this way at the yearly Feast of Firstfruits, He would bless them incredibly. The monthly firstfruits offerings are an example of these firstfruits brought at the close of the first weekly Shabbat after Passover.

Being the first is significant, and honoring the Father with your first, as a sign of your source of blessing, is important to Him and significant to you. Firstfruits: the choicest and the best.

The yearly pilgrimage of Passover to Jerusalem to be presented before ADONAI in commemoration of their corporate deliverance, salvation and provision culminates with the Feast of Firstfruits.

Israel is to bring a sheaf (omer) of the firstfruits of the harvest of the land (the first barley grain crop to ripen) to the priest. The priest would then wave the sheaf before ADONAI, as a dedication to Him, to be accepted on behalf of the people. A male lamb was then sacrificed as a burnt offering (Lev. 23:12) to ADONAI along with a food offering, a *minchah* (Strong's #H4503: a gift, tribute, an offering), of unleavened bread mixed with oil and a drink offering of wine (Lev. 23:13). The wave offering had to be performed before the crop could be used (Lev. 23:14). Did you notice the offering that accompanies the wave-sheaf offering?

- A lamb
- Unleavened bread mixed with oil
- Wine

All of the elements that represent Messiah: for the Feast of Firstfruits is when the Anointed Messiah (the Sacrificial Lamb) would rise from the dead (unleavened and oiled) as the accepted offering – paid with His Blood (the wine), to be presented before the Father for His acceptance on behalf of the people (wave-sheaf offering)! Hallelujah!!

A practical way for us to observe the Feast of Firstfruits today is to have communion (with matzah) and worship while bringing your firstfruits offering before ADONAI.

Remember the cycles and how the feasts are synonymous with God's agricultural calendar; the importance of their cyclical order; how we find these cyclical rhythms weekly (Shabbat), monthly (Rosh Chodesh), and yearly (the Feasts). We discussed how these cycles take us from harvest (Passover and Firstfruits) to harvest (Feast of Weeks) towards increase (Shavuot / Pentecost), culminating with the year-end harvest gathering of the Feast of Ingathering – all with an aspect of firstfruits along the way. We could say that firstfruits is the lifestyle indicative to Kingdom Living: "...on earth as it is in heaven."

This ever-forward yearly momentum of "further up and further in" speaks to our lifestyle participation. Our growth in understanding the wisdom of applying this "Kingdom Lifestyle" through our worship of giving and the sowing into of firstfruits will reap provision and blessing in our lives. Firstfruits is spiritual in nature, intended to produce a Kingdom mindset in us just as Torah is spiritual in nature, intended to produce Kingdom blessings in our lives. This act of honoring God with the first of what you receive is all about His cyclical rhythm of increase birthed out of your obedience to His word.

This cyclical rhythm from harvest to harvest; this "Firstfruits Lifestyle of Blessing and Provision," continues from the Feast of Firstfruits all the way to our increase with the start of the Counting of the Omer / The Feast of Weeks: the forty-nine-day countdown to the (wheat) harvest festival of Shavuot.

The Counting of the Omer / The Feast of Weeks is the count up to that wheat harvest, Shavuot / Pentecost, in anticipation and in remembrance of what He was about to do; the covenant of Torah. For seven weeks / seven Shabbats, every night at dinner during the Omer Count, we say out loud the number of the day and week that we're on, and on the 50th day, it's a High Shabbat of rejoicing.

The Passover, the exodus from Egypt, the 40-day trek through the wilderness to Mount Sinai; all with one motive behind it all:

> Say therefore to the people of Israel, 'I am ADONAI, and I will bring you out from under the burdens of the Egyptians, and I will deliver you from slavery to them, and I will redeem you with an outstretched arm and with great acts of judgment. **I will take you to be my people, and I will be your God**, and you shall know that I am ADONAI your God, who has brought you out from under the burdens of the Egyptians.'"

Exodus 6:6-7 [Emphasis mine]

Shavuot / Pentecost

Exodus 19 finds Moses and all of Israel assembled before the Living God at the base of Mount Sinai. This is when and where God established His instructions for those that would call upon His name; His instructions for mankind that make the voluntary decision to serve Him; His covenant instructions for those who call themselves "Believers" – the wedding vows, if you will, between the Bridegroom and His Bride – the vows His Bride voluntarily makes covenant promises with to be known as His. These are the instructions that "set you apart" from the rest, the covenants that make Him your God and you His people, a nation of Kings and Priests (Exodus 24).

Passover, the redemption and salvation from physical slavery and death and the resulting exodus from Egypt, was orchestrated with a single goal in mind: an encounter 50 days later with the Living God – Shavuot:

- Deliverance from spiritual slavery
- Redemption from sin
- Consecration from paganism to holiness

- Identity as His treasured people, through the
- Revelation of His Torah

All of these speak of covenant, and all of these speak of Messiah. Shavuot / Pentecost is our bridge between the deliverance of the Spring Feasts and the cleansing redemption of the Fall feasts through the marriage betrothal of Shavuot between God and Israel as His Bride (Isa. 49:18).

We saw this in Exodus 6:7 above and we saw it in Revelation 21:3 with the New Jerusalem coming out of the sky "as a bride adorned for her husband!" Here's Exodus 6:7:

> ***I will take you to be my people, and I will be your God***, *and you shall know that I am the LORD your God, who has brought you out from under the burdens of the Egyptians.* [Emphasis mine]

And then Revelation 21:3:

> *And I heard a loud voice from the throne saying, "Behold, the dwelling place of God is with man. He will dwell with them,* ***and they will be his people, and God himself will be with them as their God****.* [Emphasis mine]

This is the gospel unto salvation!

This is in effect God's "Master Plan" for humanity: The Aleph (Alpha) and the Tav (Omega); "the Wedding Feast of the Passover Lamb that was slain before the foundations of the earth!" Our future, as seen in John's Revelation, *started all the way back in Egypt!*

Because of the fulfillment of Messiah at Passover (death), the Feast of Unleavened Bread (burial) and the Feast of Firstfruits (resurrection); because of the indwelling of the Holy Spirit at Pentecost, the Covenant made at Sinai (Shavuot) is attainable: Zion!

At Sinai, Torah was given, and the covenant to keep those instructions occurred: Shavuot. Messiah rose from the dead, the power of Holy Spirit – the Fire of Sinai – fell as covenant Fire on those in the upper room to keep those instructions for Zion's sake: Pentecost (Acts 2:1-4). The writer of Hebrews says this regarding Sinai (Shavuot) and Zion (Pentecost):

> *For you have not come to what may be touched, a blazing fire and darkness and gloom and a tempest and the sound of a trumpet and a voice whose words made the hearers beg that no further messages be spoken to them. (Exod. 19 & 20)*
>
> *For they could not endure the order that was given, "If even a beast touches the mountain, it shall be stoned." Indeed, so terrifying was the sight that Moses said, "I tremble with fear."*
>
> *But you have come to Mount Zion and to the city of the living God, the heavenly Jerusalem, and to innumerable angels in festal gathering, and to the assembly of the firstborn who are enrolled in heaven, and to God, the judge of all, and to the spirits of the righteous made perfect, and to Jesus, the mediator of a new covenant, and to the sprinkled blood that speaks a better word than the blood of Abel.*
>
> Hebrews 12:18-24

The writer of Hebrews is clearly referencing, quoting and paraphrasing what occurred on Mount Sinai and uses the word "festal gathering" in describing the present reality of Mount Zion, because the writer understands the richness of the Feasts in our lives – our "New Testament" lives – and the crucial role they play in our spiritual developmental well-being. He even makes reference to the pilgrimage instruction for firstborn males as a type of "firstfruits" and the "sprinkled blood" of Yom Kippur!

So while all of Jerusalem was reaffirming their covenant with Torah during the second of the Three Pilgrimage Festivals, God was indwelling those that had aligned themselves with Him and His Word (Jesus) in the Upper Room with His Spirit – repositioning Torah to its original place: the invisible intentions of the heart, as we saw in Matthew 5.

God betrothed Himself to Israel through the giving of Torah as His marriage contract. Israel failed to consummate the wedding ceremony at Sinai, but a way for covenant was made in Messiah. We see that Jesus is the Bridegroom, and Believers are betrothed to Him. Jesus is man's final hope for that consummation; the consummation of "I will take (marry) you (the bride) to be my people (my wife), and I (the Bridegroom) will be your God (our Husband)."

Father God now calls to us with the blast of the Shofar (Yom Teruah / Feast of Trumpets) when we will ready and consecrate ourselves (Yom Kippur / Day of Atonement) as separated and presentable unto Him – for the Feast of Ingathering (Sukkot / Feast of Tabernacles) is upon us!

Feast of Trumpets (Yom Teruah) / Day of Atonement (Yom Kippur)

Sixteen weeks later, and it's the first of the three Fall Feasts: The Feast of Trumpets / Yom Teruah. Teruah literally means "shout" or "to make a loud noise." On the first day of the seventh month of Ethanim, on this specific Rosh Chodesh, it is to be a High Shabbat of remembrance, a memorial day; a solemn reminder marked or announced with shouts and blasts of the shofar.

It's a reminder of the blowing of the shofar from four months ago when we were summoned to the base of Mount Sinai by the blast of God's Shofar. Four months ago, we were summoned to the covenants of Torah. We are now being instructed to remember that call; the how, when and *why* He approached us with Life giving precepts.

We are to remember that Sinai was the reason for the exodus and it was Sinai that prophetically speaks of the marriage between man and God. Israel never consummated those marriage vows at Sinai, making Jesus man's final hope for that consummation; the consummation of "I will take (marry) you (the bride) to be my people (my wife), and I (the Bridegroom) will be your God (our Husband)."

He wants us to remember His shofar blast of Exodus 6:7!!!

He wants us to remember that this is the gospel unto salvation; His "Master Plan;" that He loves us, desires us and has taken us as our Bridegroom!

This is what we're supposed to be remembering on Yom Teruah, this holy Rosh Chodesh; this solemn day of remembrance marked with the blasts of shofars; this High Shabbat.

> *Blessed are the people who know the festal shout (teruah), who walk, O LORD, in the light of your face...*
> *Psalms 89:15*

Yom Teruah, Yom Kippur and the first day of Sukkot all happen within a two-week period. It's essentially one event. Spiritually and practically, we're being instructed to remember Sinai, repent and be prepared for the ingathering; prepare ourselves through the atonement on and of Yom Kippur for yet another opportunity to be gathered – one last time (the "end of the year") – by the blast of the shofar for Sukkot!

Atonement, or "Kippur," means "to cleanse." In Leviticus 16:12-20, this is what Moses' brother, Aaron the High Priest, is doing. He's cleansing Israel. Verse 16 says:

> Thus he shall make atonement [kippur] for the Holy Place, because of the uncleannesses of the people of Israel and because of their transgressions, all their sins. And so he shall do for the tent of meeting, which dwells with them in the midst of their uncleannesses.

Aaron is cleansing – "decontaminating" – the Holy of Holies, the Tent of Meeting and the Altar from spiritual and physical impurities (verse 20). Thus, the reason for Yom Kippur is the cleansing of our temples from our sins:

> For on this day shall atonement [kippur] be made for you to cleanse you. You shall be clean before ADONAI from all your sins. It is a Sabbath of solemn rest to you, and you shall afflict yourselves; it is a statute forever.
> Leviticus 16:30

> I will sprinkle clean water on you, and you shall be clean from all your uncleannesses, and from all your idols I will cleanse you. And I will give you a new heart, and a new spirit I will put within you. And I will remove the heart of stone from your flesh and give you a heart of flesh. And I will put my Spirit within you, and cause you to walk in my statutes and be careful to obey my rules.
> Ezekiel 36:25-27

Yom Kippur is the Day of Cleansing. It is a High Shabbat; a holy convocation when no ordinary work is done. It is a day of repentance, self-examination and atonement; "At-One-Ment" with the Living God. We are to "afflict" ourselves; busy ourselves with bowed-down humility and present a food offering to ADONAI.

Father God has called us with the blast of the Shofar (Yom Teruah / Feast of Trumpets). We have readied and consecrated ourselves through His cleansing atonement (Yom Kippur / Day of Cleansing) – separated and presentable unto Him – for the Feast of Ingathering (Sukkot / Feast of Tabernacles) has arrived!

Feast of Tabernacles / Booths – Festival of Ingathering – Sukkot

The Feast of Tabernacles, Sukkot (the plural of "sukkah"), signifies our wandering in the desert wilderness after the exodus from Egypt, His provision on our behalf and our dependence on His care all along the way (Deut. 29:5). This Feast, the third of the Three Pilgrimage Festivals, also known as "The Feast," reminds us that He had Israel "dwell in booths" after their deliverance from Egypt. These temporary dwelling places, these booths, are individually known as a "sukkah."

> "You shall dwell in booths for seven days. All native Israelites shall dwell in booths, that your generations may know that I made the people of Israel dwell in booths when I brought them out of the land of Egypt: I am ADONAI your God."
> Leviticus 23: 42-43

In remembrance, and so that future generations will also know that ADONAI made the people of Israel dwell in booths when He brought them out of the land of Egypt, we are commanded to dwell in temporary shelters for seven days. This temporary dwelling, this booth, is also called a sukkah. Think "camping." Assembling a sukkah every year is great for the entire family. It's like building a fort for the kids and the kid in you!

The theme of "temporary dwelling place" and "temporary physical body" also speaks to our temporary journey through this earth as pilgrims on our way to our final Spiritual Sukkah:

> By faith Abraham obeyed when he was called to go out to a place that he was to receive as an inheritance. And he went out, not knowing where he was going. By faith he went to live in the land of promise, as in a foreign land, living in tents with Isaac and Jacob, heirs with him of the same

promise. For he was looking forward to the city that has foundations, whose designer and builder is God.

These all died in faith, not having received the things promised, but having seen them and greeted them from afar, and having acknowledged that they were strangers and exiles on the earth. For people who speak thus make it clear that they are seeking a homeland. If they had been thinking of that land from which they had gone out, they would have had opportunity to return. But as it is, they desire a better country, that is, a heavenly one. Therefore God is not ashamed to be called their God, for he has prepared for them a city.
Hebrews 11:8-10, 13-16

The physical, prophetic and ultimately spiritual significance of Sukkot is the ingathering of God's people unto Himself – the "dwelling among" – the "being in His Rest." Sukkot brings us from the solemnest day of the year, Yom Kippur, to the most festive eight days of the year five days later – from repentance to rejoicing redemption!

Sukkot also carries the dual historical / spiritual and agricultural significance we've seen in the other Pilgrimage Festivals. Sukkot commemorates forty years of wandering in the desert wilderness while living in temporary dwellings, and agriculturally, Sukkot celebrates the gathering of the end of the year harvest known as *Chag ha-Asif*: "of the harvest," the Festival of Ingathering (Exod. 23:16).

Agriculturally, Passover paralleled the planting and harvesting of the barley season and Shavuot the wheat harvest, while Sukkot is the season for harvesting produce. Physically and spiritually, all the crops for the year have been harvested and gathered. God's cyclical provision is a time for rejoicing!

This ongoing theme of harvesting, reaping and sowing is one of God's "Love Languages" towards us; the increase of Himself, in and through us, returning to Him as fruit. Just like in the parables of the minas and the talents, He expects a return from our stewardship of His increase. Sukkot, this appointed time of "ingathering," is that reaping of the harvest in and of our lives of His sowing.

> He calls to the heavens above and to the earth, that he may judge his people: "Gather to me my faithful ones, who made a covenant with me by sacrifice!"
> Psalms 50:4-5

Final Thoughts

Fundamentally and foundationally, the Feasts are designed to aid us as individuals, families and communities, in visualizing and experiencing the life cycles God intends for us to live with, in and for Him – this side of glory. Essentially, the obedient act of keeping His appointed times, His holy convocations and rehearsals, align us with Father God.

All of the Feasts are designed to be a substantial part of our identity; individually, corporately, physically and spiritually. So one last time, I would like for you to imagine again the richness these yearly experiences, these yearly pilgrimages – the richness this yearly journey brought to communities, families and individuals and how rich your life and the lives of your family and community will become because of your desire to align yourself with God's annual covenants.

If there was one way to describe the purposes of God through religion and the biblical text, it would be the theme of God's desire to dwell with man. This theme of "dwelling together" is at the core of our Amazing Journey from Exodus to Ingathering and at the very heart of everything God has orchestrated on our behalf. It's the reason behind placing Adam in the Garden.

The Song of Moses that was sung after the victory at the Red Sea, at the very beginning of this Feast Journey, hints of it:

> You will bring them in and plant them on the mountains of your inheritance. In the place you made your dwelling, your sanctuary, established by your hands.
> Based on Exodus 15:17

> Blessed are those who do His commandments, that they may have the right to the tree of life, and may enter through the gates into the city.
> Revelation 22:14 (NKJV)

CHAPTER 10

FEAST OF DEDICATION (HANUKKAH) / PURIM
Invasion, Revolt, Lights and a Queen

At that time the Feast of Dedication took place at Jerusalem. It was winter, and Jesus was walking in the temple, in the colonnade of Solomon.
John 10:22-23

We see in the Gospels that the majority of Jesus' ministry took place in the Galil, "Galilee of the Gentiles," where He was also headquartered in Capernaum. We also saw that He made pilgrimage to Jerusalem for the Feasts but would sleep in Bethany some two miles away (Jn. 11:18; Mt. 21:17; Mk. 11:11) at the home of Martha, Mary and Lazarus.

In John chapter 10, we find that Jesus is in Jerusalem during the Feast of Dedication (Hebrew *"Hanukkah"*), also known as the Festival of Lights.

Hanukkah, or the romanized *Chanukah* or *Hanukah*, was first discussed in Chapter 2 when the Seven Rabbinic Mitzvahs (commands) not found in scripture were initially addressed.

On the 25th of Kislev are the days of Hanukkah, which are eight... these were appointed a Festival with Hallel and thanksgiving.
Gemara (Shabbat 21b)

Hanukkah / the Feast of Dedication is the Jewish festival of the rededication of the Temple. It also commemorates Israel's victory over the Greeks during the Maccabee revolt. It is an eight-day event beginning on the 25th of the Ninth Month, known by its Babylonian name of Kislev.

Chanukkah is probably one of the best known Jewish holidays because of its proximity to Christmas. Many think of this holiday as the

Jewish Christmas, adopting many of the Christmas customs. It is bitterly ironic that this holiday, which has its roots in a revolution against assimilation and the suppression of Jewish religion, has become the most assimilated, secular holiday on our calendar.
(Source: Judaism 101 "Chanukkah" http://www.jewfaq.org/holiday7.htm)

Though not found in the TaNaKh, the story of Hanukkah is found in the Apocrypha's First and Second Maccabees of the Septuagint, the Mishna and the Talmud.

A Brief History

Invasion

Alexander the Great's conquest of Persia, Syria, Egypt and Israel in 332 BCE established a moderate version of Hellenistic culture in the region. The region was allowed to continue observing their various forms of religion while the study of the Greek language, customs and dress were encouraged.

Over a century later, around 168 BCE, one of Alexander's successors, a Syrian king named Antiochus IV of the Seleucid dynasty, controlled the region and began to persecute and oppress the Jews for various reasons which are debated by biblical scholars and academics alike. What we do know is that the changes and restrictions were severe:

- A Hellenistic "High Priest" was appointed to the Temple
- A statue of Apollo was erected in the Temple
- Swine became a mandatory altar sacrifice, thereby desecrating the Temple further – the sacrificing of pigs on the altar began on Kislev / December 25th in honor of Apollo's birthday
- Torah scrolls were confiscated and burned, and the study of Torah was outlawed
- Eating pork was now mandatory, and the refusal to eat swine was punishable by death
- Circumcision was illegal and punishable by death
- The observance of Shabbat was also made illegal, and
- Pagan worship was legally forced upon Israel

It is said that a respected elder of 90 years old, Rabbi Eliezer, was ordered to eat pork to set an example for the others. When he refused, he was instructed to make it seem as if he was eating the swine by holding it to his lips. Upon that refusal, Rabbi Eliezer was executed. (Source: *The Complete Story of Chanukah* by Nissan Mindel)

Revolt

There are varying accounts of the Maccabee uprising.

Simply put, the outrageous actions of Antiochus IV incited a rebellion organized by the Hasmonean family of Mattityahu the High Priest. The Maccabees, as the resistance became to be known, were led by the five sons of Mattityahu, the eldest being named Judah. They waged a victorious three-year campaign, culminating with the Maccabees ordering of the construction of a new altar and the cleansing of the Temple for rededication. The rededication took place on the 25th of the Ninth Month known as Kislev in 165 BCE.

One account suggests two factions joined forces against Antiochus IV: the nationalists, led by Mattityahu, and the religious traditionalist Chasidim (Hasidic), forerunners of the Pharisees (no direct relation to the modern Hasidic movement).

One narrative has a Syrian army commander demanding that Mattityahu be a community example by sacrificing a pig on a pagan altar. Mattityahu not only refuses but, like Phineas, kills the Hebrew who volunteers to follow the order of making the abominable sacrifice and the Syrian commander as well. The killing of the commander and the subsequent attack on the Syrian army that followed is said to have initiated the revolt.

Another narrative notes this ragamuffin rebellion, fighting a guerilla war against well-trained and well-armed mercenary Greeks, as being made up of simple Torah-observant farmers armed with pitchforks, spears and rocks from the ground.

Lights

Tradition holds, as recorded in the Gemara, that after defeating Antiochus IV and driving his forces out from the Temple, very little of the prescribed oil (Exod. 27:20) to light and keep the Temple menorah lit (Exod. 25:31-40; Lev. 24:2) was left or undefiled by the Syrian-Greeks.

There was only one-day's worth left, and proper scriptural preparation of this oil was said to take up to eight days. The "Miracle of Lights" is that this one-day supply of oil lasted and burned for the entire eight-day period needed to prepare the fresh batch. Judah, the leader of the Maccabees and the eldest son of the now deceased High Priest Mattityahu, instituted an eight-day festival to commemorate the miracle.

Josephus, in his book *Antiquities of the Jews*, gives an account of Judah's establishing of the annual and extravagant eight-day festival memorializing the rededication of the Temple and the restoration of Torah observances referring to the feast as "Lights:"

> *Now Judas celebrated the festival of the restoration of the sacrifices of the temple for eight days, and omitted no sort of pleasures thereon; but he feasted them upon very rich and splendid sacrifices; and he honored God, and delighted them by hymns and psalms. Nay, they were so very glad at the revival of their customs, when, after a long time of intermission, they unexpectedly had regained the freedom of their worship, that they made it a law for their posterity, that they should keep a festival, on account of the restoration of their temple worship, for eight days. And from that time to this we celebrate this festival, and call it Lights.*

(Source: Josephus: *Antiquities of the Jews* 12/7:7)

A suggestion by some scholars holds that, since no mention of the miracle of lights in correlation with the rededication of the Temple is found outside of the Gemara, some 600 years after the fact, including the two books of Maccabees, is it possible that the eight day festivities founded by Judah to remember the rededication of the Temple and the restoration of Torah observance was a belated observance of Sukkot, which they had not been allowed to observe under Greek occupation?

Hanukkah Today

As stated in Chapter 2, Hanukkah is a traditional Jewish holiday, whereas all the observances we have studied thus far are scriptural and have the unique delineation of "Mine" – as in "God's" – making them "God's Holidays"; not manmade holy days.

Hanukkah is also not a "religious" holiday per se, unlike the religious foundation and significance found in all of the Feasts of Leviticus 23. The traditional candle lighting is as "religious" as Hanukkah gets but, for example, our family thanks God for the continued deliverance of His people and the Land and we pray for the continued peace of Jerusalem and Messiah's quick return during Hanukkah's candle lighting.

With Hanukkah candle lighting, the candles are displayed in a candelabrum called a "hanukkiah." Where a menorah has six branches plus a centered branch that is known as a "shamash" (servant), displaying a total of seven candles, a hanukkiah has eight branches plus the shamash, displaying a total of nine candles, one for each night of the festival.

Some other traditional parts of the celebration are eating fried foods such as latkes (woohoo!) because of the importance of oil to Hanukkah and playing the dreidel: gambling with a squared top.

The traditional explanation of this game is that during the time of Antiochus' oppression, those who wanted to study Torah (an illegal activity) would conceal their activity by playing gambling games with a top (a common and legal activity) whenever an official or inspector was within sight.
(Source: Judaism 101 "Chanukkah" http://www.jewfaq.org/holiday7.htm)

Dreidels, a widely recognized symbol representing Hanukkah, are spinning tops marked with the four Hebrew letters of Nun, Gimel, Hei and Shin, an acronym for the Hebrew phrase *"Nes Gadol Hayah Sham"* – "A great miracle happened there" in reference to the miracle of lights, the oil.

For game play, the letters also stand for the Yiddish words *"nit"* (nothing), *"gantz"* (all), *"halb"* (half) and *"shtell"* (put), also known as the rules for the game of Dreidel:

1. Everyone puts in a *"gelt"* (today, usually a large coin made out of chocolate)
2. A player spins the dreidel
3. Landing on Nun means nothing happens
4. Landing on Gimel means you get the whole pot (remember kids, this is gambling!)
5. Land on Hei, and you only get half the pot, and
6. When you land on Shin, you put a gelt into the pot

Empty pot? Everyone puts in a gelt, and you keep playing until it's time for more latkes!!

Gift giving, though not an original tradition to Hanukkah, has become as popular as playing the dreidel or the giving and receiving of gelt.

How Do You Spell H.A.N.U.K.K.A.H?

Hanukkah is not an alternative to Christmas in our community or within our family. As a family, we didn't actually celebrate Christmas, per se. Based on our understanding of the roots of Christmas, we never did the tree, ornaments, lights, wreath or nativity – all of the paraphernalia and traditions that accompany the event, because of the simple fact that the observance has absolutely nothing to do with the birth of Messiah – Sukkot does, as explained in Chapter 8. We hold to the position that "Christianizing" paganism, syncretism (the mixture of the holy and the profane,) is highly frowned upon by God (Deut. 12:1-4, 28-32). We briefly discussed this and saw this in part throughout this journey of Unlocking the Feasts, and it can be seen all throughout Israel's struggle of obedience in the TaNaKh.

Unlike the Romanized Western Church's alternative, the celebration of Hanukkah isn't a "good" religious exercise rooted in paganism. In fact, Hanukkah is rooted in aligning *with* the absolutes of God's scriptural instructions in the face of pagan worship.

Before our family started celebrating Hanukkah, what we did do during the Christmas holiday season was a traditional "Christmas Day" meal (it was actually more of a Thanksgiving Day meal) that we prepared and served for others. It started out as a way to minister to seminary students in the area that were away from home and family that did participate in Christmas. This grew to additional friends, family members and others joining us that were also away from family and who did observe "Christ's mass." We did this as a ministry for them simply because people tend to become homesick and lonely during this time. Also, not everyone around the table professed the Christian faith, so it was quite a diverse group.

We welcomed everyone with open arms, explaining that this wasn't a formal or religious gathering and that it had to do with friendship and community more than anything else. We gave a very basic and brief version of the concept behind the holiday for the benefit of those that did observe, explaining how it wasn't based on any biblical text whatsoever and pointing out what the biblical text did state. It was informative, non-judgmental, and the focus was family, friends, food and fun. We played an always-entertaining game of White Elephant, listened to the classic holiday songs – including the classic duet between David Bowie and Bing Crosby – and attempted to bring joy to their lives during what was potentially the loneliest time of the year. We do the exact same thing today with Hanukkah.

There's still no tree, no "Christmas" ornaments, lights, wreath or nativity scene. You will find typical and traditional Hanukkah decorations, music and foods (potato latkes and jelly doughnuts!!!) Since our Hanukkah Party is held toward the end of the eight days, both menorahs and hanukkiahs are alight with candles. You might see YouTube videos of Hanukkah parodies from artists like the Maccabeats and "Fiddler on the Roof" playing on a loop in the background. It's a come-and-go celebration. A sort of buffet soiree where Christians, Mormons, Jews, pagans, Buddhists and the non-affiliated in our lives can come and enjoy themselves. Everyone is welcome.

We eventually have a huge round of White Elephant gift exchange with everyone, where we explain in a very basic and brief way the origins of Hanukkah, how it isn't based on any biblical text whatsoever and what the biblical text does state. It's informative, non-judgmental, with the whole focus being family, friends, food and fun. Again, it's not a formal or religious gathering; it's about friendship and community more than anything else. We still listen to the classic duet between David Bowie and Bing Crosby, though…

In the week leading up to the party, as individual households, we light the hanukkiah each night, recount the story of the Maccabees and God's deliverance and love. We pray for the peace of Jerusalem, sing the Shema and recall the various times God has delivered Israel from her enemies; how He has delivered *us* from our enemies and proclaim the salvation and deliverance we have through Messiah's love. As far as the giving of gifts, the children receive one on each of the eight nights (usually pajamas and small items), and we have a meal / gift exchange as a community.

It is an old custom to display the hanukkiah where its light can be seen from outside. Since a window is optimal for this, we have an electric hanukkiah that we use, thus lowering the fire hazard. Heh. Like many families, we have multiple hanukkiahs around the house. There's something special about winter nights, a fire in the fireplace, a glass of wine and the glow of the hanukkiah lights.

Purim

In the Book of Esther (given name Hadassah), we find one King Ahasuerus, King of Persia – also known by his Old Persian name of Xerxes I, "the god King" – whom you may have seen depicted in the movie "300".

Chapter one finds King Ahasuerus giving a feast on behalf of the armies of Persia and Media, his nobles, governors, officials and servants. He spent 180 days showing off the vast wealth of his kingdom along with the splendor and glory of his majesty. After these six months, he gave a seven-day feast in the enclosed palace gardens for everyone in the citadel of Susa. The royal wine flowed freely and liberally.

The Queen, Vashti, also gave a banquet for the women of the palace, and on the final day of the feast, King Ahasuerus, "merry with wine," called upon the Queen to present herself with her crown so that he could publicly display her beauty for all to see, but Queen Vashti refused to obey his command. To make her insubordination an example and to ensure that all women throughout the land would honor their husbands, Queen Vashti was banned from the presence of the King and her title as Queen revoked.

Some time later, after his anger subsided, King Ahasuerus remembered what Vashti had done and how he had banished her and stripped her of her position. It was while he was having these second thoughts that the plan was hatched to find all the most beautiful virgins in the land and have them brought to the capital's harem. The most beautiful virgin that was the most pleasing to the King would become queen. This was the plan that was presented, and the King agreed and made it so.

In chapter two, we are introduced to a man named Mordecai from the Tribe of Benjamin, who lived in the capital city of Susa in those days. He had been taken from Jerusalem into Babylonian captivity at the hands of Nebuchadnezzar in the same campaign that included the prophets Daniel and Ezekiel, respectively, as we saw in Chapter 1 of this book. Mordecai had a cousin, the daughter of his uncle, named Esther. After the death of both of her parents, Mordecai adopted her as his own.

She was beautiful, lovely to look at, and when the maidens of Susa were collected on the King's order, Esther was also taken to the palace.

The Queen

Hegal, the King's eunuch, was in charge of the virgins that were being gathered at the capital's harem. Esther won his favor and was given the best place in the harem along with seven palace maids. Under Mordecai's instruction, Esther didn't reveal to anyone that she was indeed a Jewish exile. Mordecai's position as a royal official at the King's gate afforded him the opportunity to check in on Esther daily to see how she was doing.

After the allotted 12-month beautification period, each candidate was allowed to take something with them from the harem when it was their turn to be presented before the King. They would leave to be presented before the King in the evening and return the following morning to a different harem, a second harem for concubines. The candidate would never go in to the King again unless she was called for by name.

When the time arrived for Esther to go before the King, she only took with her what Hegal, the King's eunuch, advised. Out of all the virgins in his kingdom who had been presented to him, the King fell in love with Esther and made her his Queen. The King threw a banquet in Esther's honor, and she continued to keep Mordecai's instruction not to let anyone know that she was a Jewish exile.

One day, while Mordecai sat at the King's gate, he discovered an assassination plot against the King by two palace eunuchs. He immediately informed Queen Esther, who informed the King of Mordecai's discovery. An investigation revealed that there certainly was a plan to assassinate the King, and both eunuchs were sentenced to death.

Enter Haman, son of Hammedatha, the Agagite.

Chapter three opens with King Ahasuerus honoring Haman with a seat higher than all the other nobles. Under the King's orders, all royal officials at the King's gate were to kneel down and pay honor to Haman, which all did, except for Mordecai. His peers asked him daily why he wouldn't comply with the King's instruction, but he refused to obey. Mordecai told them that he was a Jew, so they informed Haman of Mordecai's reason for not bowing to him to see if that would change Mordecai's mind. The next time Mordecai refused to kneel or pay honor to Haman,

Haman was enraged. Haman's anger was so great that simply killing Mordecai wasn't enough. Every Jew in the kingdom would pay for Mordecai's disrespect with their lives!

In the first month, the Month of Abib (Babylonian: Nisan) the lot (Hebrew *"pur"*) was cast for the date of the extermination of Israel throughout the kingdom of Xerxes 1. The lot fell on the thirteenth day of the twelfth month, the Month of Adar.

> *Then Haman said to King Xerxes, "There is a certain people dispersed among the peoples in all the provinces of your kingdom who keep themselves separate. Their customs are different from those of all other people, and they do not obey the king's laws; it is not in the king's best interest to tolerate them. If it pleases the king, let a decree be issued to destroy them, and I will give ten thousand talents of silver to the king's administrators for the royal treasury."*
>
> *So the king took his signet ring from his finger and gave it to Haman son of Hammedatha, the Agagite, the enemy of the Jews. "Keep the money," the king said to Haman, "and do with the people as you please."*
>
> *Then on the thirteenth day of the first month the royal secretaries were summoned. They wrote out in the script of each province and in the language of each people all Haman's orders to the king's satraps, the governors of the various provinces and the nobles of the various peoples. These were written in the name of King Xerxes himself and sealed with his own ring. Dispatches were sent by couriers to all the king's provinces with the order to destroy, kill and annihilate all the Jews—young and old, women and children—on a single day, the thirteenth day of the twelfth month, the month of Adar, and to plunder their goods.*
>
> *A copy of the text of the edict was to be issued as law in every province and made known to the people of every nationality so they would be ready for that day. The couriers went out, spurred on by the king's command, and the edict was issued in the citadel of Susa. The king and Haman sat down to drink, but the city of Susa was bewildered.*
> Book of Esther 3:8-15 (NIV)

When Mordecai heard of Haman's plans, he tore his clothes, put on sackcloth and ashes and wailed loudly and bitterly in the city streets. All of Israel mourned, fasted, wept and wailed at the news.

Esther sent one of the King's eunuchs assigned to her to see what was troubling Mordecai. Mordecai told the eunuch everything and included a copy of the decree calling for their extermination. Mordecai also gave instructions for Esther to go before the King and beg for his mercy on behalf of Israel. Esther replied that going before the King without being summoned was punishable by death, and it had been 30 days since her last summons.

Mordecai replied.

"Do not think to yourself that in the king's palace you will escape any more than all the other Jews. For if you keep silent at this time, relief and deliverance will rise for the Jews from another place, but you and your father's house will perish. And who knows whether you have not come to the kingdom for such a time as this?"
Book of Esther 4:13-14

"For such a time as this..."

Esther asked Mordecai to gather all the Jews of Susa and to have them fast on her behalf for three days and nights, in which time she would go before the King, unsummoned, even though it was unlawful.

"And if I perish, I perish."

Now in the twelfth month, which is the month of Adar, on the thirteenth day of the same, when the king's command and edict were about to be carried out, on the very day when the enemies of the Jews hoped to gain the mastery over them, the reverse occurred: the Jews gained mastery over those who hated them. And on the fourteenth day they rested and made that a day of feasting and gladness.

And Mordecai recorded these things and sent letters to all the Jews who were in all the provinces of King Ahasuerus, both near and far, obliging them to keep the fourteenth day of the month Adar and also the fifteenth day of the same, year by year, as the days on which the Jews got relief

from their enemies, and as the month that had been turned for them from sorrow into gladness and from mourning into a holiday; that they should make them days of feasting and gladness, days for sending gifts of food to one another and gifts to the poor.
Book of Esther 9:1, 17b, 20-22

Be sure to read the entire story of Esther and Mordecai for yourselves!

Like our Hanukkah parties, we invite our friends from all walks of life to join us. Traditionally, Purim is a costume party with the retelling of the story of Esther we just read. With the children in mind, we attempt new ways of retelling of the story of Esther every year, from puppet shows to role playing. Party finger foods and traditional hamantashen are staples for us. The more the merrier, I say, when it comes to your Purim costume party!

Sorrow into gladness – mourning into a holiday – feasting and gladness – gifts of food to one another and the poor are the instructions on how to celebrate Purim as found in the Book of Esther 9:22.

In Summary

Jewish Holiday: Hanukkah
Significance: Celebrates the rededication of the Temple after being defiled by Syrian Greeks
Customs: The lighting of candles displayed on a hanukkiah for eight nights (one candle for each night). Fried foods, gift giving, gelt and playing the dreidel
Length: Eight days - Kislev (Ninth) 25 - Tevet (Tenth) 2/3

Jewish Holiday: Purim
Significance: Purim commemorates the deliverance of Israel from certain annihilation while in Persian exile
Customs: Feasting and gladness. Sending gifts of food to one another and gifts to the poor. Costume parties, eating, and triangle-shaped, fruit-filled cookies. The retelling of Queen Esther's and her cousin, Mordecai's, roles in delivering Israel as documented in the Book

of Esther

Length: Two days - Adar (Twelfth) 14 & 15

There's a lot of feasting, rejoicing – partying, to be completely honest – that we're encouraged and instructed to participate in before the Lord (Deut. 14:26). I fail to see the "legalism" in that!

In fact, a lot of this "partying" is based on His blessings in our lives (Deut. 14:24). Granted, these blessings are predicated on our obedience:

> *Be careful to obey all these regulations I am giving you, so that it may always go well with you and your children after you, because you will be doing what is good and right in the eyes of the LORD your God.*
> *Deuteronomy 12:28 (NIV)*

Blessings predicated on our obedience as also found in the Epistles of the New Testament. Remember:

Jesus is our salvation – Torah is for blessing.

Obedience to His Commandments, Torah, is the sign of *our* love towards Him…

BIBLIOGRAPHY

"Feast of Trumpets: 'A Day of Complete Rest for Remembering'.": https://messianicsabbath.com/2015/08/25/feast-of-trumpets-a-day-of-complete-rest-for-remembering

"The Day of First Fruits (The Omer)." http://biblelight.net/feasts.htm

"The Leaven of Heaven." 119 Ministries: http://c96e50a40991046dcbfa-71bc4c8fd3e50b4ee0e248e517d3026f.r87.cf2.rackcdn.com/uploaded/t/0e4616912_1445626636_the-leaven-of-heaven-transcript.pdf

Biltz, Mark. *The Feasts of the Lord*. El Shaddai Ministries, 2008.

Chumney, Eddie. "The Festival of Firstfruits (Bikkurim)," In *The Seven Festivals of the Messiah*, 71. Strasburg, OH: Hebraic Heritage Ministries Int'l, 2010. http://www.friendsofsabbath.org/Further_Research/Holy%20Days/The-Seven-Festivals-of-the-Messiah.pdf

Chumney, Eddie. "The Festival of Pentecost (Shavuot)," In *The Seven Festivals of the Messiah*, 83-87

Henderson, Jason. *The Feasts of Israel: Israel's Journey in Christ Towards God's Ultimate End*. Market Street Fellowship. https://marketstreetfellowship.com/static/assets/series/feasts-of-israel/book/01_The_Feasts_of_Israel.pdf

Lake, Michael K. TH. D. *Feasts of the Lord & Their Spiritual Significance in the Life of the Believer Study Guide,* 51. Marshfield, MO: Biblical Life Publishing, 2009. http://www.biblicallifeassembly.org/library/mp3/feasts/Feasts%20of%20the%20LORD%20Study%20Guide.pdf

Lake, Michael K. TH. D. "Hanukkah, The Feast of Dedication (Lights)," In *Feasts of the Lord & Their Spiritual Significance in the Life of the Believer Study Guide,* 114-119.

Parsons, John J. *Reishit Katzir: Messiah as the Beginning of the Harvest*. Hebrew for Christians. http://www.hebrew4christians.com/Holidays/Spring_Holidays/First_Fruits/first_fruits.html

Parsons, John J. *Sefirat HaOmer - Counting the Sheaves to Shavuot*. Hebrew for Christians. http://www.hebrew4christians.com/Holidays/Spring_

Holidays/Sefirat_HaOmer/sefirat_haomer.html

Parsons, John J. *Shavuot - Revelation and the Fruit of the Spirit*. Hebrew for Christians. http://www.hebrew4christians.com/Holidays/Spring_Holidays/Shavuot/shavuot.html

Pierce, Chuck D. & Heidler, Robert. "God's Gift of Shabbat," In *A Time to Prosper: Finding and Entering God's Realm of Blessings*, 83-92. Bloomington, Minnesota: Chosen, 2013.

Heidler, Robert. "The Calendar of God," In *A Time to Prosper: Finding and Entering God's Realm of Blessings*, 93-101.

Heidler, Robert. "Passover: Redeemed by the Blood," In *A Time to Prosper: Finding and Entering God's Realm of Blessings*, 103-118.

Heidler, Robert. "Pentecost: Celebrating God's Provision," In *A Time to Prosper: Finding and Entering God's Realm of Blessings*, 119-125.

Heidler, Robert. "Preparing for Tabernacles," In *A Time to Prosper: Finding and Entering God's Realm of Blessings*, 127-132.

Heidler, Robert. "Tabernacles: Entering God's Glory," In *A Time to Prosper: Finding and Entering God's Realm of Blessings*, 133-141.

Pierce, Chuck D. "Rosh Chodesh: Giving to God the Firstfruits," In *A Time to Prosper: Finding and Entering God's Realm of Blessings*, 143-166.

INDEX

1

18th Dynasty
   The 18th Dynasty of ancient Egypt (c. 1550–1298 BC) is the best-known ancient Egyptian dynasty. It boasts several of Egypt's most famous pharaohs, including Tutankhamun. The dynasty is also known as the Thutmosid Dynasty for the four pharaohs named Thutmosis. Famous pharaohs of Dynasty XVIII include Hatshepsut (c. 1479 BC–1458 BC), longest-reigning woman-pharaoh of an indigenous dynasty, and Akhenaten (c. 1353–1336 BC), the "heretic pharaoh," with his queen, Nefertiti 89, 92

A

Abba
   (Hebrew "Father"). Because of the Spirit of Adoption into the commonwealth of Israel, we cry "Abba"/ Father (Ro. 8:15) vi, 111

Abib
   (Hebrew) Literally, an ear of corn. Also barley as newly-ripened grain. The first of the Jewish ecclesiastical year, and the seventh of the civil year. It was renamed Nisan after the Babylonian Captivity. On the fifteenth day of the month, harvest was begun by gathering a sheaf of barley, which was offered to God 5, 10, 32, 104, 105, 106, 107, 109, 110, 112, 113, 116, 121, 123, 124, 125, 126, 127, 128, 129, 134

Abram
   Also Abraham. The first of the three patriarchs of Judaism 166

Adar
   (Hebrew) The sixth month of the civil year and the twelfth month of the ecclesiastical year on the Hebrew calendar. It is a winter month of 29 days 18, 32, 33, 105, 106, 107, 108

ADONAI
A name of God traditionally mistranslated as "Lord" v, vii, viii, 5, x, 7, xix, xxiii, xxiv, 7, 8, 9, 10, 11, 12, 13, 35, 36, 87, 88, 89, 94, 95, 56, 57, 60, 64, 36, 37, 42, 75, 76, 133, 135, 136, 137, 139, 141, 142, 96, 143, 97, 144, 98, 145, 99, 151, 152, 153, 155, 111, 113, 115, 120, 130, 131, 155, 156, 158, 161, 162, 162, 165, 167, 168, 169, 170, 188, 162, 163

Ahaz
A king of Judah, and the son and successor of Jotham. Ahaz was 20 when he became king of Judah and reigned for 16 years 142

Akitu
(Sumerian "head of the year", "barley") was a spring festival in ancient Mesopotamia. The Babylonian Akitu festival played a pivotal role in the development of theories of religion, myth and ritual 182

Aleph
The first letter of the Hebrew alphabet 174, 240

Amalek
A grandson of Esau, the descendant nation of Amalekites, and the first of all the nations to war against Israel when they came out of Egypt 153

The Amazing Journey from Exodus to Ingathering, 229

Amenhotep II
Amenhotep II was the seventh Pharaoh of the 18th Dynasty of Egypt. Amenhotep inherited a vast kingdom from his father Thutmose III 93, 94

Amenhotep III
Amenhotep III, also known as Amenhotep the Magnificent, was the ninth pharaoh of the 18th Dynasty 93, 94

The Appointed Feasts, 7

Ash Wednesday
A day of fasting, is the first day of Lent in Western Christianity. It occurs 46 days before Easter 146

Asherim
Cult objects related to the worship of the fertility goddess Asherah, the consort of Ba'al 157

B

Between the Evenings..., 112

Bikkurim. *See* Firstfruits

Building a Sukkah, 217

C

The Calendar, 30

Calvary
  also Golgatha, was a site immediately outside Jerusalem's walls where Jesus was crucified. Golgotha is the Greek transcription of the Aramaic term Gagultâ xxi

Chag ha-Asif
  Hebrew "of the harvest" 205, 245

Chametz
  (Hebrew) Ferment - leaven, leavened (bread) 118, 119, 120, 121, 122

Chuppah
  (Hebrew) Literally a canopy or covering that the couple stands under during their wedding ceremony 171, 172

Conjunction, 33

Cosplay
  the practice of dressing up as a character from a movie, book, or video game, especially one from the Japanese genres of manga and anime, 20

Council of Nicaea
  (AD 325), the first ecumenical council of the Christian church, meeting in ancient Nicaea. It was called by the emperor Constantine I, an unbaptized catechumen, or neophyte, who presided over the opening session and took part in the discussions 146

Counting of the Omer
  The seven-week count (Feast of Weeks) leading up to Shavuot starting after the Feast of Firstfruits 1, 8, 11, 31, 32, 69, 105, 145, 148, 149, 158, 163, 169

Counting of the Omer / Feast of Weeks, 8, 145

D

The Day of Atonement / Yom Kippur, 8, 193

Day of Atonement
(Hebrew "Yom Kippur"). Considered the holiest day of the year, Yom Kippur is a day of deliverance and salvation, and the only time when the High Priest could enter the Holy of Holies, call upon the Name of God and offer a blood sacrifice for the sins of the people. It is a solemn day, a Sabbath of solemn rest, marked by complete fasting and prayer 8, 9, 12, 32

Day of Preparation
The day before the High Sabbath of the First Day of the Feast of Unleavened Bread 110, 115, 116, 117, 118, 121, 123, 124, 125, 126, 127, 128, 129

Day of Preparation / Feast of Unleavened Bread, 115

The Day That Jesus Died, 123

Dietary Restrictions
Leviticus 11 lists the animals that are considered "food" by God, suitable for human consumption, clean and unclean food 22

Does the Day We Keep as a Sabbath Really Matter?, 79

Dream Stela of Thutmosis IV
Also called the Sphinx Stele, is an epigraphic stele belonging to the Ancient Egyptian Pharaoh Thutmose IV. It was erected in the first year of the king's reign, 1401 BC, during the 18th Dynasty. As was common with other New Kingdom rulers, the epigraph makes claim to a divine legitimization to pharaoh-ship 93

E

Easter
A festival celebrating the resurrection of Jesus from the dead. It is the culmination of the Passion of Jesus, preceded by Lent, a forty-day period of fasting, prayer and penance. Most Christians refer to the week before Easter as "Holy Week" - it contains the days of the

Easter Triduum, including Maundy Thursday, commemorating the Maundy and Last Supper, as well as Good Friday, commemorating the crucifixion and death of Jesus. Easter Season begins on Easter Sunday and lasts seven weeks, ending with the coming of the fiftieth day, Pentecost Sunday. In Eastern Christianity, the season of Pascha begins on Pascha and ends with the coming of the fortieth day, the Feast of the Ascension 146, 147, 148

Ēostre
(or Ostara) The Germanic goddess of fertility and the namesake of the festival of Easter in some languages 148

Erusin
the Hebrew term for betrothal. In modern Hebrew, "erusin" means engagement, but this is not the historical meaning of the term, which is the first part of marriage (the second part being nissuin) 170

Eruv
(Hebrew) An urban area enclosed by a wire boundary that symbolically extends the private domain of Jewish households into public areas, permitting activities within it that are normally forbidden in public on the Sabbath 17

Ezra
A scribe and a priest 37, 159

F

Faith Without "Works", 100

Fall Feasts
Feast of Trumpets, Day of Atonement, Feast of Tabernacles 10, 230

Fear, Doubt and Unbelief – A "Stiff-Necked" People, 154

the Feasts
The appointed times of God for His people v, viii, 1, 3, 4, 10, 12, 19, 31, 33, 35, 40, 41, 70, 143, 157

The Feasts Summarized, 233

Feast of Firstfruits
The third of the four Spring Feasts is an offering of the first agricultural produce of the barley harvest. Firstfruits were brought and given to the priests, who then offered them to God on behalf of the person

as a wave sheaf offering. Firstfruits took place immediately after the weekly Sabbath following Passover. Jesus resurrected from the dead on Firstfruits fulfilling the third part of the Passover observance 7, 105, 107, 115, 130, 134, 135, 136, 137, 138, 139, 140, 143, 145, 161, 162

The Feast of Firstfruits, 7, 135

Feast of Firstfruits / The Omer Count, 237

The Feast of Tabernacles / Sukkot, 9, 244

Feast of Tabernacles
  (Hebrew "Sukkot" or "Succot"). The seventh and final feast of the seven annual Feasts of God. It is also the third of the Three Pilgrimage Festivals on which every first born Israeli male is commanded to present himself before God in Jerusalem. Tabernacles is an eight-day feast also known as the Feast of Booths or the Feast of Ingathering where you live in temporary dwelling places (booths) for those eight days 9, 11, 12, 32, 62, 64

Feast of Tabernacles / Booths – Festival of Ingathering – Sukkot, 244

Feast of Trumpets (Yom Teruah) / Day of Atonement (Yom Kippur), 242

Feast of Trumpets / Yom Teruah (Rosh Hashanah)
  (Hebrew "Yom Teruah"). Literally "day of shouting/blasting", also known as "Rosh Hashanah" (Hebrew), literally the "beginning/head of the year" as this feast ushers in the Jewish civil calendar. The first of the "High Holy Days" and the beginning of the Fall Feasts, this feast day is a High Sabbath 8, 12, 179, 182, 183, 186, 192, 201, 202, 241, 242, 243

Feast of Unleavened Bread, 117

Feast of Unleavened Bread
  The second of the three Spring Feasts commemorates Israels hasty Passover meal which included unleavened bread. The seven-day feast is observed first by the purging of leavening agents and leaven from your home and by eating only unleavened bread (Hebrew "matzah") for those seven days. Leaven would come to represent sin and bad/unsound doctrine. This feast also speaks prophetically of Messiah's entombment 7, 11, 32, 66, 76, 87, 98, 99, 105, 106, 107, 115, 116, 117, 118, 119, 121, 122, 123, 124, 125, 126, 127, 129, 134, 136, 137, 143, 148, 162, 163

Feast of Weeks
   The seven-week Counting of the Omer leading up to Shavuot starting after the Feast of Firstfruits 8, 11, 12, 32, 40, 69, 143, 145, 148, 149, 158, 161, 163, 169, 221, 230, 233, 238

Festival of Ingathering, 205

Final Thoughts, 246

First Day of the Feast of Unleavened Bread
   A High Sabbath. The first day of this seven day feast falls on the 15th of the First month, the Month of Abib 115, 116, 117, 121, 123, 124, 125, 126, 127, 129, 133, 134, 162

Firstfruits, 35

Firstfruits
   The first agricultural produce of a season, especially when given as an offering to God; the initial results of an enterprise or endeavor; a firstfruits offering 7, 8, 10, 11, 32, 36, 37, 38, 39, 40, 41, 42, 66, 88, 89, 105, 106, 107, 109, 115, 130, 131, 133, 135, 136, 137, 138, 139, 143, 144, 145, 157, 161, 162, 165, 169, 170, 177

Firstfruits is the Resurrection *Not* a Shabbat, 138

The Four Species – Arba Minim, 214

Further up and further in
   A line from C.S. Lewis' *The Last Battle* vii, 41, 144

G

Gemara
   The component or tractate (an organizational element of Talmudic literature) of the Talmud comprising of rabbinical analysis and commentary on the Mishnah 247

Gentiles
   Non-Hebrew peoples also known as pagans in scripture viii, ix, x, xi, xv, xvi, xxiii, 24, 25, 26, 41, 64, 71, 101, 114, 122

Gershom
   First son of Moses. His mother was Zipporah, the Midianite 91

Gibeonites

Gibeon was a Canaanite city north of Jerusalem. The pre-conquest inhabitants of Gibeon, the Gibeonites, were Hivites according to Joshua or Amorites according to 2 Samuel 157

Gods commandments. *See* Torah

Golgotha
also Calvary and Gagulta, was a site immediately outside Jerusalem's walls where Jesus was crucified. Golgotha is the Greek transcription of the Aramaic term Gagultâ xxiii

H

Halakhah
(Hebrew) Literally "the way to behave" or "the way of walking." Instructions derived from Torah 25, 26

Halakhah and the Gentile Converts, 25

Hallel
A portion of the service for certain Jewish festivals, consisting of Psalms 113–118, 17

Hanukkah
(Hebrew) A traditional Jewish holiday commemorating the rededication of the Second Temple in Jerusalem at the time of the Maccabean Revolt against the Seleucid Empire. Hanukkah is observed for eight nights and days, starting on the 25th day of Kislev according to the Hebrew calendar, which may occur at any time from late November to late December in the Gregorian calendar. It is also known as the Festival of Lights and the Feast of Dedication 18, 20, 32, 211, 247, 248, 250, 251, 252, 253, 258

Hanukkah Today, 250

Hasmonean
The Hasmonean Dynasty was the ruling dynasty of Judea and surrounding regions during classical antiquity. Between 140 and 116 BCE the dynasty ruled semi-autonomously from the Seleucids in the region of Judea 249

How Do You Spell H.A.N.U.K.K.A.H?, 252

How Do You Spell S.H.A.B.B.A.T?, 72

J

Jehovah Rapha'
"I am ADONAI, who heals you" 153

Jesus and Keeping the Sabbath, 61

Jesus Calls Himself "Living Water", 62

Jesus in the Garden, 137

Jonah
 A Hebrew prophet who is sent by God to prophesy the destruction of Nineveh but tries to escape the divine mission 137

Josephus
 Titus Flavius Josephus (37 – c. 100), born Joseph ben Matityahu (Hebrew Yosef ben Matityahu). A first-century Romano-Jewish scholar, historian and hagiographer, who was born in Jerusalem to a father of priestly descent and a mother who claimed royal ancestry. Josephus recorded Jewish history, with special emphasis on the first century CE and the First Jewish–Roman War, including the Siege of Masada. His most important works were The Jewish War (c. 75) and Antiquities of the Jews (c. 94) 91

Judaize, Judaizer
 A negative term to describe rogue believing Jews that insisted Gentile converts had to keep Jewish traditions/rituals, that were based on Torah (traditions and rituals commonly and religiously confused with actual Torah), in order for Gentiles to be saved. I.e. ritual circumcision (Acts 15) 67

K

Kabbalist
 A disciple of Kabbalah (Hebrew). Literally "receiving/tradition") is an esoteric method, discipline, and school of thought that originated in Judaism 107

Karaite
 From their website:
 Karaism is the original form of Judaism as prescribed by God in the Torah. Karaite Judaism rejects later additions to the Tanach (Jewish Bible) such as the Rabbinic Oral Law and places the ultimate responsi-

bility of interpreting the Bible on each individual. Karaism does not reject Biblical interpretation but rather holds every interpretation up to the same objective scrutiny regardless of its source 107

Ketubah
(Hebrew) A special type of Jewish prenuptial agreement. It is considered an integral part of a traditional Jewish marriage, and outlines the rights and responsibilities of the groom, in relation to the bride 170, 171, 172

King Artaxerxes
Artaxerxes I was the fifth King of Persia from 465 BC to 424 BC. He was the third son of Xerxes I. He may have been the "Artasyrus" mentioned by Herodotus as being a Satrap of the royal satrapy of Bactria 159

King Asa
The third king of the Kingdom of Judah and the fifth king of the House of David. He was the son of Abijam, grandson of Rehoboam, and great-grandson of Solomon 157

King Cyrus
Cyrus II of Persia, commonly known as Cyrus the Great and also called Cyrus the Elder by the Greeks, was the founder of the Achaemenid Empire 159

King Darius
The third king of the Persian Achaemenid Empire. Also called Darius the Great, he ruled the empire at its peak and controlled the largest fraction of the world's population of any empire in history, 44% of the world's population. Darius is mentioned in the Biblical books of Haggai, Zechariah, Ezra and Nehemiah 159

King David
The second king of the United Kingdom of Israel and Judah. A valorous warrior of great renown, a poet and musician. A righteous and effective king both in battle and in providing civil and criminal justice and described as a man after God's own heart. The ancestor of the future Messiah 157

King Hezekiah
the son of Ahaz and the 13th king of Judah 157

King Josiah
Son of King Amon and Jedidah, the daughter of Adaiah of Bozkath. His grandfather, Manasseh, was one of the kings blamed for turning

away from the worship of Yahweh. Manasseh adapted the Temple for idolatrous worship while King Josiah instituted repentance and a turning back to Yahweh and His Torah 157, 158

King Solomon
Also called Jedidiah, was a fabulously wealthy and wise king of Israel and a son of David, the previous king of Israel 157

King Tutankamun
Tutankhamun was an Egyptian pharaoh of the 18th Dynasty, during the period of Egyptian history known as the New Kingdom or sometimes the New Empire Period. He has, since his discovery, been colloquially referred to as King Tut 93, 94

L

Land of Goshen
The place in Egypt given to the Hebrews by the pharaoh in Joseph's day, and the land from which they later left Egypt at the time of the Exodus. It was located in the eastern Delta of the Nile 151

the Law
The mistranslation of the Hebrew "Torah" which actually means teaching/instruction viii, ix, xi, xiii, xv, 4, 38, 47, 55, 65, 78

Leaven
A substance, typically yeast, that is added to dough to make it ferment and rise 8, 11, 98, 12, 116, 117, 118, 120, 122, 122, 165, 131

Lent
A solemn religious observance in the Christian liturgical calendar that begins on Ash Wednesday and ends approximately six weeks later, before Easter Sunday 64, 146, 147, 148

Levites, Levitical Priesthood
A member of the Hebrew tribe of Levi and worship leaders/assistants to the priests in the Temple 4, 37, 38, 39, 155, 233

M

Manasseh
A king of Judah. He was the only son of Hezekiah with Hephzibah. He became king at the age of 12 and reigned for 55 years 142

Manna
A fine as frost on the ground, flake-like thing. "Bread that ADONAI gave Israel to eat" for 40 years. It melted when the sun grew hot. It was eaten baked and/or boiled. Manna was like coriander seed, white, and the taste of it was like wafers made with honey 76, 112, 113, 153

Mardi Gras
Also called Shrove Tuesday, or Fat Tuesday, refers to events of the Carnival celebrations, beginning on or after the Christian feasts of the Epiphany (Three Kings Day) and culminating on the day before Ash Wednesday 146, 148

Matzah
Unleavened bread xxii, 10, xxii, 10, 116, 117, 118, 119, 120, 121, 122, 131

Messianic
Relating to the Messiah, "Jesus." Inspired by hope or belief in Messiah ix, xi, 107

Minas
The mina is an ancient Near Eastern unit of weight, which was divided into 50 shekels. The mina, like the shekel, was also a unit of currency 205, 245

Minchah
(Hebrew) A gift, tribute, an offering 136, 237

Miqra'
(Hebrew) A rehearsal 2

Mishna
(Hebrew) The first major written redaction of the Jewish oral traditions, the "Oral Torah". Also the first major work of Rabbinic literature 248

Mitzvahs
(Hebrew) Plural for "commandments". Refers to precepts and commandments commanded by God, i.e. the Torah 17, 55, 247

Mo'ed
: (Hebrew) An appointed place, an appointed time, or an appointed meeting; a fixed time or season; a solemn assembly 1, 3, 110, 198

Mohar
: (Hebrew) A price (for a wife) - dowry 170

Mosaic Law. *See* Torah

Moses / Egypt and the Deliverance of Israel, 95

Moses / Egyptology and the 18th Dynasty, 89

Mount Horeb
: The mountain at which the book of Deuteronomy in the Hebrew Bible states that the Ten Commandments were given to Moses. *See also* Mt. Sinai 95

Mount Sinai
: The mountain at which the book of Exodus in the Hebrew Bible states that the Ten Commandments were given to Moses. See also Mt. Hebron vii, ix, 80, 81, 166, 167, 163, 169

Mount Zion
: A hill in Jerusalem just outside the walls of the Old City. The term Mount Zion has been used in the Hebrew Bible first for the City of David and later for the entire Land of Israel 175

N

N'chushtan
: (Hebrew) the brass or bronze serpent Moses used as an oracle of healing in the desert 197

Nefure. *See* Queen Hatshepsut

Nehemiah
: The central figure of the Book of Nehemiah, which describes his work in rebuilding Jerusalem during the Second Temple period. He was governor of Persian Judea under Artaxerxes I of Persia 37, 74, 136, 159

Nephilim
: The offspring of The Watchers (the "sons of God") and the "daughters of men" before the Deluge. The "giants" of Genesis 6:4 of the Bible. According to Numbers 13:33, their descendants later inhabited Canaan

at the time of the Israelite conquest of Canaan 95, 194

Nesu'in
(Hebrew) The second stage of marriage when the couple enter their new home together (consummation) 170, 173

The New Moon / Rosh Chodesh, 33, 34

New Moon
(Hebrew "Rosh Chodesh" literally "head of the month"). Marks the head, the beginning of the month v, 31, 33, 34, 35, 104, 105, 107, 109, 41, 42, 109, 184, 110, 153

O

Old / New Testament – TaNaKh – Torah, viii

Omer
an ancient unit of measure used in the era of the ancient Temple in Jerusalem 78, 142, 250

Omer Count. *See* Counting of the Omer

One New Man
Based on Eph. 2:13-14. The inclusion and equal participation of Gentiles with Jews within the Christian faith xxiii, 138, 170

Oracles
Plural. An oracle was a person or agency considered to provide wise and insightful counsel or prophetic predictions or precognition of the future, inspired "by the gods" 56, 91

Oral Traditions, Talmud and Rabbinical Judaism vs Scripture, 16

Overview and Summary of the Seven Feasts, 10

P

Pagan
A person holding religious beliefs other than those of the main world religions, specifically a non-Christian or pre-Christian religion. Relating to pagans viii, ix, 56, 60, 147, 157

THE FEASTS UNLOCKED | **277**

Paganism
    A religion other than one of the main world religions, specifically a non-Christian or pre-Christian religion. A modern religious movement incorporating beliefs or practices from outside the main world religions, especially nature worship 26, 45, 46, 56, 60, 64, 158

Passover (Pesach), 109

Passover
    (Hebrew "Pesach"). The first of the seven annual Feasts of God and the first of the three Spring Feasts. It is also the first of the Three Pilgrimage Festivals on which every firstborn Israeli male is commanded to present himself before God in Jerusalem. Passover commemorates Israels deliverance and exodus from Egypt under the leadership of Moses 1, 7, 10, 11, 12, 18, 19, 20, 31, 32, 40, 66, 67, 68, 69, 87, 93, 94, 97, 98, 99, 105, 106, 107, 109, 110, 111, 112, 113, 114, 115, 116, 117, 118, 119, 121, 122, 123, 124, 125, 126, 127, 128, 129, 131, 133, 134, 135, 136, 137, 143, 145, 146, 147, 148, 149, 154, 156, 158, 159, 162, 163, 166, 173, 174, 175, 176, 177, 178, 187

Pentecost, 175

Pentecost
    The celebration of the descent of the Holy Spirit on the 120 disciples waiting in Jerusalem in the Upper Room. This occurred on the 50th Day of the Omer Count - the completion of the Feast of Weeks / Shavuot (Hebrew "weeks") - the fourth Feast. Shavuot is the same exact day that Moses received Torah on Mt. Sinai and it is the second of the Three Pilgrimage Festivals on which every first born Israeli male is commanded to present himself before God in Jerusalem 3, 8, 10, 11, 12, 31, 32, 40, 105, 135, 143, 148, 149, 161, 163, 166, 171, 172, 175, 176, 177, 181, 204, 206, 230, 233, 238, 239, 240,

The Promised Land
    Also known as "The Land of Milk and Honey", is the land which, according to the TaNaKh, was promised and subsequently given by God to Abraham and his descendants 36, 135, 154

Purim, 254

Purim
    (Hebrew "lots"). A traditional Jewish holiday that commemorates Esther and the saving of the Jewish people from Haman, who was planning to kill all the Jews. This took place in the ancient Achaemenid Persian Empire 18, 20, 31, 33, 34, 254, 258

Q

Queen Hatshepsut
also Hatchepsut. Meaning Foremost of Noble Ladies, (1507–1458 BC) was the fifth pharaoh of the 18th Dynasty of Egypt. She was the second historically-confirmed female pharaoh, the first being Sobekneferu. Hatshepsut came to the throne of Egypt in 1478 BC. Officially, she ruled jointly with Thutmose III, who had ascended to the throne the previous year as a child of about two years old. Hatshepsut was the chief wife of Thutmose II, Thutmose III's father. She is generally regarded by Egyptologists as one of the most successful pharaohs, reigning longer than any other woman of an indigenous Egyptian dynasty 92, 94

R

Rabbi Sha'ul
The Apostle Paul viii, 122

Removing Leaven Out of Your Houses, 118

Resurrection Sunday, 140

Reuel
Midian priest. Father of Zipporah, Moses' first wife (Exod. 2:18-20) 91

Revolt, 249

Rosh Chodesh, 33, 34

Rosh Chodesh
(Hebrew "head of the month"). Marks the head, the beginning of the month, the New Moon 31, 33, 34, 35, 40, 41, 42, 70, 104, 105, 106, 109, 110, 133, 135, 143, 161, 181, 182, 183, 184, 186, 188, 189, 191, 201, 202, 204, 233, 238, 242

Rosh Hashanah
(Hebrew "head of the year"). The Jewish Civil New Year, held on the first and second day of Tishri. It is marked by the blowing of the shofar, and begins the ten days of penitence culminating in Yom Kippur. See also Feast of Tabernacles 182, 183, 184, 185, 202

S

The Sabbath / Shabbat. See also Shabbat, 7

the Sabbath
(Hebrew "Shabbat"). The seventh day of the week, Friday sunset to Saturday sunset. A solemn and holy day of rest 1, 4, 7, 8, 9, 10, 12, 17, 18, 19, 26, 31, 34, 35, 40, 42, 43, 44, 45, 50, 54, 60, 61, 62, 63, 64, 65, 66, 67, 68, 69, 70, 71, 72, 73, 75, 76, 77, 78, 79, 80, 81, 82, 85, 87, 105, 115, 116, 117, 121, 122, 123, 124, 125, 126, 127, 130, 133, 134, 135, 138, 139, 140, 143, 145, 148, 149, 161, 162, 165, 177, 181, 182, 184, 185, 186, 193, 198, 199, 203, 208, 215, 219, 224, 225, 226, 230, 233, 235, 243

Sacred Name
Developed from the Church of God (Seventh Day) in the 1930s. The Sacred Name Movement teaches that only "Yahweh" is to be used as the name for God and only "Yahshua" is to be used as the name for Jesus. According to the Sacred Name Movement, the use of any other name is blasphemy 107

Sanhedrin
(Hebrew "sitting together", hence "assembly" or "council"). An assembly of twenty-three to seventy-one men appointed in every city in the Land of Israel 123, 124, 125, 126, 127, 129

Seder
(Hebrew "order, arrangement"). The traditional Passover meal observed by a community or by multiple generations of a family, involving the meal and the retelling of the story of the liberation of the Israelites from slavery in ancient Egypt 20, 121, 128

Senmut
Senenmut was an 18th Dynasty ancient Egyptian architect and government official. His name translates literally as "mother's brother" 96, 92, 94

Se'or
(Hebrew) Barm or yeast-cake (as swelling by fermentation) - leaven / leavening agent 118, 119, 120, 121, 122

Septuagint
The primary Greek translation of the Old Testament 248

Shabbat. *See* the Sabbath
7, 17, 18, 20, 40, 44, 45, 46, 48, 49, 50, 51, 54, 55, 56, 57, 60, 62, 64, 65, 66, 67, 68, 69, 70, 71, 72, 73, 74, 75, 76, 77, 78, 79, 81, 82, 83, 85, 105, 115, 116, 117, 121, 124, 126, 127, 129, 130, 133, 134, 135, 136, 137, 138, 143, 149, 157, 161, 162, 163, 165, 169, 177, 182, 183, 186, 188, 198, 201, 202, 216, 217, 218, 234, 235, 236, 237, 238, 239, 242, 243, 248

Shabbat Guide, 51

Shabbat Simplified, 50

Shabbat vs Sunday Church, 65

Shavuot (Hebrew "Weeks"), 169

Shavuot / Pentecost, 8

Shavuot
(Hebrew "weeks"). The culmination of the seven-week Counting of the Omer - the completion of the Feast of Weeks - the fourth Feast. Shavuot is the same exact day that Moses received Torah on Mt. Sinai, and it is the second of the Three Pilgrimage Festivals on which every firstborn Israeli male is commanded to present himself before God in Jerusalem 8, 10, 11, 12, 18, 31, 32, 40, 105, 135, 143, 145, 148, 149, 161, 163, 165, 166, 169, 170, 171, 174, 175, 176, 177, 181, 187, 194, 201, 202, 205, 221, 230, 232, 233, 238, 239, 240, 245

Shavuot: A Marriage Contract and a Bride Betrothed, 170

Shofar
An ancient musical horn made from a ram, an African Kudu, a sheep and/or a goat. Shofars come in a variety of sizes and shapes, depending on the choice of animal and level of finish. The shofar is blown every month at Rosh Chodesh, the First day of the Feast of Unleavened Bread, during Yom Teruah, at the very end of Yom Kippur and the first day of Sukkot 11, 20, 34, 35, 40, 42, 63, 109, 167, 175, 179, 182, 183, 185, 186, 187, 188, 189, 190, 191, 201, 202, 208, 218, 230, 232, 233, 241, 242, 243

Shofars and Trumpets, 188

Showbread
(Hebrew literally "Bread of the Presence"). In the King James Version shewbread, in a biblical or Jewish context, refers to the cakes or loaves of bread which were always present on a specially dedicated

two crowned table, in the Temple in Jerusalem as an offering to God. An alternative, and more appropriate, translation would be presence bread, since the Bible requires that the bread be constantly in the presence of God (Exodus 25) 61

The Sighting of the Abib, 104

Sojourner
A stranger, a foreigner, an alien. A person living out of their own country 8, 36, 44, 73, 98, 118, 122, 157, 165, 169

Spiritual Application of the Feasts, 12

Spring Equinox
The Vernal (Spring) Equinox marks the first day of astronomical spring 148

Spring Feasts
Passover, Feast of Unleavened Bread, Feast of Firstfruits, the Omer Count 3, 10, 11, 87, 108, 109, 115, 133, 204, 206, 229, 239

Sukkah
(Hebrew), also succah and often translated as booth, is a temporary hut constructed for use during the week-long festival of Sukkot 204, 206, 207, 212, 213, 214, 216, 217, 218, 219, 244

Sukkot, 9, 205

Sukkot
(Hebrew), also Succot. Literally "Feast of Booths". Commonly translated as Feast of Tabernacles, sometimes also as Feast of the Ingathering 1, 9, 11, 12, 18, 62, 63, 64, 179, 183, 189, 190, 191, 192, 198, 202, 204, 205, 206, 207, 208, 209, 212, 213, 214, 215, 216, 217, 218, 219, 230, 232, 241, 242, 243, 244, 245, 250, 252

Sukkot is Prophetic, 206

T

Tabernacles. *See* Feast of Tabernacles, *See* Sukkot

Talents
A talent was a former weight and unit of currency, used especially by the ancient Romans and Greeks 205, 245

Talmud
: The central text of Rabbinic Judaism, this body of Jewish civil and ceremonial law and legend is comprised of two components the Mishnah (c. 200 CE), a written compendium of Rabbinic Judaism's Oral Torah, and the Gemara (c. 500 CE), an elucidation of the Mishnah and related Tannaitic writings that often ventures onto other subjects and expounds broadly on the Hebrew Bible 16, 21, 119

Tammuz
: A Sumerian god of food and vegetation, also worshiped in the later Mesopotamian states of Akkad, Assyria and Babylonia 32, 142, 147

TaNaKh
: The "Old Testament". An acronym of the first Hebrew letter of each of the Masoretic Text's three traditional subdivisions vii, viii, x, xiv, xxii, xxiii, 45, xxiii, 102, 64, 138, 139, 119, 162

Tassels
: (Hebrew "tzitzit"). Knotted tassels attached to the four corners of the tallit (prayer shawl) and tallit katan (everyday undergarment). Can also be affixed to daily clothing 16, 17

Tav
: The last letter of the Hebrew alphabet 174, 240

Ten Commandments
: The Ten Commandments, also known as the Decalogue, are a set of biblical principles relating to ethics and worship ix, 79, 81, 167, 194, 221, 224, 225

Teshuvah
: (Hebrew "repentance", "turning back to God"). A special season of self examination beginning in the Month of Elul for 40 days ending on Yom Kippur,. Traditional 183

Thutmosis I
: Thutmose I was the third pharaoh of the 18th Dynasty of Egypt 92, 93

Thutmosis III
: Thutmose III was the sixth Pharaoh of the 18th Dynasty. During the first 22 years of Thutmose's reign he was co-regent with his stepmother and aunt, Hatshepsut, who was named the pharaoh 94

Thutmosis IV
: Thutmose IV was the 8th Pharaoh of the 18th Dynasty of Egypt, who ruled in approximately the 14th century BC 93, 94

Tithing, Offerings and Firstfruits, 37

Torah
  The teachings / instructions of God for His people given to Moses on Mt. Sinai. Mistranslated as "law", "the Law" v, viii, ix, x, xi, xii, xiii, xiv, xv, xvi, xvii, xviii, xix, xx, xxi, xxii, xxiii, 3, 4, 5, 6, 7, 11, 13, 16, 17, 18, 19, 20, 21, 22, 23, 24, 25, 26, 27, 28, 29, 30, 37, 38, 39, 42, 44, 45, 46, 47, 57, 60, 61, 62, 63, 66, 68, 71, 74, 76, 77, 78, 79, 82, 84, 88, 99, 100, 101, 102, 103, 104, 114, 120, 122, 130, 131, 143, 144, 149, 153, 154, 157, 158, 160, 161, 163, 166, 169, 170, 171, 172, 174, 175, 176, 177, 178, 182, 184, 185, 187, 191, 192, 194, 202, 206, 208, 214, 215, 216, 224, 225, 227, 228, 229, 230, 238, 239, 240, 241, 242, 248, 249, 250, 251, 259

Traditions Continued…, 60

Tzitzit. *See* Tassels

V

Vidcast
  A video webcast, vi

Visible Crescent Jerusalem (VCJ), 34

Visible Crescent Present (VCP), 34

W

What Does Jesus Say About It?, xiv

The Word Became Flesh and "Tabernacled" with Us, 210

Y

Yom Kippur / Day of Atonement, 193

Yom Teruah. *See* Feast of Trumpets, 185

Yom Teruah vs Rosh Hashanah, 182

Your House Is On Fire…, 57

Z

Zipporah
 Daughter of the Midian priest, Reuel. First wife of Moses and mother of Moses' first son, Gershom, 91